MATH FOR LIBERAL ARTS

DANTES/DSST* Study Guide

All rights reserved. This Study Guide, Book and Flashcards are protected under the US Copyright Law. No part of this book or study guide or flashcards may be reproduced, distributed or stored in a retrieval system, or transmitted in any form or by any means, electronic, mechanical, photocopying, recording, or otherwise, without the prior written permission of the publisher Breely Crush Publishing, LLC.

© 2019 Breely Crush Publishing, LLC

*DSST is a registered trademark of The Thomson Corporation and its affiliated companies, and does not endorse this book.

971082518143

Copyright ©2003 – 2019, Breely Crush Publishing, LLC.

All rights reserved.

This study guide/book is protected under US Copyright Law. No part of this product may be reproduced, distributed or stored in a retrieval system, or transmitted in any form or by any means, electronic, mechanical, photocopying, recording, or otherwise, without the prior written permission of the publisher Breely Crush Publishing, LLC.

Published by Breely Crush Publishing, LLC
10808 River Front Parkway
South Jordan, UT 84095
www.breelycrushpublishing.com

ISBN–10: 1-61433-551-6
ISBN–13: 978-1-61433-551-1

Printed and bound in the United States of America.

*DSST is a registered trademark of The Thomson Corporation and its affiliated companies, and does not endorse this book.

Table of Contents

Section 1: Numbers and Operations 1
   1-1: Arithmetic Word Problems 1
   1-2: Properties of Integers and Rational Numbers 11
   1-3: Sets 16
   1-4: Counting Techniques 19
   1-5: Sequences and Series 32
   1-6: Elementary Number Theory 41
Sample Test Questions 46
   Numbers and Operations Questions 46
   Numbers and Operations Key 58
Section 2: Algebra and Functions 59
   2-1: Substitution and Simplifying Algebraic Expressions 59
   2-2: Properties of Exponents 66
   2-3: Simplifying Algebraic Fractions 73
   2-4: Solutions of Linear Equations and Inequalities 77
   2-5: System of Equations and Inequalities 84
   2-6: Quadratic Equations 89
   2-7: Rational and Radical Equations 97
   2-8: Equations of Lines 109
   2-9: Absolute Value 114
   2-10: Direct and Inverse Variation 117
   2-11: Concepts of Algebraic Functions 120
Sample Test Questions 128
   Algebra and Functions Questions 128
   Algebra and Functions Key 150
Section 3: Geometry and Measurement 151
   3-1: Area and Perimeter of a Polygon and a Circle 151
   3-2: Volume of a Box, Cube, and Cylinder 156
   3-3: Pythagorean Theorem and Special Properties of Isosceles,
          Equilateral and Right Triangles 158
   3-4: Properties of Parallel and Perpendicular Lines 164
   3-5: Coordinate Geometry 169
   3-6: Slope 170
   3-7: Geometric Visualization 175
   3-8: Similarity 179
   3-9: Transformations 182
Sample Test Questions 184
   Geometry and Measurement Questions 184
   Geometry and Measurement Key 198

Section 4: Data Analysis, Statistics, and Probability *199*
    4-1: Data Interpretation *199*
    4-2: Descriptive Statistics *205*
    4-3: Probability *209*
Sample Test Questions *217*
    Data Analysis, Statistics and Probability Questions *217*
    Data Analysis, Statistics, and Probability Key *226*
Section 5: Logic, Logarithims & Exponents, Unit Conversions and Interest *227*
    5-1: Logic *227*
    5-2: Logarithms and Exponents *231*
    5-3: Unit Conversions *233*
    5-4: Interest *244*
Sample Test Questions *250*
    Unit Conversion Questions *250*
    Interest Questions *251*
    Unit Conversion Key *252*
    Interest Key *253*
Test Taking Strategies *255*
What Your Score Means *256*
Test Preparation *256*
Legal Note *257*

Section 1: Numbers and Operations

1-1: ARITHMETIC WORD PROBLEMS

One of the most common uses of arithmetic is in simple everyday situations. Arithmetic involves the four basic operations of addition, subtraction, multiplication, and division. The three most important ways that arithmetic comes into play in word problems is through percentages, ratios, proportions, and basic distance and velocity calculations.

What is a percentage? Essentially, a percentage is a fraction or proportion out of 100. This means that any percentage can be expressed as a fraction, and fractions can all be translated to percentages. For example, 30 percent is the equivalent of $\frac{30}{100}$ or .30. Alternately, $\frac{45}{100}$ is 45 percent or .45. Below are some examples of some different ways of expressing percentages.

Example 1.1:
$$20\% = .20 = \frac{20}{100} = \frac{1}{5}$$
$$33.3\% = .333 = \frac{1}{3}$$
$$105\% = 1.05 = \frac{105}{100}$$

How to find a percentage of a number: Because percentages are simply fractions, you can multiply a number by the percentage to find that percentage of the number. For example, to find 30 percent of 20, you would simply multiply 20 by 30 percent (or .30 or 30 ÷ 100).

Example 1.2: Brittney goes shopping for some new shoes. She has only $25.00 to spend. She finds some shoes that she really loves, and they cost $22.00. Will she be able to afford the shoes after adding the 8 percent sales tax?

Solution: First you have to determine what the sales tax will be. In this case it is the cost of the shoes which is 22 dollars, multiplied by the percentage sales tax of 8. Therefore, the sales tax on the shoes will be $22.00(.08) = $1.76. Based on this sales tax computation, the total cost of the shoes will be $22.00 + $1.76 = $23.76, so Brittney will have enough money to buy the shoes.

Example 1.3: Jonathan currently owns a truck which has the strength to tow up to 40,000 pounds. However, the truck doesn't get very good gas mileage so he is purchasing a smaller truck. If he purchases a truck that has 85% of the towing strength as his current truck, will he still be able to tow his 35,000 pound trailer?

Solution: If the new truck will have 85% of the towing strength as the current truck, it will be able to tow 40,000(.85) = 34,000 pounds. Jonathan's trailer weighs 35,000 pounds. Therefore, the new truck will NOT be strong enough to tow his trailer.

How to find a number from a percentage: In some cases you will be required to find a total number based on a fractional or percentage value that you are given. In this case the process is simply the opposite as before. There are two different ways to think of this process. First, you can simply divide by the percentage that you have been given. Second, you can set up an equation and solve for the original value.

Example 1.4: The sales tax on a new shirt is 43 cents. If the sales tax is 9% then what is the original cost of the shirt?

Solution 1: The first option is to simply divide the fractional total of 43 cents by the percentage. This yields that the cost of the shirt is .43/.09 = $4.78.

Solution 2: You can also find this solution by writing out an equation for the solution. In the equation below, x represents the original total of the shirt. It is multiplied by the 9% tax and set equal to 43 cents. This is because we know from the problem that the 9% tax on the total is 43 cents. From here, you simply solve for x.

$x(.09) = .43$

$x = 4.78$

How to find percent increase/decrease: Another important element of working with percentages is finding percentage change. When solving for percent change it is important to remember that the comparison is always to the original value, not the new value. To find the percent change you simply divide the amount changed by the original value. In other words the formula when working with percent change is % change = change / original.

Example 1.5: A clearance item has been marked down in price from its original sales price of 35 dollars to 20 dollars. By what percent has the price decreased?

Solution:

$$\% \text{ change} = \frac{\text{price change}}{\text{original price}}$$

$$\% \text{ change} = \frac{\$15}{\$35}$$

% change = 43%

So the price decreased by 43%

Example 1.6: A new car is increased $2,500 from its original sales price. This represents a price increase of 15%. What was the original price of the car, and what is its new price?

Solution:

$$\% \text{ change} = \frac{\text{price change}}{\text{original price}}$$

$$15\% = \frac{2500}{\text{original price}}$$

$$\text{original price} = \frac{2500}{.15}$$

original price = 16,667

So the original price of the car was $16,667

Because we know that its price was increased by $2,500, the current price of the car must be $19,167.

TRY IT YOURSELF:

Question: The sales tax on a cart full of groceries comes to $5.34. The total price that the customer had to pay was $138.84. What was the percentage sales tax on the groceries?

Answer: 4%.

Question: A car starts out going 30 mph down the road. If the car reduces its speed to 20 mph, by what percent has its speed changed?

Answer: 33%.

Question: A hot air balloon is being filled with air. At one point in time the balloon has 440 square feet of air inside of it. When it is this full, it is 65% of the way finished being filled. What amount (in square feet) remains to be filled?

Answer: 237 square feet.

How to express ratios/proportions: Ratios or proportions are used to express the amount of one type of object relative to another. Ratios are typically described in terms of one element relative to the amount of another element (the number of boys to girls, cats to dogs, or red jelly beans to green jelly beans for example). On the other hand, proportions are either used to compare the amount of one element to a total amount (for example, the amount of boys in a class, green jelly beans in a bag, or cats in a pet store), or to express things which occur at a consistent rate (such as miles per hour). There are three different ways to express proportions or ratios. They can be expressed as fractions, using a colon, or using the word "to."

Example 1.7: There are 12 boys and 8 girls in a class. Express the ratio of boys to girls in three different ways.

Solution: To express the ratio of boys to girls as a fraction, simply place the number of boys in the numerator, and the number of girls in the denominator. The ratio is

$$\frac{\# \text{ boys}}{\# \text{ girls}} = \frac{12}{8} = \frac{3}{2}$$

To express the ratio of boys to girls using a colon, simply place the number of boys on the left of the colon, and the number of girls on the right of the colon. You can simplify the ratio, or leave it as is. The ratio of boys to girls is

\# of boys: \# of girls = 12:8 = 3:2

To express the ratio of boys to girls using the word "to," simply place the number of boys before the word to, and the number of girls after. Again, this proportion can be simplified or left as is. The ratio is

12 to 8
OR
3 to 2

Example 1.8: It takes 12 hours to paint 3.5 walls. Express the relationship of walls per hours using the three different methods of expressing a proportion.

Solution: Whereas the previous example asked for the ratio to be expressed three different ways, this example uses a proportion. The number of walls painted is proportional, or relative to, the amount of time spent painting. Expressed as a fraction, this would be 3.5 ÷ 12 (because we are expressing "walls per hours," walls will be on the top of the fraction). However, 3.5 is a decimal and cannot be left in the fraction. Therefore, we must simplify it as follows.

$$\frac{3.5}{12} = \frac{\frac{7}{2}}{12} = \frac{7}{24}$$

This relationship can also be expressed using a colon. To do this, simply place the number of walls (the first element in the relationship) before the colon, and the number of hours (the second element in the relationship) after the colon. Then simplify.

#walls : #hours = 3.5:12 = 7:24

To express the relationship using the word "to" simply place the number of walls (the first element in the relationship) before the word "to" and the number of hours (the second element in the relationship) after the word "to." Then simplify. You can also think of this as simply replacing the colon in the alternate method of expressing the relationship with the word to.

#walls to #hours = 3.5 to 12 = 7 to 24
OR
7:24 = 7 to 24

Solving problems with ratios/proportions: When solving problems using proportions and ratios, the easiest thing to do is to put the ratios in fractional form and set the two proportions equal to each other. Then you can simply solve for the value that you are missing.

Example 1.9: Thomas can paint a wall in 7 hours. How long will it take Thomas to finish 2 ½ walls?

Solution: First we will express both situations using a fraction. If Thomas can paint a wall in 7 hours, he paints at a rate of $\frac{1 \text{ wall}}{7 \text{ hours}} = \frac{1}{7}$. The alternate ratio that we are trying to find is the number of hours to finish 2 ½ walls. The unknown in this situation will be the number of hours it takes, so we will express this as h. The ratio here will be $\frac{\text{\# walls}}{\text{\# hours}} = \frac{2.5}{h} = \frac{5}{2h}$. From here we must simply set the two ratios equal to each other and solve for the unknown h.

$$\frac{1}{7} = \frac{5}{2h}$$
$$2h = 35$$
$$h = 17.5$$

So it will take Thomas 17.5 hours to finish 2 ½ walls.

Example 1.10: Jeremy can paint 3 walls in 4 hours, Ryan can paint 4 walls in 3 hours, and Kody can paint 2 walls in 3 hours. If the three are working together, how long will it take them to paint the 20 walls in a particular house?

Solution: First we must express each of the different elements as fractions.

Jeremy: $\frac{3}{4}$

Ryan: $\frac{4}{3}$

Kody: $\frac{2}{3}$

Total: $\frac{20}{h}$

Now, we must simply set the sum of the three workers equal to the total amount of work that has to be done (this represents their combined work on the walls).

$$\frac{3}{4} + \frac{4}{3} + \frac{2}{3} = \frac{20}{h}$$
$$\frac{11}{4} = \frac{20}{h}$$
$$11h = 80$$
$$h = 7.3$$

Therefore, it would take Jeremy, Ryan, and Kody 7.3 hours to completely paint the house.

TRY IT YOURSELF:

Question: Jocelyn has a box full of toy blocks. The box contains 7 blue blocks, 5 yellow blocks, and 13 red blocks. Express the ratio of blue blocks to red blocks in three different ways.

Answer: $\frac{7}{13}$, 7:13, 7 to 13

Question: Jocelyn has a box full of toy blocks. The box contains 7 blue blocks, 5 yellow blocks, and 13 red blocks. Express the proportion of blocks that are yellow in three different ways.

Answer: $\frac{1}{5}$, 1:5, 1 to 5

Question: Megan's kindergarten class has a girl to boy ratio of 4:2. If there are 24 students in her class, what is the proportion of boys?

Answer: $\frac{1}{3}$, 1:3, 1 to 3

Question: Jennifer can vacuum 7 rooms in 2 hours. Assuming that all of the rooms take the same amount of time, how long would it take her to completely vacuum a house with 10 rooms?

Answer: 2.9 hours

Question: Kyle can paint 3 walls in 8 hours, Mark can paint 9 walls in 8 hours, and Tim can paint 3 walls in 4 hours. Which of the three is most efficient, and how long would it take the three of them to paint 35 walls if they were all working together?

Answer: Mark is the most efficient painter. It would take all three 15.6 hours to paint 35 walls.

How do you find average speed? Average speed is the quantity found by dividing distance by time. In other words,

$$\text{Average speed} = \frac{\text{total distance}}{\text{total time}}$$

Average speed can be found in two circumstances. The easiest case scenario is when you are given only two quantities: time and distance. In this case you simply plug the two values into the equation.

Example 1.11: A car starts on the freeway and goes 80 miles in 45 minutes. What was the car's average speed?

Solution:
$$\text{Average speed} = \frac{\text{total distance}}{\text{total time}} = \frac{80}{45} = 1.78 \text{ miles per minute} = 107 \text{ mph}$$

The more difficult situation which arises when dealing with average speed is when the speed or directions is inconsistent over time. In this case you must factor each stage into the equation individually to find the correct answer.

Example 1.12: A car begins at a starting point traveling 40 miles per hour for 3 hours. It then increases its speed for the last 2 hours, instead going 65 miles per hour. What was the car's average speed over the whole trip?

Solution: The average speed equation requires two different quantities: distance and time. Therefore, in order to find the average speed, first find the distance that the car traveled at each stage of the process.

First 3 hours: (40 mph)(3 hours)=120 miles
Final 2 hours: (65 mph)(2 hours)=130 miles

Now, simply plug the total values into the average speed equation to find the average speed for the whole trip.

$$\frac{120+130}{3+2} = \frac{250}{5} = 50 \text{ mph}$$

Note: It is essential that you calculate each stage of the trip individually. The average speed for the whole trip is 50 mph. This is different than simply averaging the two speeds, which gives an incorrect average speed of $(40+65) \div 2 = 52.5$

Example 1.13: Sally and Jane live 50 miles apart. They decide to meet each other for lunch at 1:00 PM. Sally leaves her home at noon at travels 20 miles. If the two together had an average speed of 30 mph, how fast must Jane have driven and at what time must she have left her house?

Solution: First consider the average speed equation and plug in the values that are given in the problem. From the problem, it can be determined that

Sally's distance = 20 miles
Sally's time = 1 hour
Jane's distance = (50 – 20) = 30 miles
Jane's time = ?

$$\text{Average speed} = \frac{\text{Jane distance} + \text{Sally distance}}{\text{Jane time} + \text{Sally time}}$$

$$30 = \frac{30 + 20}{x + 1}$$

$$30(x+1) = 50$$

$$30x = 20$$

$x = .67$ hours or 40 minutes

Therefore, Jane must have driven for .67 hours or 40 minutes. In order to travel 30 miles in 40 minutes, Jane must have driven at a speed of

$$\text{speed} = \frac{\text{distance}}{\text{time}}$$

$$\text{speed} = \frac{30 \text{ mi.}}{.67 \text{ hrs}} = 45 mph$$

Also, she must have left her house at 12:20 p.m.

How do you solve problems with rates? The best way to solve problems that involve rates, or most word problems in general, is to write an equation that will describe the situation you are dealing with. From there it is a simple matter of using the information that you have been given to find the solution the question asks for.

Example 1.14: Write an equation to describe the amount of water to have emptied out of a bucket if the bucket empties at a rate of 20 cm^3 of water per minute. Using the equation, determine how much water will have emptied out of the bucket after 7 minutes.

Solution: First, pick variables that will describe each of the elements of the equation. Such as:

e = amount of water to have emptied
r = rate at which water empties
m = minutes that have passed

The equation describing the situation will be a simple rate multiplied by time equation:

$e = (r)(m)$ Note: $r = 20$ is given in the question
$e = 20m$

Now that the equation has been written, simply plug in $m = 7$ to determine how much water has emptied after 7 minutes.

$e = 20(7) = 140$ cm^3

Example 1.15: John and Bill live 120 miles apart. They are having a business meeting and have agreed that they will both drive part of the way and meet somewhere in the middle. If John leaves his home at 6 AM and travels at a speed of 40 mph and Bill leaves his home at 6 AM and travels a speed of 50 mph at what point and time will they meet? Assume that you are measuring in miles from John's home.

Solution: First, create equations to describe John's and Bill's traveling distance.

We know that distance = speed(time), therefore

John's distance = $40t$
Bill's distance = $50t$
Total distance = 120

Note: The same variable t can be used to describe the traveling time of both Bill and John because they will be traveling for the same amount of time (they left at the same time, and will stop traveling at the same time when they meet each other).

Now we can combine each of these elements into a single equation to describe the situation.

John's distance + Bill's distance = Total distance
$40t + 50t = 120$

Using this equation, solve for the time that each was traveling

$40t + 50t = 120$
$90t = 120$
$t = 1.33$ hours

Now that we know how long the two were traveling for, we can use the equation for John's traveling distance to determine how far each traveled:

John's distance = $40t$
John's distance = $40(1.33) = 53$ miles

Therefore, they met 53 miles from John's home at 7:20 AM.

How to solve other word problems: The most important thing to remember when solving word problems is to write an equation that describes the situation. Then simply solve for the quantity that is unknown in the equation.

TRY IT YOURSELF:

Question: Melissa leaves her home traveling 20 miles per hour until reaching the freeway 15 minutes from her home. She then increases her speed for 30 minutes on the freeway, traveling 65 miles per hour. Finally, she reaches her work after another 20 minutes of driving 40 miles per hour. What is her average speed?

Answer: 47 miles per hour

Question: Tasha borrows money from her cousin and agrees that she will pay back the original sum, plus one seventh in interest and $30 as a 'thank you.' If she paid him $200, what was the amount that she borrowed?

Answer: $148.75

Question: A hot air balloon requires 750 cubic feet of air to be completely filled. A machine can pump air into the balloon at a rate of 20 ft^3/min. However, air is also leaking out of the top of the balloon at a rate of 5 ft^3/min as it fills. How long will it take the balloon to fill?

Answer: 50 minutes

1-2: PROPERTIES OF INTEGERS AND RATIONAL NUMBERS

What is the real number system? The real number system consists of many different types of numbers including:

- Natural numbers
- Whole numbers
- Integers
- Rational numbers
- Irrational numbers

Natural Numbers can best be described as all whole numbers (i.e., numbers without fractions or decimals) 1 and greater. In other words, natural numbers can be defined as the set {1, 2, 3, 4, 5,…}.

Whole Numbers include all natural numbers (so all non-decimal numbers greater than one) but also includes 0. In other words, whole numbers can be defined as the set {0, 1,

2, 3, 4, 5,…}. Another way to think about the relationship between natural numbers and whole numbers is that natural numbers are a subset of whole numbers.

Integers include all whole numbers (and, by extension, all natural numbers), but with the addition of all negative whole numbers as well. In other words, integers are any numbers that can be expressed without a decimal or fraction whether they are positive or negative. Integers can be defined as the set {…, –4, –3, –2, –1, 0, 1, 2, 3, 4,…}. Just like natural numbers are a subset of whole numbers, natural numbers and whole numbers are each subsets of integers.

In addition to being able to identify whether or not a number is an integer, it is important to also understand some different classifications of integers. For example, consecutive integers, odd integers, even integers, prime numbers, and digits.

Consecutive Integers: Consecutive integers, as the name implies, are integers that appear consecutively. In other words, consecutive integers appear sequentially on the number line.

> Example 2.1: The following numbers are consecutive integers
>
> 2, 3, 4, 5
> 24, 25, 26, 27
> 101, 102, 103, 104
> Etc.
>
> Example 2.2: The following are NOT consecutive integers
>
> 2, 4, 6, 8
> 1, 3, 4, 8, 9
> 1, 2, 3, 5, 8, 13
> Etc.

Odd Integers: There are a few different ways that odd integers can be described. Firstly, odd integers are any integer $2k + 1$, where k is an integer. What this is essentially saying is that any number multiplied by 2, plus 1 is odd. This means that odd integers are never divisible by two. Odd integers are described by the set {… 1, 3, 5, 7, 9, …}.

> Example 2.3: Determine whether 10 is an odd integer.
>
> Solution 1: If 10 is an odd integer, the formula $2k + 1$ will result in an integer value for k when set equal to 10.
>
> $2k + 1 = 10$
> $k = 4.5$

4.5 is NOT an integer, therefore 10 cannot be an odd integer.

Solution 2: If 10 is an odd integer it will not be divisible by 2. 10 ÷ 2 = 5; therefore, 10 is not an odd integer.

Even Integers: Even integers are essentially any integers that aren't odd. They can also be thought of as the "counterpart" to the odd integers set. You will notice that odd integers start at one and skip every other integer. All of the integers that are skipped are even integers. Even integers are described by the formula $2k$, where k is an integer. In other words, even integers will always be divisible by two. Even integers are described by the set {… 0, 2, 4, 6, 8, …}. Note: "0" is an even integer.

Example 2.4: Determine whether 22 is an even integer.

Solution: If 22 is an even integer, the formula $2k$ will yield an integer value for k when set equal to 22.

$2k = 22$
$k = 11$

11 IS an integer, therefore 22 must be an even integer.

Prime Numbers: A prime number is a number greater than 1 that is only divisible by itself and 1. When we say "divisible" we mean that the answer will come out to be an integer (i.e., it will NOT have a decimal or fractional value). Prime numbers are so called because they are in their simplest form, and can't be broken down any farther.

Examples of Prime Numbers: 2, 3, 5, 7, 11, 13, 17, …

Common Mistakes: Remember that even numbers can NEVER be prime with the exception of the number 2. This is because every other even number must, by definition, be divisible by two. A second common mistake is that one is NOT considered to be a prime number.

Composite Numbers: A composite number is essentially the counterpart to a prime number. A composite number is any number that is NOT prime. This means that composite numbers are always divisible by at least one number other than itself and one.

Example 2.5: Determine whether 15 is a prime number or a composite number.

Solution: For 15 to be a composite number it must have factors (numbers that it is divisible by) other than one and itself. Therefore, to determine whether 15 is prime or composite, we must list all of its factors. The factors of 15 are:

$1 \times 15 = 15$ 1, 15
$3 \times 5 = 15$ 3, 5

Therefore, 15 is a composite number.

Additional Examples of Composite Numbers: 4, 6, 8, 10, 12, 15, 16 …

<u>Digits</u>: The term "digits" is often used when referring to integers. The number of digits in an integer basically refers to the number of decimal places that it takes up, or the number of integers that must be used to express it. For example single-digit integers are those integers that can be represented using a single integer. Single-digit integers are the numbers 0-9. However, the number 10 requires two digits to be expressed, 1 and 0. Further, the number 1400 requires four digits to be expressed (1, 4, and two 0's). In cases such as these the final digit in the number is referred to as the units digit, or one's digit.

Example 2.6: Determine the units digit of the following numbers:

Number	Units digit
1	1
13	3
135	5
16	6
18	8

TRY IT YOURSELF:

Question: Identify all of the composite numbers in the set {−6, −1, 0, 5, 6, 8}

    Answer: {−6, 6, 8}

Question: Identify at least two prime numbers greater than 15

    Answer: Many examples exist, a few of which are 17, 19, 23, 29, 31, etc.

Question: Identify the relationships among the following sets of numbers: whole numbers, even numbers, integers, odd numbers, rational numbers.

    Answer: Whole numbers, even numbers, odd numbers and integers are all subsets of rational numbers. Whole numbers, odd numbers, and even numbers are subsets of rational numbers. Odd numbers and even numbers are disjoint sets, and their union is the set of integers.

Rational numbers are numbers that can be expressed as a fraction or decimal. This includes all natural, numbers, whole numbers, and integers. That is, where natural numbers and whole numbers are a subset of integers, integers, whole numbers, and natural numbers are each subsets of the rational numbers category.

The fraction describing a rational number can be proper or improper (greater than one) and positive or negative. Also, remember that whole numbers CAN be expressed as fractions (by putting them over 1) so they are rational.

Because there exists an infinite number of fractions between any two given whole numbers, the set of rational numbers is essentially limitless. However, some examples of rational numbers include:

$$\frac{3}{4}, -\frac{3}{4}, \frac{11}{2}, \frac{6}{1}, 3.114, 7.8, \ldots$$

Irrational numbers are numbers that can't be expressed as a fraction. Irrational numbers exist outside the regular number system because they are not related to any other group of numbers. In other words, whereas rational numbers, integers, whole numbers, and natural numbers are subsets of each other, irrational numbers exist as a separate group. Irrational numbers include numbers with decimals that continue on forever. If a number is not rational then it is irrational.

The two most common examples of irrational numbers are π and e (which is commonly used in calculating interest).

$\pi = 3.14159265358979\ldots$
$e = 2.71828182845904523\ldots$

It can be extremely difficult to prove definitively whether or not a number is actually irrational. This is because by definition it is a decimal which goes on infinitely (which can't be reached). However, some general tips for determining whether a number is rational or irrational follow.

1. Square roots, cube roots, fourth roots, etc. will all result in irrational numbers UNLESS they come out perfectly and evenly.

   Rational: $\sqrt{169} = 13, \sqrt[3]{8} = 2$
   Irrational: $\sqrt{5} = 2.236067977499\ldots$

2. A decimal that goes on indefinitely will be rational if it repeats (if a decimal is a repeating decimal then it CAN be expressed as a fraction).

$$\text{Rational: } .\overline{97} = \frac{97}{99}, .\overline{06589} = \frac{6589}{99999}, .01010101... = \frac{1}{99}$$

$$\text{Irrational: } \frac{\pi}{6}, \pi^2, \pi + e$$

3. A whole number, integer, natural number, etc. will always be rational.

TRY IT YOURSELF:

Question: Is 3.121212… Rational or Irrational?

    Answer: Rational

Question: Is $\sqrt[5]{32}$ Rational or Irrational?

    Answer: Rational

Question: Is $\sqrt[4]{156}$ Rational or Irrational?

    Answer: Irrational

1-3: SETS

What is a "set"? A set is a collection of elements. Elements can be any type of number. A finite set has a specific number of elements while an infinite set as an unlimited number of elements.

What are examples of sets? Elements of a set are placed within braces { } and each element is separated by a comma.

    Example of a finite set: $A = \{3,4,5,6,7,8\}$
    This is a finite set because it has a specific number of elements. There are six elements in this set.

    Example of an infinite set: $W = \{0,1,2,3,4,...\}$
    The "…" denotes that the elements in the set continue on infinitely.
    In this case, the set W represents all the Whole numbers.

What notation do you use with sets?
Set notation uses symbols for each definition. Following is a list of relationships between sets and their symbols.

Empty set: An empty set is also referred to as a null set. An empty set does NOT have any elements in it and is represented by {} or ∅.

>Common Mistake: It may be tempting to identify {0} as an empty set. However, {0} is not an empty set because it contains one element which is the number 0.

Union of two sets: A union of two sets means that you combine the elements of one set with the elements of the other set to create one, larger set. A union of two sets is denoted by ∪.

>Example of a union: Let's say you have two sets, set A and set B.
>$A = \{1,2,3,4\}$ and $B = \{2,4,6,8\}$
>$A \cup B = \{1,2,3,4,6,8\}$
>
>Note: You don't write the numbers A and B have in common twice. For example, both A and B had "2" and "4" in common. You only write "2" and "4" ONCE in the union of sets A and B.

Intersection of two sets: An intersection of two sets means that you only write the elements that are common to both sets. An intersection of two sets is denoted by ∪.

>Example of an Intersection: Let's say you have two sets, set C and set D.
>$C = \{2,3,4,5,6,7,8\}$ and $D = \{6,7,8,9\}$.
>
>$C \cup D = \{6,7,8\}$ because these are the only numbers that are in both set C and set D.
>Note: What if the two sets have no elements in common? For example, what if you had $A = \{1,3,5\}$ and $B = \{2,4,6,8\}$? They don't have any numbers in common. In this case, the two sets are disjoint and you write their intersection as the empty set {}.

Subset: The ⊂ symbol is used to denote a subset. $A \subset B$ means that A is a subset of B.

>Example of a Subset: $A = \{1,2,3\}$ and $B = \{1,2,3,4,5,6\}$
>Every number in set A is in set B therefore, A is a subset of B, $A \subset B$.
>
>However, B is NOT a subset of A. Why not? $B \not\subset A$ because set B has more elements than set A and therefore can't be a subset of set A.

Disjoint sets: Disjoint sets are sets which have none of the same numbers. In other words, disjoint sets are sets which result in an empty set when intersected.

Example of disjoint sets:
$A = \{2,4,6\}$ and $B = \{1,3,5\}$
Therefore $A \cap B = \{\}$

Equivalent Sets: Equivalent sets are sets which have all of the same numbers. In other words, if two sets are equivalent, then the intersection of the two sets is equal to each of the sets.

Example of equivalent sets:
$A = \{1,14,21\}$ and $B = \{1,14,21\}$
Therefore $A \cap B = \{1,14,21\}$

Example 3.1: Determine the set resulting from an intersection of set A and B

$A = \{2,3,4,5,6,7,8,9\}$
$B = \{0,2,4,6,8\}$

Answer: An intersection of two sets is the elements that the two sets have in common. That is, where they "intersect." In this case the elements that the two have in common are 2, 4, 6, and 8. Therefore,

$A \cap B = \{2,4,6,8\}$

Example 3.2: The union of two sets is as follows: $C \cup D = \{\}$. What can you determine about the two sets?

Answer: A union is created by combining all of the elements in either of the sets (this includes those that they have in common and those which they do not). However, in this problem, the union of sets C and D results in an empty set. For this to happen both of the sets must have been empty sets as well. Therefore, you can determine that

$C = \{\}$
$D = \{\}$

Example 3.3: Describe the most logical relationship between set C and sets A and B if

$A = \{13,16,23,45,60,81\}$
$B = \{7,13,15,44,60,71\}$
$C = \{13,60\}$

Answer: *A* union describes the set resulting from compiling all of the elements in two sets. If set *C* were the union of *A* and *B* it would have to additionally contain the elements 7, 15, 16, 23, 44, 45, 71, and 81. Therefore, *C* cannot be the union of *A* and *B*.

An intersection describes the set resulting from compiling the common numbers between two sets. This describes set *C*, so this is the most logical relationship between the three sets.

TRY IT YOURSELF:

Question: Determine $A \cup B$ if $A = \{1,2,3,4,5,6\}$ and $B = \{2,4,6,8\}$

Solution: $\{1,2,3,4,5,6,8\}$

Question: Determine $A \cup B$ if $A = \{1,2,3,4,5,6\}$ and $B = \{2,4,6,8\}$

Solution: $\{2,4,6\}$

Question: If $A \cup B = \{2,6,7,8,16,29,33,34\}$ and $A = \{2,6,6,7,29\}$, find *B*.

Solution: $B = \{8,16,33,34\}$. Note: the set *B* could also contain multiples of any of these elements, and could include any of the elements also found in set *A*. However, it must at the very least contain the elements indicated.

1-4: COUNTING TECHNIQUES

When most people think of counting, the first thing that comes to mind is sitting in a kindergarten class and learning their numbers. However, there is really much more to counting than this. In math, there is always a purpose to counting, typically to find a number of outcomes or situations, but also in terms of sequences and series. Counting can involve summing different figures, using equations, and other techniques. Some basic vocabulary terms associated with counting are the addition principle, tree diagrams (multiplication rule/principle), factorials, permutations, and combinations.

Addition principle: The addition principle states that if there are *x* options in one group, and *y* options in a second group, then the total number of options between the two groups is $x + y$. Of course, this requires that the groups be disjoint (i.e., that no elements are the same between the groups). The addition principle is a simple way to save yourself from having to count options individually in situations where you must determine the number of options with two disjoint sets.

Example 4.1: Ashley has thirteen different shirts and twenty different pairs of pants. Assuming that they are all mixed together in the same drawer, how many items of clothing are in the drawer?

Solution: In this case the addition principle can be used with the shirts representing group x and the pants representing group y. Based on the information given in the problem we can determine that

$x = 13$
$y = 20$

Therefore, the total number of clothing items is

$x + y = 13 + 20 = 33$

Example 4.2: Thomas has 13 tennis balls, 20 baseballs, 32 golf balls, and 2 ping-pong balls. How many balls does he have total?

Solution: This can be answered using the addition principle. Group x is represented by the number of tennis balls, group y by the number of baseballs, z represents the number of golf balls and p can represent the number of ping-pong balls. Based on the information in the equation we can determine that

$x = 13$
$y = 20$
$z = 32$
$p = 2$

Therefore, the total number of balls owned by Thomas is

$x + y + z + p = 13 + 20 + 32 + 2 = 67$

A second way to think of this problem is as a simple union of sets, but instead of simply joining the two sets you are determining the number of elements between the two sets. Again, remember that the addition principle begins by assuming that the two sets are disjoint.

Example 4.3: Sally is combining a bunch of different jars of coins that she found lying around her house. She combines three different jars which have only pennies in them. After she combines the jars she has $150.33. She realizes that one of the jars was actually her sister's, but she doesn't know how much money was in it. She knows that the two jars of hers held $33.44 and $76.90 respectively. How many pennies were in her sister's jar?

Solution: This problem can be solved using the addition principle. First, consider that each of the jars is its own "set" of pennies. We will call them sets A, B, and C respectively. Combining each of the jars is the equivalent of the union of sets A, B, and C, with the resulting total being a new set, D. (In other words, $D = A \cup B \cup C$.) Because no penny can be in multiple jars at once, we know that the three sets are all disjoint. Therefore, the addition principle can be used. Based on the information in the problem we can determine that

A held 3344 pennies
B held 7690 pennies
D held 15033 pennies

Therefore, using the addition principle we know that C must have held 3999 pennies.

The addition principle is a very simple way of determining the number of possible options when only one option is being chosen, and in no particular order. Other forms of counting require more complex counting techniques.

TRY IT YOURSELF:

Question: Jerika has 20 blue poker chips and 20 red poker chips. When she mixes the two colors of poker chips together how many poker chips will she have?

Answer: 40

Question: Alex has three bags of letters. The first bag has 3 letters, the second bag has 12 letters, and the third bag has 9 letters. Assuming no letter appears twice, how many different letters could be chosen out of the bags?

Answer: 24

Tree diagrams: Whereas the addition principle applies only when there is a single step involved, tree diagrams are used when there is more than one step involved in a process. Tree diagrams are so named because they appear as a sideways opening tree, and diagram all of the possible options and sequences of options that can occur. Tree diagrams work in situations where one and only one option is chosen at each step. For example, you walk into a sandwich shop and you are given a number of different options to construct your own sandwich. First, there are three different types of bread (white, wheat, and flatbread). Second, there are two different types of meat (turkey and ham). And lastly there are three different condiment options (mayo, mustard, and ranch). For a tree diagram to be used, you must choose one option from each group, and you cannot choose more than one.

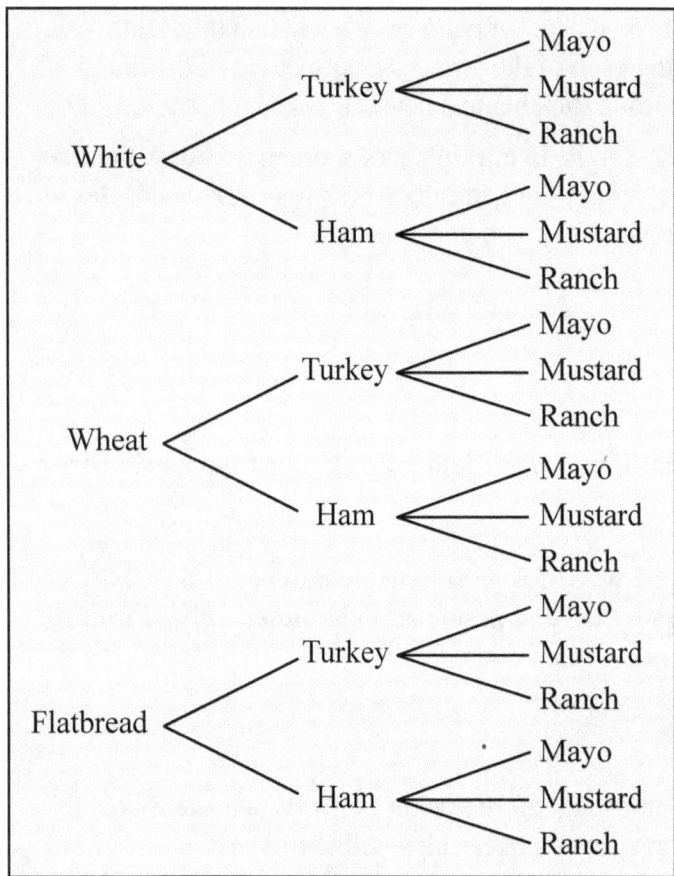

As you can see, it could become very tedious and frustrating to count out each individual pathway that could be taken regarding sandwich types at the shop. The solution is the multiplication principle, or the fundamental counting principle.

Tree diagrams make use of the multiplication principle. The multiplication principle states that when a task involves multiple steps, the total number of ways in which the task can be completed can be determined by multiplying the number of possibilities at each step.

For example, in the case of the sandwich shop there are three options for bread, two options for meat, and three options for condiments. Therefore, the total number of available sandwich options is

(3)(2)(3) = 18

That there are 18 possible options can be verified by listing out each of the options individually; however, it will typically be much more beneficial for you to simply multiply the number of options when the conditions for the multiplication principle are met.

Example 4.4: Jonathan must decide what to wear to a friend's birthday party. He must choose a shirt, a pair of pants, and a pair of shoes. He has narrowed it down to a few options. For shirts he must choose between a blue shirt and a green shirt. For pants he must choose between jeans and a pair of shorts. For shoes he must choose between flip flops and sneakers. How many different outfit options does he have?

There are two different ways of answering this question:

Solution 1: The first way to solve this problem is by creating a tree diagram and mapping out the various options individually. The tree diagram is shown below.

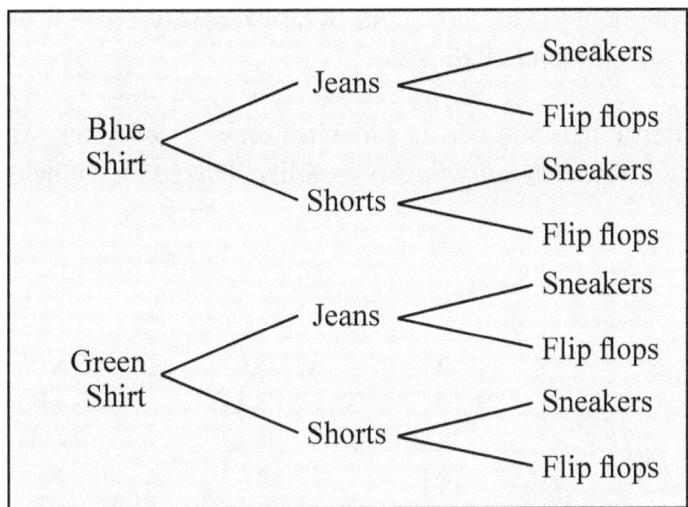

Based on the tree diagram, the available options are:

Blue shirt – jeans – sneakers
Blue shirt – jeans – flip flops
Blue shirt – shorts – sneakers
Blue shirt – shorts – flip flops
Green shirt – jeans – sneakers
Green shirt – jeans – flip flops
Green shirt – shorts – sneakers
Green shirt – shorts – flip flops

Therefore, there are 8 different outfit options.

Solution 2: The second way to solve this problem is using the multiplication principles, and multiplying the number of options at each step. According to the multiplication principles, the number of outfit options is

(2 shirts)(2 pants)(2 shoes) = 8 outfits

Example 4.5: Wendy is picking letters out of hats. She has three different hats. The first hat contains the letters c, b, and s. The second hat contains the letters a and e. The third hat contains the letters t, d, and b. (Notice that "b" appears in both the first and third hats. The sets of letters do NOT have to be completely disjoint when doing tree diagrams, as they do with the addition principle.) Determine the number of letter combinations that exist if Wendy picks a letter first from hat one, then hat two, then hat three.

This problem can be solved in two different ways; using the multiplication principle and using a tree diagram.

Solution 1: The first way to solve this problem is by creating a tree diagram and determining each individual possibility. This is shown below.

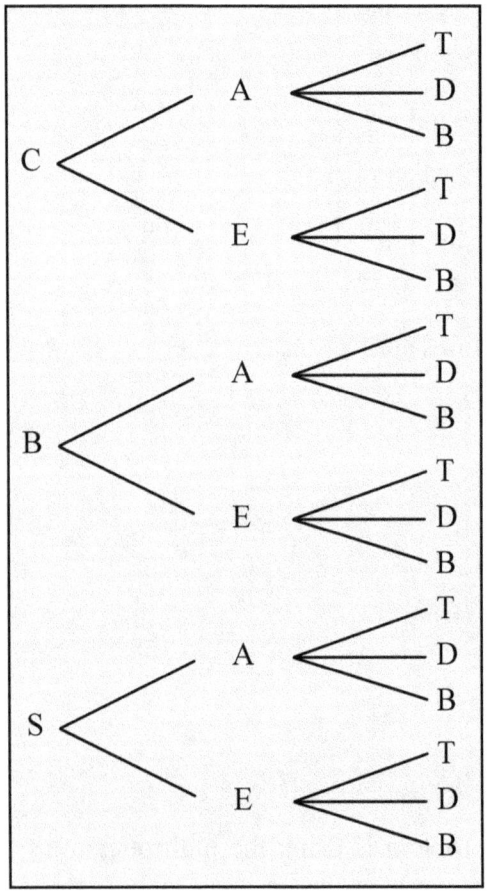

Based on the tree diagram, the possible letter combinations are:

CAT	BAT	SAT
CAD	BAD	SAD
CAB	BAB	SAB
CET	BET	SET
CED	BED	SED
CEB	BEB	SEB

Therefore, there are 18 letter combinations.

Solution 2: The second way to solve this problem is by applying the multiplication principle.

Possibilities = (3 letters in hat one)(2 letters in hat two)(3 letters in hat three) = 18 letter combinations.

TRY IT YOURSELF:

Question: A custom jewelry shop offers a simple three step process for designing your own jewelry shop. First you select one of 5 different metals. Then you select one of 14 different patterns. How many different jewelry combinations are possible?

Answer: 70

Question: A cleaning-supply store custom builds mops to customer specifications. Customers first select one of their 3 different handle options (wood, plastic, or metal), and then select one of their two end options (rag style or sponge style). Draw a tree diagram to outline the available options.

Answer:

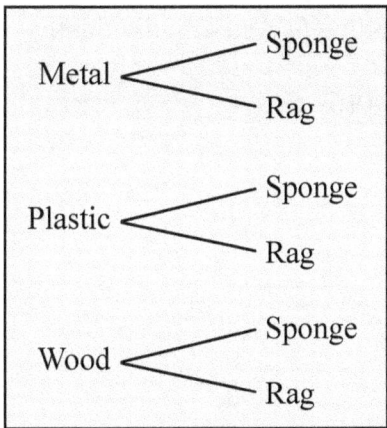

Question: Jenna has 7 different shirts, 4 different pairs of jeans, 3 different necklaces, 9 different pairs of shoes, and is debating between 2 hairstyles. How many different ways can she get ready?

Answer: 1512

Factorials: The third counting technique to be familiar with are factorials. Factorials are fairly straightforward because they can really only be done one way. Essentially, a factorial is just a compact way of expressing the multiplication of consecutive integers (remember that consecutive integers are in sequence with each other).

A factorial is denoted by the ! symbol, and is defined as $n! = n(n-1)(n-2)...(1)$ where n is any natural number. In other words, factorials can only be calculated for whole numbers that are 1 and greater. The following examples show the calculation of a few common factorials.

Example 4.6: Find 4!

Solution: Using the formula for a factorial given in the example above, we can calculate the value of 4! (said "four factorial") as

$4! = 4(4-1)(4-2)(4-3)$
$4! = 4(3)(2)(1)$
$4! = 24$

Example 4.7: Find 6!−4!

Solution: We can solve by finding 6! And 4! individually.

$6! = 6(6-1)(6-2)(6-3)(6-4)(6-5)$
$6! = 6(5)(4)(3)(2)(1)$
$6! = 720$

$4! = 4(4-1)(4-2)(4-3)$
$4! = 4(3)(2)(1)$
$4! = 24$

Therefore,

$6!-4!$
$= 720 - 24$
$= 696$

It is very important that you recognize that 6!−4! DOES NOT simplify to the same as (6−4)!, and it is very important to be aware of the location of parenthesis when working with factorials. The difference between these two patterns of logic is shown below.

$6!-4!$	$(6-4)!$
$= 720 - 24$	$= (2)!$
$= 696$	$= 2(1)$
	$= 2$

There are two additional rules to be aware of when working with factorials. These two special cases are taking the factorial of zero, and multiplying numbers by factorials. The two special cases are explained below.

Zero factorial – The factorial of zero is always equal to one. In other words, $0! = 1$.

Multiplication – The second property of factorials to be familiar with is that $n(n-1)! = n!$. For example,

$6(6-1)! = 6(5!)$
$= 6(5*4*3*2*1)$
$= 6!$

Example 4.8: Evaluate 4!−3(2)!

Solution:
4!−3(2!)
= 4!−3!
= 4*3*2*1−3*2*1
= 24−6
= 18

Example 4.9: Evaluate $(7-2)!(0!)+3(2!)$

Solution:
$(7-2)!(0!)+3(2!)$
= (5!)(0!)+3!
= (120)(1)+(6)
= 126

TRY IT YOURSELF:

Question: Evaluate 7!−2!

    Answer: 5038

Question: Evaluate (8−5)!(0!)−4!(2)

    Answer: −42

Question: Evaluate 5(4)!−16

    Answer: 104

Permutations: The reason that it is important to understand the use of factorials is because they are used in the next important counting technique: permutations. A permutation is an ordered sequence of items taken from a set of distinct items <u>without replacement</u>. Stated more plainly, a permutation is a count of the number of possible arrangements of a specific set of elements. Because the arrangement is of specific elements, each element can only be used once (hence, they are taken without replacement). Furthermore, each element must be used in the arrangement.

There are two different ways to denote a permutation. They are

$$_nP_r \text{ or } P(n,r)$$

so

$$P(6,4) = {_6P_4}$$

n = number of distinct items
r = number of items in each group
Note, $r \leq n$.

The formula used in calculating permutations is

$$\frac{n!}{(n-r)!}$$

so,

$$P(6,4) = {_6P_4} = \frac{6!}{(6-4)!}$$

When you are calculating a permutation there are essentially two different cases that may arise. First, you could be making sets that use all of the available elements. For example, if you have six racers and wish to know how many different arrangements can be made for their finishing order in a race, the situation would have the following setup:

n = number of distinct items = 6 different racers
r = number of items in each group = 6 racers

In this example $n = r$ because we wish to make "sets" or arrangements which use each of the different elements. Therefore

$$P(6,6) = {_6P_6} = \frac{6!}{(6-6)!} = \frac{6!}{0!} = \frac{6!}{1} = 6! = 720$$

Note: You can see that in the special case where you have a permutation in which $n = r$, the result will simply be $n!$. In other words, an interesting property of permutations is that

$$P(n,n) = n! \text{ or } {_nP_n} = n!$$

The second situation of permutations that you could be asked to consider is when only a subset of items is being selected from the total group. For example, if you wanted to know how many ways you could arrange three letters when choosing them from a bag containing all of the letters of the alphabet. In this case $n = 26$ because of the twenty six letters in the bag and $r = 3$ because that is the size of groups that you are creating.

Example 4.10: Find the number of permutations of the numbers 2, 4, 6 taken two at a time.

Solution:

n = number of distinct items = 3
r = number of numbers in each group = 2

$$_3P_2 = \frac{3!}{(3-2)!} = \frac{3!}{1!} = 6$$

Technically, you can also find the number of permutations by listing all the possibilities. Generally this will be more time consuming, but you can see below that it results in the same answer as the formula:

2, 4   2, 6   4, 2
4, 6   6, 2   6, 4

Note: In permutations that 2,6 and 6,2 are considered to be separate results.

Example 4.11: Six friends are all competing with each other in an eating competition. How many combinations of first, second, and third place exist among the six friends?

Solution:

n = 6 different friends = 6
r = 3 awards (first, second, and third) = 3

$$_6P_3 = \frac{6!}{(6-3)!} = \frac{6!}{3!} = 120$$

TRY IT YOURSELF:

Question: A group of friends is starting a band and they want the title of their band to be an arrangement of the first letters of each of their names. The letters are A, N, Y, B, and D. How many options are there for their band name?

Answer: 120

Question: There are twenty six runners in an upcoming city-wide marathon. The city is going to give special awards to the first, second, and third place winners. How many possible combinations of first, second, and third place winners are there (Note: this question does want to know how many combinations in that specific order exist)?

Answer: 15,600

Question: $_5P_2 = ?$

Answer: 20

Combinations: The final counting strategy that this section addresses is combinations. Combinations and permutations are often confused, and it is important for you to understand the difference between them and in what situations each is used.

A combination is an unordered subset of items taken from a group of distinct items without replacement. You will notice that in the case of both combinations and permutations the items must be chosen without replacement. In other words, neither permutations nor combinations allow repeating elements. The difference between the two is that a combination counts the number of unordered subsets, whereas a permutation looks at the ordered subsets. Essentially, permutations are used when you want to the number of specific arrangements. Combinations are used when you just need to know the number of possible groups.

As with permutations, there are multiple notations used for combinations. The three notions for a combination are

$$_nC_k \text{ or } C(n,k) \text{ or } \binom{n}{k}$$

n = number of distinct items
k = number of items in each group

Note: although combinations use "k" and permutations use "r" the two are basically the same.

The formula used in calculating combinations is

$$_nC = C(n,k) = \binom{n}{k} = \frac{n!}{k!(n-k)!}$$

As you can see, the formula is quite similar to that used for permutations, but with an extra element multiplied in the denominator.

> Example 4.12: Find the number of combinations for the numbers 2, 4, and 6 taken two at a time.
>
> n = number of distinct items = 3
> k = number of numbers in each group = 2
>
> $$_3C_2 = C(3,2) = \binom{3}{2} = \frac{3!}{2!(3-2)!} = \frac{3!}{2!1!} = 3$$

As with permutations, it is also possible to simply write out all of the possible combinations. Again, however, as the numbers become more complex this becomes increasingly difficult and the formula is much more straightforward.

In this example, there are only three combinations which include:

2,4   2,6   4,6

Note: 2,4 and 4,2 are considered the same result and are NOT counted twice – this is what is meant by the fact that order doesn't matter with combinations.

Example 4.13: A magician is picking cards out of a full deck (Note: a full deck is 52 cards). If he is picking out sets of 4 cards randomly, how many different 4-card combinations could he possibly pull out?

Solution: This would be a combination and not a permutation because the question is asking about how many different 4-card combinations are possible. This means that order does not matter, and we just need to find the number of possible "groups." In this case

n = number of items = 52 cards
k = size of groups = 4 cards

Therefore,

$$_{52}C_4 = \frac{52!}{4!(52-4)!} = \frac{52!}{4!48!} = 270,725$$

TRY IT YOURSELF:

Question: A license plate manufacture gets a special order for new license plates. These license plates can use any combination of letters A-Z or numbers 0-9. However, no two license plates can have the same set of letters and numbers used (even if they are in a different order). If each license plate needs to have 7 figures, how many license plates can be made?

Answer: 8,347,680

Question: Evaluate $\binom{14}{3}$

Answer: 364

Question: A teacher needs to choose a group of three students to send to the office and pick up papers. If there are 40 students in the class, how many different groups of students could possibly be chosen?

Answer: 9,880

1-5: SEQUENCES AND SERIES

What is a sequence? A sequence of numbers is a function defined on the set of positive integers. Stated most simply, a sequence is a list of numbers. The numbers can be determined based on some specific rule or formula. The numbers in the sequence are called "terms." In terms of terminology associated with sequences, they are fairly similar to sets. However, sequences can have the same number multiple times and sequences always have an order (sets typically have a term only once and order is unimportant). A few ways to describe sequences are as:

Finite: a specific a number of terms {1, 2, 3, 4}
Infinite: the terms continue on to infinity {1, 2, 3, 4, …}
Backwards: the terms go from high to low {4, 3, 2, 1}
Alternating: the terms alternate between two values {0, 1, 0, 1, 0, 1}

Sequences can be as simple as 1, 2, 3, 4,… or can be fairly complex and difficult to work with. For example, the sequence $\frac{-1}{3}, \frac{1}{6}, \frac{-1}{11}, \frac{1}{18}...$ does in fact follow a specific rule, but this is much more difficult to pinpoint and work with. There are two important types of sequences that you should be familiar with: arithmetic sequences and geometric sequences.

Arithmetic sequences: An arithmetic sequence is a sequence of numbers that are determined by adding a constant to the preceding number. For example: 4, 8, 12, 16… is an arithmetic sequence. This particular sequence has the number four added to each additional term. The general formula that can be applied to arithmetic sequences is

$$a_n = a + d(n-1)$$

a = first number in the series
d = difference between each term
n = indicates the terms position in the sequence (e.g., $n = 1$ is the first term)

Although this formula may look complex on the surface, it is truly fairly straightforward. For example, consider a sequence where $a = 1$ and $d = 3$. The first 5 terms in the series would be

$$a_1 = 1 + 3(1-1) = 1$$
$$a_2 = 1 + 3(2-1) = 4$$
$$a_3 = 1 + 3(3-1) = 7$$
$$a_4 = 1 + 3(4-1) = 10$$
$$a_5 = 1 + 3(5-1) = 13$$

As you can see, the terms simply increase by 3 each successive term. In cases where the first term in the sequence is 0, the formula can even be simplified to $a_n = d(n-1)$.

Example 5.1: Find the 15th term in the sequence described by $a_n = 8 + 2(n-1)$.

Solution: Because we are given the formula for the sequence, we can use it to find any nth value that we need. In this case we will solve for the 15th term by substituting 15 for n.

$$a_n = 8 + 2(n-1)$$
$$a_{15} = 8 + 2(15-1)$$
$$a_{15} = 36$$

Example 5.2: Write a formula to describe the sequence 2, 5, 8, 11, 14, ...

Solution: We can see from the formula that each successive term is three higher than the previous term. Therefore, we know that $d = 3$. We can determine that $a = 2$ because 2 is the first term in the sequence. Based on this information we simply insert these values into the general formula for an arithmetic sequence and find the following formula:

$$a_n = a + d(n-1)$$
$$a_n = 2 + 3(n-1)$$

Example 5.3: Find the first five terms of the arithmetic sequence given by the formula $a_n = 3n$.

Solution:
$$a_n = 3n$$
$$a_1 = 3(1) = 3$$
$$a_2 = 3(2) = 6$$
$$a_3 = 3(3) = 9$$
$$a_4 = 3(4) = 12$$
$$a_5 = 3(5) = 15$$

Notice that in this particular case $a = d$ (the difference between terms is three, and the first term of the sequence is also three). When this occurs the formula for the sequence is simply dn.

TRY IT YOURSELF:

Question: Find the first five numbers in an arithmetic sequence which begins with the number 7 and follows the rule $d = 2$.

Answer: 7, 9, 11, 13, 15

Question: Write a formula to describe the following sequence 5, 9, 13, 17, 21, ...

Answer: $a_n = 5 + 4(n-1)$ or $a_n = 1 + 4n$

Question: Find the 18th term in the following sequence 6, 16, 26, 36, 46, ...

Answer: 176

Geometric sequences: A geometric sequence is a sequence of numbers that are obtained by multiplying a constant by the preceding number. For example, 5, 10, 20, 40, 80…is a geometric sequence. Because each successive term is simply multiplied by a constant, the ratio between terms is also a constant. In the previous example this ratio is 2:

$10 \div 5 = 2$
$20 \div 10 = 2$
$40 \div 20 = 2$
And so on…

The constant ratio between the successive terms is denoted in a geometric sequence as "r," which stands for "common ratio." As with arithmetic sequences, the first term in a sequence is denoted as "a." The general formula for a geometric sequence is $a_n = ar^n$.

To illustrate the difference between these two general formulas, consider the following equations:

$a_n = 2(2)^n$ $\qquad\qquad a_n = 2(2)^{n-1}$

In each case the ratio between numbers is 2, in addition to "a" being equal to 2. However, when you begin working out the two sequences, notice what happens:

$a_n = 2(2)^n$ $\qquad\qquad a_n = 2(2)^{n-1}$
$a_1 = 2(2)^1 = 4$ $\qquad\qquad a_1 = 2(2)^{1-1} = 2$
$a_2 = 2(2)^2 = 8$ $\qquad\qquad a_2 = 2(2)^{2-1} = 4$
$a_3 = 2(2)^3 = 16$ $\qquad\qquad a_3 = 2(2)^{3-1} = 8$
$a_4 = 2(2)^4 = 32$ $\qquad\qquad a_4 = 2(2)^{4-1} = 16$

Although each is a geometric series which increases in multiples of 2, one equation is shifted "up" a term. While there isn't an incorrect way to write the formulas, just be sure to check that you use either "n" or "$n - 1$" appropriately to get the right starting point.

Example 5.4: Derive the formula for the following sequence 9, 27, 81, 243,…

Solution: First we must determine whether the sequence is arithmetic or geometric. If it is arithmetic the difference between terms will be constant. If it is geometric, the ratio will be.

Difference:
27 − 9 = 18   81 − 27 = 54   IS NOT constant, therefore IS NOT arithmetic

Ratio:
27 ÷ 9 = 3   81 ÷ 27 = 3 etc.   IS constant, therefore IS geometric

Having determined that the sequence is geometric, we proceed to gather information to create the formula. We know that the first term is "9" and that the ratio between terms is "3." Knowing this, there are two possible correct formulas. One of the form ar^{n-1} and the other $\left(\dfrac{a}{r}\right)r^n$. You can see below that both formulas will yield the same sequence:

$a_n = 3(3^n)$
$a_1 = 3(3) = 9$
$a_2 = 3(9) = 27$
$a_3 = 3(27) = 81$
…

$a_n = 9(3)^{n-1}$
$a_1 = 9(1) = 9$
$a_2 = 9(3) = 27$
$a_3 = 9(9) = 81$
…

Example 5.5: Find the 15th term in the sequence 2, 4, 8, 16 …

Solution: First we determine that the sequence is a geometric sequence with a ratio of two between terms, and a first term of 2. From here there are two possible ways to solve the problem.

First, we can simply continue multiplying by 2 until we reach the 15th term of the sequence. This method is shown below:

16*2 = 32   32*2 = 64   64*2 = 128   128*2 = 256
256*2 = 512   512*2 = 1024   1024*2 = 2048   2048*2 = 4096
4096*2 = 8192   8192*2 = 16384   16384*2 = 32768

Therefore, the fifteenth term in the sequence is 32,768. While this method does work, it is much easier to make errors when so many calculations must be made, and it can be time consuming when higher numbers must be used.

The second way to solve the problem is by creating the formula for the sequence and simply solving for the nth term of 15. We have already determined that $a = 2$ and $r = 2$. Therefore, the formula for the sequence is $a_n = 2(2)^{n-1}$ and

$$a_{15} = 2(2)^{14}$$
$$a_{15} = 2(16384) = 32768$$

TRY IT YOURSELF:

Question: Find the first five numbers in the sequence given by $a_n = 5^n$.

Answer: 5, 25, 125, 625, 3125

Question: Derive a formula to describe the sequence given by 9, 18, 36, 72, …

Answer: $a_n = 9(2)^{n-1}$ or $a_n = 4.5(2)^n$

Question: Find the 13th term in the series 1, 3, 9, 27, …

Answer: 531,441

Series: Stated most simply, a series is the sum of the terms of a sequence. In other words, while a sequence may be noted as 1, 2, 3, 4, … a series will appear as 1 + 2 + 3 + 4 + …. Just like a sequence, a series can be described by a formula noted a_n. A series can be the sum of a geometric sequence, an arithmetic sequence, or any other sequence of numbers. A common notation to use for a sequence is the capital "s" in Greek, Σ, which is referred to as "sigma." This notation is displayed below:

$$\sum_{n=1}^{10} a_n$$

This notation indicates that you will be summing (or adding together) the terms in the sequence given by the formula a_n. The lower bounds, or the number underneath the sigma, is $n = 1$. This indicates that you are to begin adding with the first term of the sequence. The upper bounds of the series, or the number above the sigma, is 10. This indicates that you are to stop adding with the tenth term of the sequence. Any combination of upper and lower bounds can be used in calculating a series, as the case demands.

Example 5.6: Evaluate $\sum_{n=3}^{7} 2n+3$

Solution: The notation indicates that we are to begin the series at the 3rd term of the sequence (this is indicated by the lower bounds of $n = 3$), and that we are to finish the series at the 7th term of the sequence (this is indicated by the upper bounds of 7). Therefore,

$$\sum_{n=3}^{7} 2n+3 = a_3 + a_4 + a_5 + a_6 + a_7$$

$$\sum_{n=3}^{7} 2n+3 = [2(3)+3]+[2(4)+3]+[2(5)+3]+[2(6)+3]+[2(7)+3]$$

$$\sum_{n=3}^{7} 2n+3 = [9]+[11]+[13]+[15]+[17]$$

$$\sum_{n=3}^{7} 2n+3 = 65$$

Note: The form of the equation with each term of the sequence to be summed is called an expansion.

Example 5.7: Evaluate $\sum_{n=2}^{6} 1+2^{n-1}$

Solution: The notation indicates that we are to begin the series at the 2nd term of the sequence (indicated by the lower bounds of $n = 2$) and that we are to finish the series at the 6th term of the sequence (indicated by the upper bounds of 6). Therefore,

$$\sum_{n=2}^{6} 1+2^{n-1} = a_2 + a_3 + a_4 + a_5 + a_6$$

$$\sum_{n=2}^{6} 1+2^{n-1} = [1+2^1]+[1+2^2]+[1+2^3]+[1+2^4]+[1+2^5]$$

$$\sum_{n=2}^{6} 1+2^{n-1} = [3]+[5]+[9]+[17]+[33]$$

$$\sum_{n=2}^{6} 1+2^{n-1} = 67$$

An interesting scenario arises when you take the series of a geometric sequence for which $0 < r < 1$ (i.e., when "r" is a fractional value, or is between zero and one). Consider the series $\sum \left(\frac{1}{2}\right)^n$.

$$\sum_{n=1}^{1}\left(\frac{1}{2}\right)^n = \frac{1}{2}$$

$$\sum_{n=1}^{2}\left(\frac{1}{2}\right)^n = \frac{1}{2} + \frac{1}{4} = \frac{3}{4}$$

$$\sum_{n=1}^{3}\left(\frac{1}{2}\right)^n = \frac{1}{2} + \frac{1}{4} + \frac{1}{8} = \frac{7}{8}$$

$$\sum_{n=1}^{4}\left(\frac{1}{2}\right)^n = \frac{1}{2} + \frac{1}{4} + \frac{1}{8} + \frac{1}{16} = \frac{15}{16}$$

$$\sum_{n=1}^{5}\left(\frac{1}{2}\right)^n = \frac{1}{2} + \frac{1}{4} + \frac{1}{8} + \frac{1}{16} + \frac{1}{32} = \frac{31}{32}$$

Notice that as progressive terms are added to the series, the sum of the series grows closer and closer to 1, without ever going over it. In fact, the sum of the series to the term infinity can be calculated. This is referred to as a "sum to infinity," or an "infinite geometric series." There are two notations for this which are displayed below.

$$\sum_{n=1}^{\infty}\left(\frac{1}{2}\right)^n = S\infty\left(\frac{1}{2}\right)^n = 1$$

When these specific conditions are met (i.e., when $0 < r < 1$ and the series is geometric) the following formula can be used to calculate the sum as the series approaches infinity.

$$\sum_{n=1}^{\infty} a_n = S\infty = \frac{a}{1-r}$$

Example 5.8: Evaluate $\sum_{n=1}^{\infty} 2\left(\frac{2}{3}\right)^n$

Solution: Because we know that the series is a geometric series, and we can see that the "r" value is $\frac{2}{3}$ we know that the general formula given above can be used to find the sum of the series. Based on the equation, $a = 2$. Therefore the sum is calculated as

$$\sum_{n=1}^{\infty} 2\left(\frac{2}{3}\right)^n = \frac{2}{1-\left(\frac{2}{3}\right)} = \frac{2}{\left(\frac{1}{3}\right)} = 6$$

Example 5.9: Evaluate the sum to infinity of the following series $\sum_{n=1}^{\infty} 3+\left(\frac{3}{4}\right)^n$

Solution: This example is different from previous examples because it has the number 3 added to the geometric part of the series. In cases such as this, you simply solve for the sum of the geometric part of the series, and add that same number to the result. This is demonstrated below:

$$\sum_{n=1}^{\infty} 3+\left(\frac{3}{4}\right)^n = 3+\frac{1}{1-(3/4)} = 3+\frac{1}{1/4} = 3+4 = 7$$

You may be asked to calculate the sum to infinity of other types of series as well; however, in many cases the sum of the series will simply be infinity because the numbers in the series will simply increase as the series progresses. For example, $2n - 1$, $1 + 3n$, n^2, and many others.

Another trick to remember when working with series and sequences is when series alternate between positive and negative values. This effect can be created by simply multiplying the series by $(-1)^n$ or when the series uses a negative "r" value. For example, below is demonstrated the effect of multiplying a series by $(-1)^n$.

$$\sum_{n=1}^{\infty} 3^n = 3, 9, 27, 81$$

$$\sum_{n=1}^{\infty} (-1)^n 3^n = 3, -9, 27, -81$$

This same effect results from a negative "r" value (because it is essentially the same as multiplying by $(-1)^n$, but it has been distributed through the parenthesis). Note: the general formula to find the sum of an infinite geometric series is true both when $0 < r < 1$ AND when $-1 < r < 0$.

Example 5.10: Evaluate $\sum_{n=1}^{\infty} 5\left(-\frac{1}{4}\right)^n$

Solution: $\sum_{n=1}^{\infty} 5\left(-\frac{1}{4}\right)^n = \frac{5}{1-(-1/4)} = \frac{5}{5/4} = 4$

Example 5.11: Evaluate $\sum_{n=1}^{\infty} 13 + 2\left(-\frac{1}{5}\right)^n$

Solution: $\sum_{n=1}^{\infty} 13 + 2\left(-\frac{1}{5}\right)^n = 13 + \frac{2}{1-(-1/5)} = 13 + \frac{2}{(6/5)} = 13 + \frac{10}{6} = \frac{88}{6} \approx 14.67$

TRY IT YOURSELF:

Question: Evaluate $\sum_{n=2}^{5} 5n - 10$

Answer: 30

Question: Expand $\sum_{n=6}^{9} 9 + \frac{1}{2}n$

Answer: 12 + 12.5 + 13 + 13.5

Question: Evaluate $\sum_{n=1}^{\infty} 7 + 2\left(\frac{5}{6}\right)^n$

Answer: 19

1-6: ELEMENTARY NUMBER THEORY

What is a factor? A number *a* is a factor of another number *b* if their quotient $b \div a$ is an integer (that is, dividing them does not leave a remainder).

Example 6.1: Is 3 a factor of 14?

Solution: If 3 is a factor of 14 then $14 \div 3$ will have no remainder. However, $14 \div 3 = 4.67$. Therefore 3 is NOT a factor of 14.

Example 6.2: Is 4 a factor of 24?

Solution: If 4 is a factor of 24 then $24 \div 4$ will be an integer, or have no remainder.
$24 \div 4 = 6$ so 4 IS a factor of 24.

What is a multiple? A number *a* is a multiple of another number *b*, if *b* is a factor of *a*. In other words, multiples of a number are numbers that that number can be multiplied to become.

Example 6.3: Is 8 a multiple of 2?

Solution: Based on the definition above, 8 is a multiple of 2 if 2 is a factor of 8. $8 \div 2 = 4$, which has no remainder. Therefore, 2 is a factor of 8 and 8 must be a factor of 2.

Notice that you can also determine that 8 is a multiple of 2 because 2 can be multiplied to become 8. This is possible either by multiplying it by 2 twice, or multiplying it by 4.

Example 6.4: Is 64 a multiple of 13?

Solution: 64 is a multiple of 13 if 13 is a factor of 64. 64 ÷ 13 = 4.9. Therefore 64 is NOT a multiple of 13.

What is prime factorization? One of the fundamental theorems of arithmetic is that every number can be broken down into a unique multiple of primes. In other words, every number is simply a multiplied series of prime numbers. Finding this string of prime numbers is referred to as prime factorization.

Example 6.5: 2*2*3*5 is the prime factorization of which number?

Solution: The prime factorization is simply a breakdown of the multiples of a number. Multiplying the numbers together will therefore give the number that they are a prime factorization of. In this case 2*2*3*5 = 60

How is a prime factorization found? The easiest way to find the prime factorization of a number is by using a factor tree. To create a factor tree, simply break a number into two of its factors. For example, 20 can be broken down into 10 and 2 (because 10*2 is 20). While 2 is a prime number, 10 is not. Continue factoring until all prime numbers are reached. This method is called a factor tree because it is easiest when completed visually, and looks like a tree as shown below:

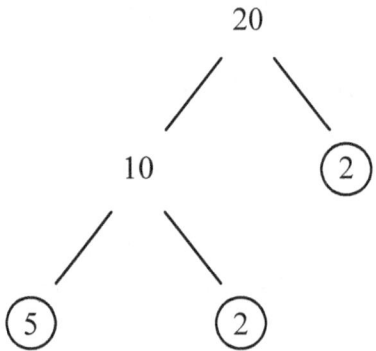

Notice that eventually all of the numbers factor down to primes. In this example the primes have all been circled. The prime factorization is therefore 2*2*5.

Example 6.6: Find the prime factorization of 36.

Solution: 2*2*3*3

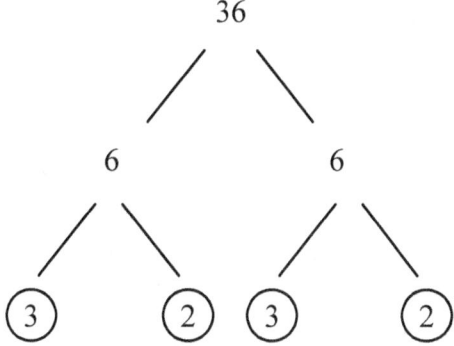

Notice that it doesn't matter how you choose to factor a number. It will still always break down to the same prime factorization.

Example 6.7: Find the prime factorization of 30

Solution:

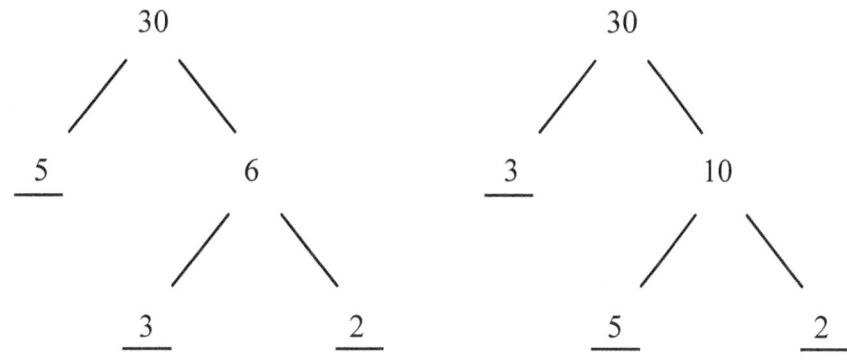

TRY IT YOURSELF:

Question: Find the prime factorization of 45

Answer: 3*3*5

Question: Find the prime factorization of 96

Answer: 2*2*2*2*2*3

Question: Is 21 a multiple of 3?

Answer: Yes

Question: List all of the possible factors of 26

Answer: 1, 2, 13, 26

What is a Greatest Common Divisor (GCD)? The greatest common divisor of two numbers is the largest number that is a factor of both numbers. For this reason it is also referred to as the Greatest Common Factor (GCF). To find the GCF, either list all of the possible factors of a number, and see which ones they have in common, or utilize the common elements of their prime factorizations.

Example 6.8: Find the GCF of 54 and 80

Solution: First, list the factors of 54 and 80:

54: 1, 2, 3, 6, 9, 18, 27, 54
80: 1, 2, 4, 5, 8, 10, 16, 20, 40, 80

The only factors in common are 1 and 2, so 2 is the GCF.

Second, utilize the common elements of their prime factorizations. To do this, first determine the prime factorizations of both 54 and 80:

54: 2*3*3*3
80: 2*2*2*2*5

The only element that is common between the two factorizations is the number 2. Therefore, 2 is the GCF.

Example 6.9: Find the GCF of 36 and 48

Solution: First, list the factors of 36 and 48:

36: 1, 2, 3, 4, 6, 9, 12, 18, 36
48: 1, 2, 4, 6, 8, 12, 24, 48

The factors they have in common are 1, 2, 4, 6, and 12 so 12 is the GCD.

Or second, find the prime factorizations of each number:

36: 2*2*3*3
48: 2*2*2*2*3

The elements that are common between the two are 2*2*3 and 2*2*3 = 12 so 12 will be the GCD.

What is a Least Common Multiple (LCM)? The least common multiple of two numbers is the lowest number that they are both a factor of. In other words, the smallest number that is a multiple of both numbers. The LCM can be found by listing all of the multiples of two numbers until a common one is reached.

Example 6.10: Find the LCM of 3 and 4.

Solution: Simply list all of the multiples of 3 and 4 until a common multiple is reached:

3: 3, 6, 9, 12
4: 4, 8, 12

Therefore, the LCM of 3 and 4 is 12.

Example 6.11: Find the LCM of 11 and 7

Solution: Simply list all of the multiples of 7 and 11 until a common multiple is reached:

7: 7, 14, 21, 28, 35, 42, 49, 56, 63, 70, 77
11: 11, 22, 33, 44, 55, 66, 77

Therefore, the least common multiple is 77.

TRY IT YOURSELF:

Question: Find the GCD of 64 and 48

Answer: 16

Question: Find the LCM of 5 and 7

Answer: 35

Question: Find the GCF of 48 and 12

Answer: 12

Question: Find the LCM of 6 and 8

Answer: 24

 Sample Test Questions

NUMBERS AND OPERATIONS QUESTIONS

1. A water tank can hold 40,000 gallons of water. When the tank is 45% full, how much water is in the tank?

   A. 10,000 gallons
   B. 15,000 gallons
   C. 18,000 gallons
   D. 22,000 gallons
   E. 30,000 gallons

2. A large balloon is being filled with water. As it is being filled it expands from having 25 cubic centimeters of water, to having 250 cubic centimeters of water. By what percent has the volume of the balloon increased?

   A. 10%
   B. 50%
   C. 100%
   D. 900%
   E. 1000%

3. Which of the following is NOT an alternate way to express the percentage 40%?

   A. .40
   B. $\frac{3}{7}$
   C. $\frac{40}{100}$
   D. $\frac{2}{5}$
   E. All of the above are correct expressions of 40%

4. Sales tax on a particular item comes to 57 cents. If the tax is 4.32%, what is the price of the item?

   A. $10.25
   B. $12.51
   C. $13.19
   D. $14.24
   E. $15.13

5. Which of the following does NOT express the same proportion as the others?

   A. 3:4
   B. 4:3
   C. $\frac{3}{4}$
   D. 3 to 4
   E. All of the above express the same proportion

6. Ryan, Kyle, and Bryce own a lawn mowing business together. Ryan can mow 3 lawns in 2 hours, Kyle can mow 2 lawns in 5 hours, and Bryce can mow 4 lawns in 3 hours. On a particular day, they must mow 33 lawns. Assuming that each lawn takes the same amount of time and ignoring traveling time, how long will it take the three to complete their work for the day?

   A. 8.4 hours
   B. 9.6 hours
   C. 10.2 hours
   D. 10.8 hours
   E. 13.5 hours

7. Jocelyn and Megan own a film developing business where they develop pictures for their neighbors and friends. They have a special process that they use and it takes Jocelyn 40 minutes to develop 3 pictures, and Megan 35 minutes to develop 3 pictures. If the two have an order for 14 pictures, how long will it take the two of them (working together) to develop all of the pictures?

   A. 75 minutes
   B. 80 minutes
   C. 84 minutes
   D. 87 minutes
   E. 92 minutes

8. Sam borrowed money from his parents and agrees that in one week he will pay back half of the money plus an extra three eighths in interest. Two weeks after he pays the remaining half with an added eighth in interest plus five dollars. If on the second week Sam pays his parents 55 dollars, what was the initial amount that he borrowed?

    A. 65 dollars
    B. 70 dollars
    C. 80 dollars
    D. 88 dollars
    E. 92 dollars

9. Valerie leaves her school going 45 mph heading straight south. At the same time, her brother Ryan leaves their home heading straight north (towards the school) at 30 mph. If their home and school are 50 miles apart, at what distance from their home will the two meet?

    A. 15 miles
    B. 20 miles
    C. 25 miles
    D. 30 miles
    E. 35 miles

10. The water flows out of a bucket at a rate of 3 cubic centimeters per second. Simultaneously the water flows into the bucket at a rate proportional to the square of the number of seconds. Which of the following equations correctly models the amount a of water in the bucket at any given time t?

    A. $a = 2t + 3t^2$
    B. $a = t + t^2$
    C. $a^2 = 2t + 3$
    D. $a = 2t - 3$
    E. $a = t^2 - 3t$

11. Which of the following is TRUE about the relationship between number systems?

    A. Whole numbers are a subset of even numbers
    B. Even numbers are a subset of natural numbers
    C. Integers are a subset of rational numbers
    D. Rational numbers are a subset of irrational numbers
    E. Natural numbers are a subset of irrational numbers

12. What is the units digit of 1387?

    A. 1
    B. 3
    C. 8
    D. 7
    E. Thousands

13. Which of the following is NOT prime?

    A. 1
    B. 2
    C. 3
    D. 5
    E. 7

14. To which set of integers does zero belong?

    A. Even integers
    B. Composite integers
    C. Consecutive integers
    D. Odd integers
    E. Prime integers

15. Consider the following set and determine which elements, if any, are irrational

    $$\{-\frac{\pi}{2}, -2, \sqrt{225}, 2.\overline{13}, -\sqrt{7}\}$$

    A. $\{-\frac{\pi}{2}, -2, \sqrt{225}, 2.\overline{13}, -\sqrt{7}\}$
    B. $\{-\frac{\pi}{2}, \sqrt{225}, -\sqrt{7}\}$
    C. $\{-\frac{\pi}{2}, -\sqrt{7}\}$
    D. $\{-\frac{\pi}{2}\}$
    E. None of the elements are irrational

16. Which of the following is a subset of irrational numbers?

    A. Natural numbers
    B. Whole numbers
    C. Rational numbers
    D. Integers
    E. None of the above

17. 3.095609560956... is

    A. Natural
    B. Whole
    C. Irrational
    D. Rational
    E. None of the above

18. Determine $A \cap B$ where

    $A = \{1, 3, 5, 7, 9, 11, 13\}$
    $B = \{1, 2, 4, 6, 8, 10, 11\}$

    A. $\{1, 2, 3, 4, 5, 6, 7, 8, 9, 10, 11, 13\}$
    B. $\{1, 3, 5, 7, 9, 11, 13\}$
    C. $\{2, 4, 6, 8, 10\}$
    D. $\{1, 11\}$
    E. $\{\}$

19. What are the individual numbers in a set referred to as?

    A. Elements
    B. Properties
    C. Proportions
    D. Figures
    E. Integers

20. The set $\{2, 3, 4, 5, \ldots\}$ can be described as a(n)

    A. Null set
    B. Finite set
    C. Intersecting set
    D. Unified set
    E. Infinite set

21. If A = {Even Integers} and B = {Odd Integers} and $A \cap B$, which of the following must be true?

    A. C = {Natural Numbers}
    B. C = { }
    C. C = {Prime Integers}
    D. C = {Integers}
    E. C = {Rational Numbers}

22. Janalee has twelve dogs and six cats. She is allowed to take only one of her pets with her on vacation. How many options does she have?

    A. 12
    B. 6
    C. 18
    D. 72
    E. 9

23. The principle that states "that if there are x options in one group, and y options in a second group, then the total number of options between the two groups is $x + y$" is which principle?

    A. Additive property
    B. Multiplication property
    C. Tree diagram
    D. Permutation principle
    E. Addition principle

24. There are two boxes filled with different letters of the alphabet. The first box holds 12 different letters and the second box holds 26 different letters. If a person pulls a letter first from the first box, and then from the second box, how many different combinations of letters are possible?

    A. 12
    B. 26
    C. 38
    D. 312
    E. 517

25. Sarah is selling meals at her local baseball field to pick up some extra money during the summer. Each meal comes with an option of three different entrees (a hamburger, a hot dog, or a salad), accompanied by a choice of three different sides (chips, nachos, or fruit) and a choice of three different drinks (juice, soda, or water). How many different meal combinations can be made at her stand?

   A. 27
   B. 32
   C. 9
   D. 18
   E. 3

26. Evaluate $(3 - 1)!(0!) - 2! + 4! - 0!$

   A. 24
   B. 23
   C. 22
   D. 17
   E. 28

27. Which of the following is equal to $7(6!) - 3! + 1$?

   A. $7! - 3! + 0!$
   B. $(7 - 3 + 1)!$
   C. $(7 - 6)! + 6$
   D. 105
   E. None of the above

28. A prison is having inmates manufacture license plates in order to make some extra money while they are in prison. The license plates can use only the first 12 letters of the alphabet, and repeat letters are NOT allowed on the license plates. If each plate has 7 letters, how many license plate combinations are possible?

   A. 3,218,091
   B. 2,186,514
   C. 1,800,000
   D. 3,991,680
   E. None of the above

29. A teacher needs volunteers for a demonstration he is doing. He puts the names of each of his 35 students in a hat and picks out 4 of them. Each of the students is assigned a specific job based on the order in which their name is selected. Which of the following would be used to calculate the number of possible volunteer arrangements?

   A. $_4P_{35}$
   B. $_4C_{35}$
   C. $_{35}C_4$
   D. $_{35}P_{35}$
   E. $_{35}P_4$

30. Sally is an avid coin collector. She has put all of her 72 unique collector coins in a bag. If she wishes to choose 4 of them randomly to share with friends, how many possibilities are there?

   A. 1,664,498
   B. 1,028,790
   C. 165,678
   D. 24690960
   E. None of the above

31. Jason is learning a new magic trick where he pulls cards out of a hat. He starts with half of a deck of cards dumped into the hat. Then he chooses out 3 different cards and attempts to guess what they are. How many possibilities are there for the 3 cards he could choose?

   A. 9880
   B. 1800
   C. 1560
   D. 2400
   E. 2600

32. The permutation $P(8,3)$ would be evaluated as

   A. $\dfrac{8!}{3!(8-3)!}$
   B. $\dfrac{3!}{8!(8-3)!}$
   C. $\dfrac{8!}{(8-3)!}$
   D. $\dfrac{3!}{(8-3)!}$
   E. $\dfrac{3!}{8!-3!}$

33. Which of the following is a correct formula for the sequence $\{3, 5, 7, 9,...\}$?

   A. $a_n = 3 + 2n$
   B. $a_n = 3(n-1)$
   C. $a_n = 2 + 3(n-1)$
   D. $a_n = 3 + 2(n-1)$
   E. $a_n = (3)2^{n-1}$

34. Find the 112th term in the sequence $\{12, 16, 20, 24, ...\}$

   A. 488
   B. 452
   C. 456
   D. 460
   E. 464

35. Which of the following is a correct formula for the sequence 1, 4, 16, 64, ...?

   A. $a_n = 4 + (4)^{n-1}$
   B. $a_n = (4)^{n-1}$
   C. $a_n = 4(1)^{n-1}$
   D. $a_n = 4(1)^n$
   E. $a_n = 4(4)^n$

36. Find the 20th term in the sequence 1, 2, 4, 8, …

    A. 2,096,541
    B. 1,048,576
    C. 131,072
    D. 262,144
    E. 524,288

37. The sequence given by the formula $a_n = 3(2)^{n-1}$ is

    A. Geometric
    B. Indefinite
    C. Arithmetic
    D. Consecutive
    E. Finite

38. Evaluate $\sum_{n=1}^{\infty} 1 + 5(.5)^n$

    A. 1
    B. 11
    C. 15
    D. ∞
    E. Cannot be determined

39. Which of the following is the correct expansion of $\sum_{n=4}^{6} n+6$?

    A. 7 + 8 + 9
    B. 9 + 10 + 11
    C. 10 + 11 + 12
    D. 11 + 12 + 13
    E. None of the above

40. Evaluate $\sum_{n=1}^{\infty} 2^n + 1$

    A. 0
    B. 11
    C. 17
    D. ∞
    E. Cannot be determined

41. What is the prime factorization of 40?

   A. 2 × 2 × 3 × 5
   B. 2 × 2 × 2 × 3 × 7
   C. 2 × 2 × 2 × 5
   D. 2 × 3 × 5
   E. None of the above

42. Which of the following is NOT included in the prime factorization of 50?

   A. 2
   B. 3
   C. 5
   D. Neither 2 nor 5
   E. All of the above are included in the prime factorization

43. Which of the following is NOT a multiple of 7?

   A. 14
   B. 28
   C. 47
   D. 56
   E. All of the above are multiples of 7

44. The smallest number that two numbers are both a factor of is called the

   A. Lowest common factor
   B. Least common multiple
   C. Lowest common denominator
   D. Least common divisor
   E. None of the above

45. The LCM of 12 and 6 is

   A. 3
   B. 6
   C. 12
   D. 24
   E. 72

46. The GCD of 35 and 40 is

    A. 5
    B. 3
    C. 2
    D. 7
    E. 15

47. The LCM of 6 and 14

    A. 42
    B. 84
    C. 8
    D. 2
    E. None

48. Find the 10th term in the sequence: 5, 8, 11, 14, …

    A. 23
    B. 26
    C. 29
    D. 32
    E. 35

49. Find the LCM of 4 and 13

    A. 4
    B. 26
    C. 16
    D. 43
    E. 52

50. Find the GCD of 150 and 250

    A. 4
    B. 20
    C. 50
    D. 75
    E. 125

NUMBERS AND OPERATIONS KEY

1. C
2. D
3. B
4. C
5. B
6. C
7. D
8. C
9. B
10. E
11. C
12. D
13. A
14. A
15. C
16. E
17. D
18. D
19. A
20. E
21. B
22. C
23. E
24. D
25. A
26. B
27. A
28. D
29. E
30. B
31. E
32. C
33. D
34. C
35. B
36. E
37. A
38. B
39. C
40. D
41. C
42. B
43. C
44. B
45. C
46. A
47. A
48. D
49. E
50. C

Section 2: Algebra and Functions

2-1: SUBSTITUTION AND SIMPLIFYING ALGEBRAIC EXPRESSIONS

What is an algebraic expression? Expressions contain numbers and variables that are called "terms." An algebraic expression does **NOT** have an equal sign. It is simply a collection of terms that are separated by arithmetic operations including addition, subtraction, multiplication, and division.

How do you combine algebraic expressions? There are three main steps involved in combining (or simplifying) an algebraic expression. The three steps include:

1. Identify "like" terms.
2. Add or subtract the coefficients of "like" terms.
3. Multiply the number found in Step 2 by the common variable(s).

In order to complete these three steps, you need to understand a few definitions:

"Like" terms: Two terms are considered "like" terms if they have the **SAME** variable with the **SAME** exponent. For example, $2x$ and $3x$ are like terms because they have the same variable "x" and this variable has the same exponent of 1.

Following is a table that contains "like" terms and "unlike" terms:

"LIKE" TERMS	"UNLIKE" TERMS
$2y, -14y$	$2y, -14x$
$3x^2, 12x^2$	$3x^2, 3x$
$14, -14$	$14, -14z$
$\frac{1}{2}x^4, 2x^4$	$\frac{1}{2}y^4, 2x^4$
$0.75x, 15x$	$0.75x, 15xy^2$

Coefficient of the variable: The coefficient of the variable is the number that is multiplied by the variable. In other words, the coefficient of the variable is the number directly in front of the variable. For example, the coefficient of $3x$ is 3 and the coefficient of $0.75y$ is 0.75.

The coefficient of the variable is sometimes referred to as the "numerical coefficient" and it can be positive, negative, an integer, fraction, or decimal.

Examples of Combining Algebraic Expressions:

1. $2x + 3x$ Answer: $5x$

2. $10y + 9 + 14y - 5$ Answer: $24y + 4$

3. $3x^2 + 2x - 5x^2 + 6y$ Answer: $-2x^2 + 2x + 6y$

What are polynomials? A polynomial is an expression containing the sum of a finite number of terms of the form ax^n, for any real number a and any whole number n.

Examples of Polynomials:

$x^2 + 6x + 5$

$2x^3 + 3x^2 + 4x + 16$

How do you ADD and SUBTRACT two polynomials?
There are two general steps you take to add and subtract polynomials. The two steps include:

Step #1: Remove parentheses (if applicable)

Step #2: Combine "like" terms

Question: Evaluate $(x^2 + 8x + 12) + (2x^2 - 3x + 13)$
This is an ADDITION problem.

1. Remove the parentheses
Note: There is a positive 1 on the outside of each parenthesis.
Therefore, you multiply a positive 1 by each term to remove the parentheses.

$1(x^2 + 8x + 12) + 1(2x^2 - 3x + 13)$
$x^2 + 8x + 12 + 2x^2 - 3x + 13$

2. Combine "like" terms
$x^2 + 2x^2 + 8x - 3x + 12 + 13$
Answer: $3x^2 + 5x + 25$

Question: Evaluate $(x^2 + 8x + 12) - (2x^2 - 3x + 13)$
This is a SUBTRACTION problem.

1. Remove the parentheses

Note: There is a positive one by the first set of parentheses, but a NEGATIVE one by the second set of parentheses because you are dealing with subtraction. The signs of the first polynomial remain the same and change the signs of the second polynomial to their opposites.

$(x^2 + 8x + 12) - (2x^2 - 3x + 13)$
$1(x^2 + 8x + 12) - 1(2x^2 - 3x + 13)$
$x^2 + 8x + 12 - 2x^2 + 3x - 13$

2. Combine "like" terms

$x^2 - 2x^2 + 8x + 3x + 12 - 13$
Answer: $-x^2 + 11x - 1$

TRY IT YOURSELF:

Question: Add $3(2x^2 + 6x + 8) + (5x^2 + 2x + 1)$

Answer: $11x^2 + 20x + 25$

Question: Subtract $(12x^3 - 4x + 1) - (3x^2 + 2x - 1)$

Answer: $12x^3 - 3x^2 - 6x + 2$

Question: Combine $2(x^2 + 6x + 3) - 3(x^2 + x + 1) + (4x^2 - 2x + 7)$

Answer: $3x^2 + 7x + 10$

How do you MULTIPLY AND DIVIDE two polynomials?

Two types of multiplication include:

- Multiplication using the distributive property.
- Multiplication of two binomials using the FOIL method.

How to multiply terms using the Distributive Property:

Evaluate: $2x(x + 14)$

Multiply the term "$2x$" by **EACH** term on the inside of the parentheses.

Example 1.1:

$2x(x + 14)$
$2x(x) + 2x(14)$

Solution: $2x^2 + 28x$

How do you multiply two binomials using the "FOIL" method?

Use the FOIL method to multiply two binomials.

Example 1.2: Evaluate $(x + 3)(x + 4)$
Multiply **F**irst Terms: $(\mathbf{x} + 3)(\mathbf{x} + 4) = x^2$
Multiply **O**uter Terms: $(\mathbf{x} + 3)(x + \mathbf{4}) = 4x$
Multiply **I**nner Terms: $(x + \mathbf{3})(\mathbf{x} + 4) = 3x$
Multiply **L**ast Terms: $(x + \mathbf{3})(x + \mathbf{4}) = 12$

Solution:
Therefore, $x^2 + 4x + 3x + 12$
Combine "like" terms:
Answer: $x^2 + 7x + 12$

What does it mean to "FACTOR" a polynomial? Remember how to factor a number? Factors are two numbers or terms that when multiplied together yield the original term. You will be given a polynomial in Standard Form such as $x^2 + 7x + 12$. Factoring this polynomial is the reverse of applying the distributive property.

For example, factors of the number 12 include:
 1×12
 2×6
 3×4

The same method applies to polynomials; however you have to take into account the Rules of Exponents.

For example, the factors of $2x^2$ can be 2 and x^2 because when you multiply the two factors together you end up with your original $2x^2$.

How do you factor a polynomial (trinomial) of the form $x^2 + bx + c$?
Follow these two steps:

1. Find all possible pairs of integers whose product is *c*.
2. For each pair, test whether its sum is *b*.

> Example 1.3: Factor $x^2 + 7x + 12$
> What factors of "12" add up to "7"? The factors 3 and 4 fit the criteria.
>
> Solution: $(x + 3)(x + 4)$

How do you factor a polynomial (trinomial) of the form $ax^2 + bx + c$?

Follow these three steps:

1. Compute *ac* for all the possible factors of *a* and *c*. Find all the possible pairs of integers (positive and negative) whose product is *ac*.
2. For each pair of integers, test if its sum is *b*.
3. If the pair of integers satisfies both step 1 and step 2 then you will use those factors.

> Example 1.4: Factor $2x^2 + 11x + 5$
> *ac* = 10. The factors of 5 are 1 and 5. Therefore, you must put the factors in the correct order. You can double check your answer by using the foil method.
>
> Solution: $(2x + 1)(x + 5)$

Some additional examples of factoring: Factoring can take time and practice to get used to. There are essentially four different types of factoring that you need to be familiar with. The first type is pulling a single common term out of a polynomial in which all of the terms have the same factor.

> Example 1.5: Consider the polynomial expression $3x^2 + 6x + 33$.
>
> Solution: Notice that the leading coefficient (the coefficient of the highest powered exponent) is a 3. It is generally much easier to factor and work with equations that have a leading coefficient of 1. Because all of the terms in the polynomial are divisible by 3, simply factor out the 3 to simplify the expression. This results in the polynomial $3(x^2 + 2x + 11)$. Notice that you can still multiply the 3 back through the polynomial and get the same answer. Factoring doesn't change the polynomial, it simply converts it to a form that is easier to understand and work with.

Example 1.6: Consider the polynomial expression $4x^4 + 2x^3 + 8x^2$.

Solution: The first thing to do when working with polynomials is to factor them and simplify to the most basic form. In this case, notice that each of the terms in the polynomial have 2 and x^2 as factors. Therefore, the polynomial can factor to $2x^2(2x^2 + x + 4)$.

The second type of factoring is taking a trinomial (a polynomial with three terms) and turning it into two binomials. This is the most common form of factoring, with the trinomial being in the form $ax^2 + bx + c$ where $a = 1$.

Example 1.7: Factor $x^2 + 2x + 1$

Solution: Because this polynomial has a leading coefficient (*a*) of 1, we can begin by placing "*x*" as the first term in each of the binomials. We can do this because the only way to get a single x^2 as the leading coefficient is to multiply *x* by itself. In other words, we immediately know that the polynomial will have $(x+?)(x+?)$. To finish factoring, simply consider all of the factors of the remaining two coefficients, *b* and *c*. Look for a pair of numbers that will ADD to *b* and MULTIPLY to *c*. In this case, 1 and 1. Therefore, the factored form of the polynomial is $(x+1)(x+1)$ OR $(x+1)^2$.

Example 1.8: Factor $2x^2 + 14x + 24$

Solution: Because this polynomial has a leading coefficient of 2, the first step is to see if there is any way to factor that 2 out of the equation. In this polynomial, you can factor the two out of each term to get the expression $2(x^2 + 7x + 12)$. Again, because the polynomial that we are working with has a leading coefficient of 1, we know that the first element of each binomial will be *x*. In other words, we know that

$2(x+?)(x+?)$

Now, simply factor the rest of the polynomial by finding a pair of integers which ADD to 7 and MULTIPLY to 12. The pairs which multiply to 12 are 1 and 12, 2 and 6, and 3 and 4. The 3 and 4 also add to 7, therefore the polynomial factors to.

$2(x+3)(x+4)$

The third type of factoring to be familiar with is a special case referred to as the difference of squares. This describes polynomials where there are two terms, both of which are squares and one of which is being subtracted. In other words, the difference of squares appears as: $x^2 - a^2$. When this occurs, the factored form will simply be the multiplied conjugates of the two terms. A conjugate is the same term, but with an opposite sign. Therefore, the factored form of $x^2 - a^2$ is $(x+a)(x-a)$. Notice that the factorization is simply the first degree (first power) form of each of the terms, in one case added and in one case subtracted.

Example 1.9:
$x^2 - 4 = (x+2)(x-2)$
$y^2 - 25 = (y+5)(y-5)$
$x^2 - 9y^2 = (x+3y)(x-3y)$

The final form of factoring to be familiar with is the trinomial form $ax^2 + bx + c$, where the leading coefficient is not one. In other words, where $a \neq 1$. The process to factor these has been described, and below are some additional examples:

Example 1.10: Factor $2x^2 + 5x - 3$

Solution: First we must find all of the factors of *a* and all of the factors of *c*. In this example the factors of *a* are 1 and 2, and the factors of *c* are –1 and 3 or 1 and –3.

Now we test each of the combinations by multiplying the factors of *a* and *c* together to find a combination that will have the sum of *b*, or 5.

a = 1, 2	*c* = –1, 3	1(–1) + 2(3) = 5
a = 2, 1	*c* = –1, 3	2(–1) + 1(3) = 1
a = 1, 2	*c* = 1, –3	1(1) + 2(–3) = –5
a = 2, 1	*c* = 1, –3	2(1) + 1(–3) = –1

As you can see, only the combination of *a* = 1, 2 and *c* = –1, 3 will work. Now, simply arrange the numbers in the correct order in the binomials. The answer is $(2x-1)(x+3)$.

Example 1.11: Factor $4x^2 + 8x + 3$

Solution: First we must find all of the factors of *a* and all of the factors of *c*.

Factors of *a*	Factors of *c*
1, 4	1, 3
2, 2	

Second, we test all the possible combinations of *ac* to find the one that will multiply to *b*.

$a = 1, 4 \quad c = 1, 3 \quad\quad 1(1) + 4(3) = 13$
$a = 1, 4 \quad c = 3, 1 \quad\quad 1(3) + 4(1) = 7$
$a = 2, 2 \quad c = 1, 3 \quad\quad 2(1) + 2(3) = 8$

Therefore, the combination $a = 2, 2$ and $c = 1, 3$ is the correct combination because the product of *ac* is 8, which is *b* in the polynomial. Therefore, the factored form of $4x^2 + 8x + 3$ is

$(2x+1)(2x+3)$

TRY IT YOURSELF:

Question: Factor $x^2 + 14x + 13$

Answer: $(x+13)(x+1)$

Question: Factor $x^2 - 169$

Answer: $(x+13)(x-13)$

Question: Factor $3x^2 - 5x - 2$

Answer: $(3x+1)(x-2)$

Question: Factor $3x^2 + 9x + 6$

Answer: $3(x+1)(x+2)$

2-2: PROPERTIES OF EXPONENTS

What is an exponent? An exponent is used when the same number or variable is multiplied by itself. Exponents are noted with a smaller number in the upper right-hand corner of the number or variable which is being multiplied by itself. The number that is used as the exponent indicates the number of times that the number or variable is being multiplied by itself. Any number is equal to itself raised to an exponent of 1.

Examples of Exponents:
$3 = 3^1$

$(2)(2) = 2^2$

$(y)(3)(y)(y) = 3y^3$

$2(x)(x)(y)(3)(y) = 6x^2 y^2$

What are the parts of an exponent? Elements with exponents are composed of three different parts. These parts are the coefficient, the base, and the actual exponent. The exponent, as explained above, is the number in the upper right hand corner. The number that is being raised to the exponent is referred to as the base. The number that is in front of the base/exponent combination is referred to as the coefficient. This indicates the number of times that the entire exponent appears in the expression.

Example 2.1: Identify the coefficient, base, and exponent in the following algebraic terms.

$$4x, \quad 2x^5, \quad \frac{1}{2}(3)^7$$

Solution: $4x$: coefficient = 4, base = x, exponent = 1
$2x^5$: coefficient = 2, base = x, exponent = 5
$\frac{1}{2}(3)^7$: coefficient = $(\frac{1}{2})$, base = 3, exponent = 7

What are the rules of exponents when simplifying? When you are dealing with exponents it is important to get them in their simplest form. There are a number of rules that you need to be familiar with when combining exponents and working with them within algebraic expressions and functions. These are the product rule, quotient rule, power rule, and zero exponent.

Product Rule: The product rule describes situations when an exponent is multiplied by an exponent with the same base. When multiplying the two terms, just add their exponents and multiply their coefficients.

Example 2.2: Simplify $(2x^4)(4x^5)$

Solution: There are two ways to think about simplifying this problem. The first is to simply remember to add exponents and multiply coefficients, which yields the solution.

$(2x^4)(4x^5)$

$(2 \cdot 4)(x^{4+5})$

$8x^9$

The second way to think of this is to break down the problem and consider each multiplication within the exponent separately, then combine all of the "like terms." For example, if you deconstruct the exponents, they would appear

$(2x^4)(4x^5)$

$(2 \cdot x \cdot x \cdot x \cdot x)(4 \cdot x \cdot x \cdot x \cdot x \cdot x)$

Then, combining "like" terms would mean to multiply all of the "x" variables together, and the coefficients "2" and "4" together. Because exponents represent the number of times that the variable is multiplied by itself, this yields the same solution of $8x^9$.

Example 2.3: Simplify $(3y^2)(12y^5)(y)$

Solution: Again, there are two ways of considering the expression. First, simply add all of the exponents and multiply all of the coefficients:

$(3y^2)(12y^5)(y)$

$(3 \cdot 12 \cdot 1)(y^{2+5+1})$

$36y^8$

Second, deconstruct the problem and then move it into exponential form:

$(3y^2)(12y^5)(y)$

$(3 \cdot y \cdot y)(12 \cdot y \cdot y \cdot y \cdot y \cdot y)(y)$

$36y^8$

Example 2.4: Simplify $(3w^2)(4y^5)(wy^3)$

Solution: In this example there are two different variables to work with. In this case the expression will be simplified in essentially the same manner. Still multiply the coefficients and add the exponents, just be careful to keep the different exponents separate when you are combining them.

$(3w^2)(4y^5)(wy^3)$

$(3 \cdot 4 \cdot 1)(w^{2+1})(y^{5+3})$

$(12)(w^3)(y^8)$

$12w^3y^8$

You can also still deconstruct the problem before moving it into exponential form. This makes it quite clear what each exponent should be when there are two different variables in question.

$(3w^2)(4y^5)(wy^3)$

$(3 \cdot w \cdot w)(4 \cdot y \cdot y \cdot y \cdot y \cdot y)(w \cdot y \cdot y \cdot y)$

$12w^3y^8$

Quotient Rule: The quotient rule comes into play when you are dividing two exponential terms with the same base. When dividing the terms, just subtract the exponents and divide the coefficients. Note: It is extremely important that you subtract the bottom exponent from the top exponent and not the other way around.

Example 2.5: Simplify $\dfrac{4x^5}{2x^2}$

Solution: As with the product rule you can think of simplifying exponential terms in fractions in two different ways. The simplest way is to simply remember to subtract the exponents and divide the coefficients.

$$\dfrac{4x^5}{2x^2} = \left(\dfrac{4}{2}\right)(x^{5-2}) = 2x^3$$

However, you can also deconstruct the exponents. By doing this you can see which numbers "cancel" each other out and see what the simplified version is.

$$\dfrac{4x^5}{2x^2} = \left(\dfrac{4 \cdot x \cdot x \cdot x \cdot x \cdot x}{2 \cdot x \cdot x}\right) = \left(\dfrac{2 \cdot x \cdot x \cdot x}{1}\right) = 2x^3$$

Example 2.6: Simplify $\dfrac{9y^9}{3y^{15}}$

Solution: Again, you can simply divide the coefficients and subtract the exponents, as shown below:

$$\frac{9y^9}{3y^{15}} = \left(\frac{9}{3}\right)(y^{9-15}) = 3y^{-6} = \frac{3}{y^6}$$

Note: If you get a positive number when you subtract, the remaining exponent is in the numerator. If you get a negative number when you subtract, the remaining exponent is in the denominator. In this case, it is negative and in the denominator. Also notice that the coefficient remained in the numerator.

Or you can deconstruct the different exponential elements and see which ones cancel. This method is particularly effective if you can't remember whether the remaining exponent should be on the top or bottom of the equation – it goes on whichever side has "more" of the variable.

$$\frac{9y^9}{3y^{15}} = \left(\frac{9 \cdot y \cdot y \cdot y \cdot y \cdot y \cdot y \cdot y \cdot y \cdot y}{3 \cdot y \cdot y \cdot y \cdot y \cdot y \cdot y \cdot y \cdot y \cdot y \cdot y \cdot y \cdot y \cdot y \cdot y \cdot y}\right) = \left(\frac{3}{y \cdot y \cdot y \cdot y \cdot y \cdot y}\right) = \frac{3}{y^6}$$

Example 2.7: Simplify $\frac{3y^2 w^6}{7yw^7}$

Solution: You will notice that in this example there are two variables to deal with. In cases such as this, follow the same rules, but be careful to consider each variable separately. Also notice that unlike the other examples, dividing the coefficient does NOT come out evenly. Therefore, we will leave the 3 in the numerator and the 7 in the denominator because they are already in simplest form.

$$\frac{3y^2 w^6}{7yw^7} = \left(\frac{3}{7}\right)(y^{2-1})(w^{6-7}) = \left(\frac{3}{7}\right)(y^1)(w^{-1}) = \frac{3y}{7w}$$

OR

$$\frac{3y^2 w^6}{7yw^7} = \left(\frac{3 \cdot y \cdot y \cdot w \cdot w \cdot w \cdot w \cdot w \cdot w}{7 \cdot y \cdot w \cdot w \cdot w \cdot w \cdot w \cdot w \cdot w}\right) = \left(\frac{3y}{7w}\right)$$

<u>Power Rule</u>: The power rule is used in situations where the exponential term is in parenthesis and raised to an exponent itself. To simplify, simply multiply by exponent in the parenthesis by the exponent outside the parenthesis. You can think of this in two different ways. First, simply remember this rule and multiply the numbers. Second, remember that second exponent outside the parenthesis as indicating that the entire figure is being multiplied by itself. Then simply apply the product rule and simplify.

Example 2.8: Simplify $3(x^2)^3$

Solution: Notice that when a term is in parenthesis and raised to an exponent, the exponent must be distributed to all of the terms inside the parenthesis, but not those on the outside. Both methods of simplifying the expression are shown below.

$$3(x^2)^3 = 3(x^2)(x^2)(x^2) = 3(x^{2+2+2}) = 3x^6$$
OR
$$3(x^2)^3 = 3(x^{2 \cdot 3}) = 3x^6$$

Example 2.9: Simplify $12(2z^3)^2$

Solution: In this example there are coefficients both inside and outside of the parenthesis. It is important that they are not combined until the last stage of simplifying to ensure that the exponent is properly distributed to all elements of the expression.

$$12(2z^3)^2 = 12(2^2 \cdot z^{3 \cdot 2}) = 12(4z^6) = 48z^6$$
OR
$$12(2z^3)^2 = 12(2z^3)(2z^3) = (12 \cdot 2 \cdot 2)(z^{3+3}) = 48z^6$$

Example 2.10: Simplify $\left(\dfrac{2x^2}{yw}\right)^3$

Solution: In this example there is an entire fraction in the parenthesis. Notice that the exponent is applied to every term in the parenthesis – in both the numerator and the denominator.

$$\left(\frac{2x^2}{yw}\right)^3 = \left(\frac{2^3 x^{2 \cdot 3}}{y^3 w^3}\right) = \frac{8x^6}{y^3 w^3}$$
OR
$$\left(\frac{2x^2}{yw}\right)^3 = \left(\frac{2x^2}{yw}\right)\left(\frac{2x^2}{yw}\right)\left(\frac{2x^2}{yw}\right) = \frac{(2 \cdot 2 \cdot 2)(x^{2+2+2})}{(y^{1+1+1})(w^{1+1+1})} = \frac{8x^6}{y^3 w^3}$$

Math for Liberal Arts

<u>Zero Power</u>: This rule is really just a matter of memorization. It is that whenever a number or exponent is raised to the zero power, it is equal to one.

Example 2.11:
$3^0 = 1$
$1^0 = 1$
$x^0 = 1$
$(xyz)^0 = 1$

<u>Fractions as Exponents</u>: Remember that the inverse or opposite operation to an exponent is a "root." I.e., a square is the inverse of a square root and vice versa. This means that a root can also be expressed as a fractional exponent, or a fractional exponent as a square root.

Example:
$\sqrt[3]{5} = 5^{\frac{1}{3}}$
$(xy)^{\frac{1}{2}} = \sqrt{xy}$
$(4wz)^{\frac{3}{4}} = \sqrt[4]{(4wz)^3} = \sqrt[4]{64(wz)^3} = 2\sqrt[4]{4w^3z^3}$

TRY IT YOURSELF:

Question: Identify the coefficient, base, and exponent of the following: $21x^3$

Answer: Coefficient: 21, Base: x, Exponent 3

Question: Simplify $\left(\dfrac{4y^7x^2w}{2y^3xw^6}\right)^2$

Answer: $\dfrac{4y^8x^2}{w^{10}}$

Question: Simplify $2(3x^2yz)^3(xy^2)$

Answer: $54x^7y^5z^3$

Question: Rewrite $6\sqrt[5]{2^x}$

Answer: $6(2)^{\frac{x}{5}}$

Question: Rewrite $wz(y^3x)^{\frac{7}{2}}$

Answer $wzy^{10}x^6\sqrt{xy}$

2-3: SIMPLIFYING ALGEBRAIC FRACTIONS

How do you simplify algebraic fractions? An algebraic fraction occurs when you have one algebraic expression above another algebraic expression. In other words, the algebraic expressions are expressed as a quotient.

For example, $\dfrac{2x^2 + 12x}{2x}$ and $\dfrac{x^2 + 4x + 3}{x + 1}$.

If the algebraic fraction has a one term (a monomial) in the denominator then you simply divide EACH term in the numerator expression by the denominator. Note: Use the quotient rule for the exponents.

Example 3.1:

$$\dfrac{2x^2 + 12x}{2x} \rightarrow \dfrac{2x^2}{2x} + \dfrac{12x}{2x}$$

Solution: $x + 6$

If the algebraic fraction has two terms (a binomial) in the denominator then you will need to simplify using long division.

Example 3.2:

$$\dfrac{x^2 + 6x + 3}{x + 2}$$

$x^2 + 6x + 3$ is the "dividend". $x + 2$ is the "divisor".

Solution:
Write the fraction as a division problem in the following form:

$$x + 2 \overline{\smash{)}x^2 + 6x + 8}$$

Divide x^2 (the first term in the dividend) by x (the first term in the divisor).

$$\dfrac{x^2}{x} = x \quad \rightarrow \quad x + 2 \overline{\smash{)}x^2 + 6x + 8}^{\,x}$$

Multiply x by $x + 2$ and subtract this from the dividend. Bring down the next term.

$$\begin{array}{r} x \\ x+2\overline{)x^2 + 6x + 8} \\ \underline{-x^2 - 2x} \\ 4x + 8 \end{array}$$

Repeat the process.

$$\begin{array}{r} x + 4 \\ x+2\overline{)x^2 + 6x + 8} \\ \underline{-x^2 - 2x} \\ 4x + 8 \\ \underline{-4x - 8} \\ 0 \end{array}$$

Answer: $x + 4$

The second option when the denominator is a binomial and the numerator is a trinomial is to attempt to factor the numerator and see if any of the elements are the same (if the binomials are the same after it has been factored, they will simplify to "1" and no division is necessary).

$$\frac{x^2 + 6x + 8}{x + 2} = \frac{(x+2)(x+4)}{x+2} = x + 4$$

Notice that the same answer resulted from either the long division process, or by simply simplifying the quotient using factoring. This method can be much more efficient when the numerator factors, but this will not always be the case.

Example 3.3: Simplify $\dfrac{x^2 + 7x + 12}{x + 2}$

Solution: Note that $\dfrac{x^2 + 7x + 12}{x + 2} = \dfrac{(x+3)(x+4)}{x+2}$. Therefore, although the numerator does factor, it does not simplify by canceling out the denominator. Therefore, the long division process must be used to simplify the expression.

First, rewrite the expression in long division form: $x+2\overline{)x^2 + 7x + 12}$

Second, divide the first term in the dividend (x^2) by the first term in the divisor (x): $x^2 \div x = x$

Third, multiply the divisor by the result in the previous step (x) and subtract from the dividend. The x that you multiplied by goes above the x^2 in the long division symbol.

$$\begin{array}{r} x \\ x+2 \overline{\big)\, x^2+7x+12} \\ -(x^2+2x) \\ \hline \end{array}$$

Fourth, bring down the next element in the dividend and repeat the process with the first term of the divisor and the first term of the new polynomial.

$$\begin{array}{r} x\, +\, 5 \\ x+2 \overline{\big)\, x^2+7x+12} \\ -(x^2+2x) \\ \hline 5x+12 \\ -(5x+10) \\ \hline 2 \end{array}$$

Because there are no additional terms to pull down out of the dividend, the remaining "2" becomes the remainder. Therefore, the simplified form would be expressed as

$$x+5+\frac{2}{x+2}$$

Example 3.4: Simplify the algebraic fraction $\dfrac{2x^2+8x-10}{x+3}$

Solution: Note that $\dfrac{2x^2+8x-10}{x+3} = \dfrac{2(x+5)(x-1)}{(x+3)}$. Therefore, once again, although the numerator does factor, it does not cancel with the denominator to simplify. Long division must be used to simplify the algebraic fraction.

First, rewrite the expression in long division form: $x+3 \overline{\big)\, 2x^2+8x-10}$

Second, divide the first term in the dividend ($2x^2$) by the first term in the divisor (x): $2x^2 \div x = 2x$.

Third, multiply the divisor by the result in the previous step ($2x$) and subtract from the dividend. Place the "$2x$" above the long division symbol.

$$\begin{array}{r} 2x \\ x+3\overline{)2x^2+8x-10} \\ -(2x^2+6x) \\ \hline 2x \end{array}$$

Fourth, bring down the next element in the dividend and repeat the process with the first term of the divisor and the first term of the new polynomial.

$$\begin{array}{r} 2x+2 \\ x+3\overline{)2x^2+8x-10} \\ -(2x^2+6x) \\ \hline 2x-10 \\ -(2x+6) \\ \hline -16 \end{array}$$

Because there is no additional term to pull down out of the dividend, the remaining "−16" becomes the remainder. Therefore, the simplified form would be expressed as

$$2x+2-\frac{16}{x+3}$$

TRY IT YOURSELF:

Question: Simplify $\dfrac{12x^3-6x^2+3x}{3x}$

Answer: $4x^2-2x+1$

Question: Simplify $\dfrac{2x^2+2x+1}{x+7}$

Answer: $2x-12+\dfrac{85}{x+7}$

Question: Simplify $\dfrac{x^4 + 3x^3 + 4x^2 + 8x + 17}{x^2 + 4x + 2}$

Answer: $x^2 - x + 6 - \dfrac{14x + 5}{x^2 + 4x + 2}$

2-4: SOLUTIONS OF LINEAR EQUATIONS AND INEQUALITIES

What is a linear equation? A linear equation is the most basic type of equations. Linear equations contain variables, but cannot have root symbols, squares/exponents greater than one, and cannot have x and y being multiplied or divided by each other. For example, $x + 7$, $2x + 1$, and $3x + 4y - 1$ are all linear terms. However, xy, $1 + x \div y$, and $4 + 3x^2$ are all NOT linear.

What is an algebraic equation? Equations contain numbers and variables that are called "terms". An algebraic equation must have an equal sign. Equations must always be in "balance" meaning that the value of each side of the equation is the same.

How do you solve a linear equation? You need to follow specific procedures when solving an equation. The two main goals you need to accomplish include moving the variable to one side of the equal sign and setting the coefficient of the variable equal to 1.

Example of a "One Step" linear equation: Solve $x + 10 = 28$

The variable "x" already has a coefficient of 1 so we need to move 10 to the other side of the equation. Therefore, you will add the opposite of 10 to each side of the equation. Remember: When you complete an operation on one side of the equation you MUST do the exact same operation to the other side of the equation.

$x + 10 = 28$
$x + (10 - 10) = (28 - 10)$
$x + 0 = 18$
$x = 18$

Example of a "Two Step" linear equation: Solve $2x + 15 = 45$

First, move 15 to the other side of the equation so that $2x$ is by itself on one side.

$2x + 15 = 45$
$2x + (15 - 15) = (45 - 15)$
$2x = 30$

The second step is to make the coefficient of the variable 1. Therefore, divide each side by 2.

$$2x = 30$$

$$\frac{2x}{2} = \frac{30x}{2} = 15$$

Therefore, $x = 15$

Note: Dividing by 2 is the equivalent to multiplying its reciprocal of ½.

Example of "Two" Step Linear Equation using a Reciprocal: Solve $\frac{2}{3}x + 2 = 8$

$$\frac{2}{3}x + 2 = 8$$

$$\frac{2}{3}x + (2-2) = (8-2)$$

$$\frac{2}{3}x = 6$$

$$\frac{3}{2} * \frac{2}{3}x = 6 * \frac{3}{2}$$

$$x = 9$$

TRY IT YOURSELF:

Question: Solve $2x + 3 = x + 1$

Answer: $x = -2$

Question: Solve $4x + 3x - 1 = \frac{1}{2}x - 2$

Answer: $x = -\frac{2}{13}$

Question: Solve $x + 2.5 = 4x - .5$

Answer: $x = 1$

Linear equations with two variables: Linear equations can also have two variables. When this is the case, you solve the equation by choosing which variable to solve for.

Then, simply treat it like any other equation and solve by isolating the chosen variable on one side of the equation.

Example 4.1: Solve $2x+3y+1=x+6y-5$ for y

Solution: To solve for y, simply isolate y on one side of the equation. To do this we will subtract $3y$ from both sides of the equation to get all of the "y's" on the same side of the equals sign. Next, subtract x and add 5 to both sides to get the "y's" alone.

$$\begin{array}{rl} 2x+3y+1 & =x+6y-5 \\ -3y & \quad -3y \\ \hline 2x+1 & =x+3y-5 \\ -x+5 & \quad -x+5 \\ \hline x+6 & =3y \end{array}$$

Now simply divide by 3 to set the coefficient of the y variable equal to 1 so that it is completely isolated. This answer can be verified by plugging it back into the original equation:

$$3y = x+6$$
$$y = \frac{1}{3}x+2$$

Verify:
$$2x+3y+1 = x+6y-5$$
$$2x+3(\frac{1}{3}x+2)+1 = x+6(\frac{1}{3}x+2)-5$$
$$2x+x+6+1 = x+2x+12-5$$
$$3x+7 = 3x+7$$
$$3x = 3x$$
$$x = x$$

Example 4.2: Solve $2x+3y+1=x+6y-5$ for x

Solution: This time we must solve the equation for x. To do this, isolate the x variable on one side of the equation, rather than the y variable. To do this, subtract x from each side of the equation. Then subtract $3y$ and subtract 1 to get the "x's" alone.

$$3y = x + 6$$
$$y = \frac{1}{3}x + 2$$

Now simply verify by substituting $3y + 6$ for x in the original equation:

$$2x + 3y + 1 = x + 6y - 5$$
$$2(3y - 6) + 3y + 1 = (3y - 6) + 6y - 5$$
$$6y - 12 + 3y + 1 = 3y - 6 + 6y - 5$$
$$9y - 11 = 9y - 11$$
$$9y = 9y$$
$$y = y$$

TRY IT YOURSELF:

Question: Solve $2(x + y) - 1 = 4x + 10$ for x

Answer: $x = y - \frac{11}{2}$

Question: Solve $4(m + 2r) - 2 = 3m + 5r - 1$ for r

Answer: $r = -\frac{1}{3}m + \frac{1}{3}$

What is an inequality? Some equations that you will encounter will not be described using the regular equals sign. Rather, one side of the equation will be related to the other using one of the four basic inequality symbols. The four inequality symbols are

< is "less than"
> is "greater than"
≤ is "less than or equal to"
≥ is "greater than or equal to"

For example, all of the following are basic examples of linear inequalities:

$x + 2 < -4$
$\frac{1}{2}x - 3 \geq 14$
$8x + 4 > 9$
$2x - 1 \leq x - 1$

Inequalities are not much more difficult than regular algebraic equations. To solve an algebraic inequality, simply solve it as you would a regular algebraic equation: i.e., get the variable alone, and set its coefficient to 1.

Example 4.3: Solve the inequality $3x - 1 < 4x + 2$

Solution: First we will get all of the terms with variables in them on the same side of the equation, and alone. To do this, subtract 2 from both sides and subtract $3x$ from both sides

$$3x - 1 < 4x + 2$$
$$\underline{-2-2}$$
$$3x - 3 < 4x$$
$$\underline{-3x -3x}$$
$$-3 < 4x$$
$$-3 < x \text{ or } x > -3$$

In this example, this is all that is required to solve the inequality. The answer is

$x > -3$ or x is greater than negative three.

This answer can be verified by testing different values, to see whether they result in a correct statement. The solution means that a correct statement will result when values greater than -3 are substituted into the equation. Picking the arbitrary values of $x = 3$ and $x = -5$:

If $x = 3$; $\quad 3(3) - 1 < 4(3) + 2 \rightarrow 8 < 14$ TRUE

If $x = -5$; $3(-5) - 1 < 4(-5) - 2 \rightarrow -16 < -22$ FALSE

Example 4.4: Solve the inequality $4x + 1 \leq 7 + x$

Solution: First, get all of the terms with variables in them on one side of the inequality and all of the terms without variables on the opposite side of the inequality. To do this, subtract a one from each side of the equation and subtract "x" from each side of the equation.

$$4x + 1 \leq x + 7$$
$$\underline{-1-1}$$
$$4x \leq x + 6$$
$$\underline{-x -x}$$
$$3x \leq 6$$

Second, finish solving the equation by setting the coefficient of the variable equal to zero. In this example, this is done by dividing by 3 (or multiplying by one-third).

$$\frac{3x}{3} \leq \frac{6}{3}$$ or x is less than or equal to 2
$$x \leq 2$$

This solution can be verified by testing different values to see whether they result in the true statement. According to the solution, any answer less than or equal to 2 will result in a true answer, while any number greater than 3 will result in a false answer. Picking the arbitrary values of $x = 1$, $x = 2$, and $x = 3$ results in:

If $x = 1$ $4(1)+1 \leq (1)+7$ → $6 \leq 8$ TRUE
If $x = 2$ $4(2)+1 \leq (2)+7$ → $9 \leq 9$ TRUE
If $x = 3$ $4(3)+1 \leq (3)+7$ → $13 \leq 10$ FALSE

Special Rule when solving inequalities: There is one special rule that you need to use when you have a negative coefficient value for the variable to begin with. Remember that we want x to be positive and have a coefficient of 1. To achieve this with a negative coefficient, in the very last step of the solution you will have to divide each side of the inequality by a negative number. This means that you need to change the direction of the inequality sign to the opposite direction. This is ONLY when dividing (or multiplying by a reciprocal) by a NEGATIVE number.

Example 4.5: Solve the inequality $14 - x \geq 15 - 2x$

Solution: To solve the equality, first get all of the terms with variables on one side of the inequality, and all terms without variables on the opposite side of the inequality. In this example, this is done by adding "x" to both sides and subtracting "15" from both sides.

$$14 - x \geq 15 - 2x$$
$$\underline{-15 + x \quad -15 + x}$$
$$-1 \quad \geq \quad -x$$

Now, to finish solving the coefficient of the variable must be set equal to "1" This is done by dividing by "–1." Because we are dividing by a negative number, the inequality must be reversed, changing from "is greater than or equal to" to is "less than or equal to."

$$-1 \geq -x$$
$$\frac{-1}{-1} \geq \frac{-x}{-1}$$
$$1 \leq x \quad OR \quad x \geq 1$$

Therefore, x is greater than or equal to one. This can be verified by substituting in arbitrary values to test the inequality. For example, the arbitrary values of $x = 0$ and $x = 2$ yield:

If $x = 0$ $14 - (0) \geq 15 - 2(0) \quad \rightarrow \quad 14 \geq 15 \quad$ FALSE

If $x = 2$ $14 - (2) \geq 15 - 2(2) \quad \rightarrow \quad 12 \geq 11 \quad$ TRUE

Example 4.6: Solve the inequality $5x - 5 \leq 10x + 15$

Solution: First, solve the inequality by getting all of the terms with variables on one side of the inequality and all terms without on the opposite side:

$$5x - 5 \leq 10x + 15$$
$$5x \leq 10x + 20$$
$$-5x \leq 20$$

Finishing solving by setting the coefficient equal to zero. Remember that because we are dividing by a negative number, the inequality must be flipped.

$$-5x \leq 20$$
$$x \geq -4$$

Verifying with the arbitrary values of $x = -5$ and $x = -3$:

If $x = -3$ $5(-3) - 5 \leq 10(-3) + 15 \quad \rightarrow \quad -20 \leq -15 \quad$ TRUE

If $x = -5$ $5(-5) - 5 \leq 10(-5) + 15 \quad \rightarrow \quad -30 \leq -35 \quad$ FALSE

TRY IT YOURSELF:

Question: Solve the inequality $-5x + 15 > 20$

Answer: $x < -1$

Question: Solve the inequality $-8x + 6 > 12 + x$

Answer: $x < -\dfrac{2}{3}$

Question: Solve the inequality $-\dfrac{2}{3}x + 1 > 4$

Answer: $x < -\dfrac{9}{2}$

2-5: SYSTEM OF EQUATIONS AND INEQUALITIES

What is a system of equations? A system of equations is just another way of saying a group of equations. Although a system of equations can include more than two equations, the term generally refers to just two. An equation with two variables (such as $x + y = 1$) has infinitely many solutions, but when studying systems of linear equations there is only one set of coordinates that solves both equations. In other words, it is the point at which the graphs of the two equations intersect. This is called a simultaneous solution, because it applies to both equations.

How do you find a simultaneous solution? Finding the simultaneous solution is called solving the system. You do this by solving one equation and substituting it into the other.

Example 5.1: Find the simultaneous solution for $\begin{array}{l} x + y = 5 \\ x - y = 1 \end{array}$

Solution: We must first solve for one variable in one equation. In this example we will solve for x.

$x - y = 1$
$x = (1 + y)$

Next, substitute the value of "x" into the opposite equation and solve for y. Note: If you substitute $x = (1 + y)$ in the same equation, you will simply find that $x = x$, therefore you MUST substitute it into the opposite equation in order to solve for y.

$x + y = 5$
$(1 + y) + y = 5$
$1 + 2y = 5$
$2y = 4$
$y = 2$

We now know that $y = 2$. We can use this answer to solve for x. As you can see, it doesn't matter which equation we plug $y = 2$ into. Because the simultaneous solution holds true for both equations they will have the same answer.

$x + y = 5$
$x + (2) = 5$
$x = 3$
OR
$x - y = 1$
$x - (2) = 1$
$x = 3$

Therefore, the simultaneous solution for the system is the point $(3, 2)$. This means that the graphs of the two functions intersect at this point.

Example 5.2: Find the simultaneous solution for $\begin{array}{l} 2x + y = 1 \\ y - 2x = 3 \end{array}$

Solution: First solve for one variable in one equation. In this example we will solve for y first instead of x.

$y - 2x = 3$
$y = 3 + 2x$

Next, substitute the value of "y" into the opposite equation and solve for x.

$2x + y = 1$
$2x + (3 + 2x) = 1$
$4x + 3 = 1$
$4x = -2$
$x = -\dfrac{1}{2}$

Now that we know what x is, we can plug it into either of the equations to find the corresponding y value, and complete the simultaneous solution.

$$2(-\frac{1}{2}) + y = 1$$
$$-1 + y = 1$$
$$y = 2$$

OR

$$y - 2(-\frac{1}{2}) = 3$$
$$y + 1 = 3$$
$$y = 2$$

Therefore, the simultaneous solution, or the solution to this system of equations, is the point $(-\frac{1}{2}, 2)$. This means that the graphs of the two equations intersect at this point.

Addition method to solving a system: There is a second method you can use when solving a system of equations. This method is referred to as the "Addition Method." With the addition method, you simply add or subtract the two equations in the system in order to eliminate one of the variables and solve for the remaining variable. To use the addition method, following these six steps:

1. If necessary, rewrite each equation so that the terms containing variables appear on the left hand side of the equal sign and any constants appear on the right side of the equal sign.
2. If necessary, multiply one or both equations by a constant(s) so that when the equations are added the resulting sum will contain only one variable.
3. Add the equations. This will yield a single equation containing only one variable.
4. Solve for the variable in the equation from step 3.
5. a) Substitute the value found in step 4 into either of the original equations. Solve that equation to find the value of the remaining variable.
   OR
   b) Repeat steps 2-4 to eliminate the other variable.
6. Check the values obtained in all original equations.

Example 5.3: Solve the system $\begin{array}{l} x + 3y = 13 \\ x + 4y = 18 \end{array}$ using the addition method

Solution: First, ensure that each equation has the variables on the left hand side of the equation and the constants on the right hand. Note how this differs from the first method in which you attempt to solve for one of the variables. In this example, the equations are already set up properly.

Second, multiply one of the equations by a constant so that when they are added the result will have only one variable. In this case we will multiply the second equation by "–1" so that the "x" variables will cancel out.

$x + 3y = 13$
$(x + 4y = 18)(-1) = (-x - 4y = -18)$

Third, add the equations to get a single equation with one variable.

$$\begin{array}{r} x + 3y = 13 \\ -x - 4y = -18 \\ \hline -y = -5 \end{array}$$

Fourth, solve for the variable in the equation above. In this case $y = 5$.

Fifth, substitute the variable found in the fourth step into either of the equations, and substitute for the remaining variable. Notice that at this step, the two methods for solving the system are the same. Also notice that you can still substitute the known variable value into either of the equations to find the remaining variable.

$x + 3y = 13$
$x + 3(5) = 13$
$x = -2$
OR
$x + 4y = 18$
$x + 4(5) = 18$
$x = -2$

Therefore, the solution is $(-2, 5)$

Example 5.4: Solve the system $\begin{array}{l} 2x + 1 = y \\ 2y + 4 = x \end{array}$ using the addition method

Solution: First, ensure that each equation has the variables on the left hand side of the equation and the constant on the right hand. The rewritten equations appear:

$2x - y = -1$
$-x + 2y = -4$

Second, multiply one of the equations by a constant so that when they are added the result will have only one variable. In this case, we will multiply the second equation by 2, resulting in the two equations appearing as:

$2x - y = -1$
$-2x + 4y = -8$

Third, add the equations to get a single equation with one variable.

$$\begin{array}{r} 2x - y = -1 \\ -2x + 4y = -8 \\ \hline 3y = -9 \end{array}$$

Fourth, solve for the variable in the resulting equation.

$3y = -9$
$y = -3$

Fifth, substitute the variable found in the fourth step into the original equation to find the remaining variable.

$2x - y = 1$
$2x - (-3) = -1$
$2x = -4$
$x = -2$

Therefore, the simultaneous solution is $(-2, -3)$

TRY IT YOURSELF:

Question: Solve the system $\begin{array}{l} 3x + 6 = 2y \\ y + 2x = 4 \end{array}$

Answer: $(\dfrac{2}{7}, \dfrac{24}{7})$

Question: Solve the system $\begin{array}{l} 3x + 1 = y \\ 2y + 3x = 4 \end{array}$

Answer: $\left(\dfrac{2}{9}, \dfrac{5}{3}\right)$

Question: Find the simultaneous solution to $\begin{aligned} x+1 &= y \\ y-5 &= 2x \end{aligned}$

Answer: $(-4, -3)$

2-6: QUADRATIC EQUATIONS

What is a quadratic equation? A quadratic equation in one variable is an equation that can be changed into the form $ax^2 + bx + c = 0$, where a, b, and c are real constants. A **solution** to a quadratic equation is always a **root** of the polynomial $ax^2 + bx + c = 0$.

How do you find the "root" of a polynomial? The roots of a polynomial can be found by **factoring** the polynomial. Set each factor equal to "0" and solve the equation.

Question: Find the solutions to the quadratic equation: $x^2 + 7x + 12$
Factor to find: $(x + 3)(x + 4)$
$x + 3 = 0$ Therefore $x = -3$
$x + 4 = 0$ Therefore $x = -4$
The solutions are -3 and -4.

Example 6.1: Solve $2x - x - 1$

Solution: Because the equation is quadratic, we will solve by setting it equal to zero, and attempting to factor.

$2x - x - 1 = 0$
$(2x + 1)(x - 1) = 0$

Because the equation factors, we will now solve by simply setting each of the factors, or binomials, equal to zero and solving for x. Note: This works because in order for the equation to equal zero either the first or the second binomial MUST be equal to zero.

$2x + 1 = 0 \qquad x - 1 = 0$
$2x = -1 \qquad x = 1$
$x = -\dfrac{1}{2}$

Therefore, $x = -\dfrac{1}{2}, 1$

Example 6.2: Solve $x^2 + x - 6$

Solution: Because the equation is quadratic, we will solve by setting the equation equal to zero, and attempting to factor.

$x^2 + x - 6 = 0$

$(x+3)(x-2) = 0$

Because the equation factors, we will now solve by simply setting each of the binomials equal to zero and solving for x.

$x + 3 = 0 \quad\quad x - 2 = 0$

$x = -3 \quad\quad\quad x = 2$

Therefore, $x = 2, -3$

TRY IT YOURSELF:

Question: Solve $x^2 + 3x - 4$

Answer: $x = -4, 1$

Question: Solve $6x^2 + 5x - 4$

Answer: $x = -\dfrac{4}{3}, \dfrac{1}{2}$

How do you solve a quadratic equation using the "square root" property? The square root property says that if you set $x^2 = a$ then $x = \pm\sqrt{a}$.

Question: Solve $x^2 = 36$
Answer: $x = \pm\sqrt{36} = \pm 6$

How do you solve a quadratic equation by completing the square? When you solve a quadratic equation by completing the square you are creating a trinomial that can be expressed as a square of a binomial.

Follow these seven steps to solve a quadratic equation by completing the square.

1. Use the multiplication (or division) property of equality if necessary to make the numerical coefficient of the squared term equal to 1.

2. Rewrite the equation with the constant by itself on the right side of the equation.

3. Take one-half the numerical coefficient of the first-degree term, square it, and add this quantity to both sides of the equation.

4. Replace the trinomial with its equivalent squared binomial.

5. Use the square root property.

6. Solve for the variable.

7. Check your answers with the original equation.

Question: Solve $x^2 - 10x + 21$ by completing the square.

1. $x^2 - 10x + 21 = 0$
2. $x^2 - 10x = -21$
3. $\frac{1}{2}(-10) = -5$ and $(-5)^2 = 25$

    $x^2 - 10x + 25 = -21 + 25$

    $x^2 - 10x + 25 = 4$
4. $(x - 5)^2 = 4$
5. $x - 5 = \pm\sqrt{4}$ Therefore $x - 5 = \pm 2$ or $x = 3, 7$

Example 6.3: Solve $x^2 = 169$

Solution: According to the "square root" property, the result will be both a positive and a negative answer. This is because a negative number squared will be positive, as will a positive number squared. In most cases, it is just assumed that the positive answer is needed. However, when working with quadratic equations it is important that both values are considered.

$x^2 = 169$

$x = \pm\sqrt{169}$

$x = \pm 13$

Example 6.4: Solve $x^2 + 6x - 160$ by completing the square.

Solution: Some quadratic equations cannot be solved by factoring. In this example, the equation does not factor. Instead, we will solve by completing the square. Essentially, completing the square involves forcing the equation to factor into a perfect square so that it can be solved. Of course, it isn't as accurate/perfect as factoring, but it is still a useful technique.

First, ensure that the leading coefficient (the *a* value of a quadratic equation in standard form) is equal to 1 (in this example this is already the case), and set the equation equal to zero.

$$x^2 + 6x - 160 = 0$$

Second, rewrite the equation with the constant (i.e., the *c* value of a quadratic equation in standard form, or the value without a variable attached to it) on the right side of the equation.

$$x^2 + 6x = 160$$

Third, add $\left(\frac{b}{2}\right)^2$ to each side of the equation. (Remember that *b* is the numerical coefficient of the first-degree term of a quadratic equation in standard form.) Adding this to both sides of the equation keeps the equation in balance and makes it so that the left side of the equation will now factor to a perfect square, achieving the goal of factoring.

$$x^2 + 6x + \left(\frac{b}{2}\right)^2 = 160 + \left(\frac{b}{2}\right)^2$$

$$x^2 + 6x + \left(\frac{6}{2}\right)^2 = 160 + \left(\frac{6}{2}\right)^2$$

$$x^2 + 6x + 9 = 169$$

Fourth, factor the left side of the equation. Notice that we now have a perfect square, and that because in step 3 we added $\left(\frac{b}{2}\right)^2$ to each side of the equation, the factored binomials have the quantity $b \div 2$ in them.

$$(x+3)^2 = 169$$

Fifth, use the square root property to solve for possible solutions to the equation

$(x+3)^2 = 169$

$x + 3 = \pm\sqrt{169} = \pm 13$

$x = -3 + 13, -3 - 13$
OR
$x = 10, -16$

Finally, verify the solutions by substituting them into the original equation.

If $x = 10$ $(10)^2 + 6(10) - 160 = 0$ TRUE
If $x = -16$ $(-16)^2 + 6(-16) - 160 = 0$ TRUE

Example 6.5: Solve $x^2 + 4x - 12$ by completing the square

Solution: First, ensure that the leading coefficient is equal to 1 and set the equation equal to zero

$x^2 + 4x - 12 = 0$

Second, rewrite the equation with the constant on the right side of the equation

$x^2 + 4x = 12$

Third, add $\left(\dfrac{b}{2}\right)^2$ to each side of the equation. In this case,

$x^2 + 4x + \left(\dfrac{4}{2}\right)^2 = 12 + \left(\dfrac{4}{2}\right)^2$

$x^2 + 4x + 4 = 16$

Fourth, factor the left side of the equation (it will be a perfect square with binomials $x + (b \div 2)$).

$(x + 2)^2 = 16$

Fifth, solve the equation using the square root property

$(x+2)^2 = 16$

$x + 2 = \pm\sqrt{16} = \pm 4$

$x = -2 \pm 4 = 2, -6$

Finally, verify the solutions by substituting them into the original equation

If $x = 2$ $\quad (2)^2 + 4(2) - 12 = 0 \quad$ TRUE
If $x = -6$ $\quad (-6)^2 + 4(-6) - 12 = 0 \quad$ TRUE

TRY IT YOURSELF:

Question: Solve by completing the square $2x^2 + 4x - 8$

Answer: $x = -1 \pm \sqrt{5}$

Question: Solve by completing the square $3x^2 + 5x - 6$

Answer: $x = \dfrac{30 \pm \sqrt{97}}{36}$

Question: Complete the square of $x^2 - 7x - 31$

Answer: $\left(x - \dfrac{7}{2}\right)^2 - \dfrac{173}{4}$

What is the quadratic equation/formula? The quadratic formula, which is also referred to as the quadratic equation, is the final way to solve a quadratic equation. The quadratic formula, like completing the square, can be used to find solutions to equations which will not factor.

How do you solve a quadratic equation by using the quadratic formula?
Follow these two steps:

1. Write the equation in standard form, $ax^2 + bx + c = 0$, and determine the numerical values for *a, b*, and *c*.

2. Substitute the values for *a, b*, and *c* from Step 1 in the quadratic formula below and then evaluate to obtain the solution.

THE QUADRATIC FORMULA:

$$x = \frac{-b \pm \sqrt{b^2 - 4ac}}{2a}$$

Example 6.6: Solve $4x^2 - 71x = -1$

Solution: Because this equation does not factor, we will use the quadratic equation to solve. First we will get it in standard form:

$4x^2 - 71x + 1 = 0$

Now that it is in standard form we can see that
$a = 4$
$b = -71$
$c = 1$

Knowing this, simply substitute the numbers into the quadratic formula, and simplify as much as possible.

$$x = \frac{-b \pm \sqrt{b^2 - 4ac}}{2a}$$

$$x = \frac{-(-71) \pm \sqrt{(-71)^2 - 4(4)(1)}}{2(4)}$$

$$x = \frac{-(-71) \pm \sqrt{(-71)^2 - 4(4)(1)}}{2(4)}$$

$$x = \frac{71 \pm \sqrt{5025}}{8}$$

$$x = \frac{71 \pm 5\sqrt{201}}{8} \approx 17.74, .01$$

Example 6.7: Solve using the quadratic equation $7x^2 - 13x + 5 = x^2 - 2$

Solution: First, get the equation in standard form

$$7x^2 - 13x + 5 = x - 2$$
$$6x^2 - 13x + 7 = 0$$

$a = 6$
$b = -13$
$c = 7$

Second, substitute the numbers into the quadratic formula and simplify

$$x = \frac{-(-13) \pm \sqrt{(-13)^2 - 4(6)(7)}}{2(6)}$$

$$x = \frac{13 \pm \sqrt{169 - 168}}{12}$$

$$x = \frac{13 \pm \sqrt{1}}{12} = \frac{13 \pm 1}{12}$$

$$x = \frac{7}{6}, 1$$

Example 6.8: Solve using the quadratic equation $4x^2 + x + 2 = 0$

Solution:
$a = 4$
$b = 1$
$c = 2$

$$x = \frac{-1 \pm \sqrt{(1)^2 - 4(4)(2)}}{2(2)}$$

$$x = \frac{-1 \pm \sqrt{-30}}{4}$$

Notice that in this example, substituting into the quadratic formula resulted in an answer with a negative value under the square root. This means that the equation cannot be solved, and that the equation has no roots (the graph of the equation does not cross the x axis).

TRY IT YOURSELF:

Question: Solve $x^2 - 1 = -x$ using the quadratic equation.

Answer: $x = \dfrac{-1 \pm \sqrt{5}}{2} \approx 0.62, -1.62$

Question: Solve $-2x^2 - 2x + 7$ using the quadratic equation.

Answer: $x = \dfrac{1 \pm \sqrt{15}}{-2} \approx -2.44, 1.44$

Question: How many real roots does the equation $2x^2 + x + 4 = 0$ have?

Answer: None

2-7: RATIONAL AND RADICAL EQUATIONS

What is a radical equation? A "radical" is essentially a square root, except that radical is the overarching term which can describe any type of "root"; i.e., square roots $\sqrt{}$, cube roots $\sqrt[3]{}$, fourth roots $\sqrt[4]{}$, and so on. A radical equation, therefore, is any equation that has a radical in it. Note: an expression is only a radical equation if the x-variable is inside the square root. $\sqrt{x} + 2$ IS a radical expression. $\sqrt{2} + x$ IS NOT a radical expression.

How do you solve radical equations? Radical equations are closely related to polynomial and quadratic equations because the two are opposite operations. In other words, a radical "undoes" an exponent. Therefore, exponents can be used in solving radical equations. To solve a radical equation, first use exponents to eliminate the radical, and then solve for x algebraically.

Example 7.1: Solve $\sqrt[4]{x+2} = 2$

Solution: First, eliminate the radical (i.e., the "root"). To do this we will raise both sides of the equation to an exponent of 4 because the radical is a "fourth" root.

$\sqrt[4]{x+2} = 2$
$(\sqrt[4]{x+2})^4 = 2^4$

Now, simply finish solving the equation algebraically

$x + 2 = 16$

$x = 14$

Example 7.2: Solve the radical equation $\sqrt[3]{2 + 2x} = 4$

Solution: First, eliminate the radical by cubing both sides of the equation.

$(\sqrt[3]{2 + 2x})^3 = (4)^3$

$2 + 2x = 64$

Now, simply finishing solving the equation algebraically

$2 + 2x = 64$

$2x = 62$

$x = 31$

TRY IT YOURSELF:

Question: Solve the radical equation $\sqrt[5]{5x + 2} = 2$

Answer: $x = 6$

Question: Solve the radical equation $\dfrac{\sqrt[4]{12x + 5}}{7} = 2$

Answer: $x = \dfrac{38411}{12} \approx 3200.9$

Solving radical equations may seem fairly straightforward, but there are a couple of tips to be aware of to help you avoid making mistakes.

Tip #1 Extraneous Solutions: Be aware of extraneous solutions. Extraneous solutions are solutions that emerge as mathematically correct, but which are actually false or irrelevant to the question at hand. These often emerge when working with radicals and exponents because of the "±" which you put in front of a square root. It creates an extra answer that won't actually work in the original equation. The following example will demonstrate this.

Example 7.3: Solve $\sqrt{x-1} = x-7$

Solution: The two functions represented by this equation are $y = x - 7$ and $y = \sqrt{x-1}$ and when graphed they will appear as:

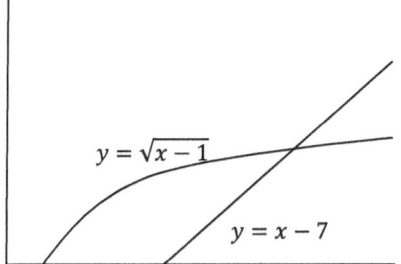

Remember that the solution to the equation will be the point at which these two graphs intersect. As you can see the graph has a single intersection point; therefore, the equation should result in a single solution. Moving back to the original equation, we can proceed to solve it algebraically.

$$\sqrt{x-1} = x-7$$
$$\sqrt{x-1}^2 = (x-7)^2$$
$$x-1 = x^2 - 14x + 49$$
$$0 = x^2 - 15x + 50$$
$$0 = (x-5)(x-10)$$
Therefore, $x = 5, 10$

The algebraic method provided two solutions, when we know that only one exists based on the graph. We can conclude, therefore, that one of the results must be extraneous. This is why it is important that whenever you finish solving an equation, you plug both numbers back into your original equation and ensure that they are, in fact, true solutions.

$x = 5$, FALSE $x = 10$, TRUE

$\sqrt{(5)-1} = (5) - 7$ $\sqrt{(10)-1} = (10) - 7$
$\sqrt{4} = -2$ $\sqrt{9} = 3$
$2 = -2$ $3 = 3$

Therefore $x = 10$ is the only correct solution to the equation.

Example 7.4: Solve the equation $\sqrt{2-x} = x$

Solution: First eliminate the radical from the equation by squaring both sides

$2 - x = x^2$

Next, continue solving algebraically.

$2 - x = x^2$

Notice that in this example, the equation CAN be moved into standard quadratic form, and does factor. This makes solving relatively simple. Note: If it's unclear whether the solution will factor, the quadratic formula will yield the same result as factoring.

$2 - x = x^2$
$x^2 + x - 2 = 0$

Now, simply substitute each answer into the original equation to determine whether or not it is a valid or an extraneous solution.

If $x = 1$ $\sqrt{2-(1)} = (1)$ TRUE
If $x = -2$ $\sqrt{2-(-2)} = (-2)$ FALSE

Therefore, $x = 1$ is the only solution to the equation

Tip #2 Common Sense Check: Use common sense. Many times people will overlook that there is not a solution to a radical expression and solve for an incorrect solution. Remember, an even exponent will NEVER yield a negative result.

Example 7.5: $\sqrt{x} = -2$ yields the solution $x = 4$, which is extraneous.

However,

$\sqrt[3]{x} = -1$ yields the solution $x = -1$ which IS possible because ODD roots CAN yield negative answers.

Tip #3 Be Careful with Algebra: Make sure that you deal with SIDES when solving equations and not individual TERMS.

Example 7.6: Solve $\sqrt{x+5} - 1 = 4$

Incorrect Solution:

$\sqrt{x+5}^2 - 1^2 = 4^2$
$x + 5 - 1 = 16$
$x = 20$

Correct Solution:

$(\sqrt{x+5} - 1)^2 = 4^2$
$(x+5) - 2\sqrt{x+5} + 1 = 16$
etc.

Clearly these two methods will yield different solutions to the equation.

Tip #4 Isolate the Radical First: Whenever possible, get the radical ALONE before raising to an exponent. Otherwise the equation may simply become more complex or yield false answers as a result. This is true in the case of the above equation, and is further illustrated below.

Example 7.7: Solve $\sqrt{x+5} - 1 = 4$

Simpler way:

$\sqrt{x+5} - 1 = 4$
$\sqrt{x+5} = 5$
$\sqrt{x+5}^2 = 5^2$
$x + 5 = 25$
$x = 20$

Harder way:

$(\sqrt{x+5} - 1)^2 = (4)^2$
$(x+5) - 2\sqrt{x+5} + 1 = 16$
$x - 10 = 2\sqrt{x+5}$
etc.

TRY IT YOURSELF:

Question: Solve $x - 6 = \sqrt{x}$

Answer: $x = 9$ Note: $x = 4$ is an extraneous solution

Question: Solve $\sqrt{10 - x} - 2 = x$

Answer: $x = 1, -6$

What is a rational expression? A rational expression is simply a rational number. Recall that rational numbers are numbers which can be expressed as fractions. Therefore, rational expressions are fractions. Rational expressions can have different operations within them, and variables. For example, all of the following are rational expressions:

$$\frac{2x+5}{x^2+1} \quad \frac{2-5x}{4} \quad \frac{\sqrt{3x}}{4-x} \quad \frac{1}{2x-1}$$

How do you combine rational expressions? Rational expressions are combined the same way that regular fractions are combined. If the expressions are being added or subtracted with each other, simply get a common denominator and add or subtract the numerators. If they are being multiplied, simply multiply straight across to get your answer.

Example 7.8: Combine $\frac{2x+1}{15} + \frac{3x-1}{5}$

Solution: In order to add the two rational expressions, they must first have a common denominator. This problem is fairly simple because the denominators do not contain variables or other complex operations. In order to get a common denominator we can simply multiply the second expression by ($\frac{3}{3}$). This is a valid operation because it is technically equal to multiplying by one.

$$\frac{2x+1}{15} + \frac{3x-1}{5}\left(\frac{3}{3}\right) = \frac{2x+1}{15} + \frac{9x-3}{15}$$

Now that the two have common denominators, simply add straight across the numerator and simplify.

$$\frac{2x+1}{15} + \frac{9x-3}{15} = \frac{2x+1+9x-3}{15} = \frac{11x-2}{15}$$

Example 7.9: Combine $\left(\frac{2x}{x+1}\right)\left(\frac{3x-1}{4}\right)$

Solution: In this example the two rational expressions are being multiplied together. To combine them, simply multiply straight across both the numerator and the denominator and simplify. Note: No common denominator is needed when multiplying rational expressions.

$$\left(\frac{2x}{x+1}\right)\left(\frac{3x-1}{4}\right) = \frac{(2x)(3x-1)}{4(x+1)} = \frac{6x^2-2x}{4x+4}$$

Example 7.10: Combine $\left(\dfrac{4x}{x+1}\right)+\left(\dfrac{3x-5}{4}\right)$

Solution: First the two expressions must have a common denominator. In this case we can find a common denominator by multiplying the two. In other words, the common denominator is $4(x+1)$. In order to achieve this denominator, multiply the first term by $\left(\dfrac{4}{4}\right)$ and the second term by $\left(\dfrac{x+1}{x+1}\right)$.

$$\left(\dfrac{4x}{x+1}\right)\left(\dfrac{4}{4}\right)+\left(\dfrac{3x-5}{4}\right)\left(\dfrac{x+1}{x+1}\right)$$

Now, simply add across the rational expressions and simplify

$$\dfrac{16x}{4(x+1)}+\dfrac{(3x-5)(x+1)}{4(x+1)}$$

$$\dfrac{16x+(3x^2-5x+3x-5)}{4(x+1)}$$

$$\dfrac{3x^2+14x-5}{4(x+1)}$$

How do you solve rational equations by cross-multiplying? A rational equation is an equation which deals with rational expressions. In other words, rational equations are equations with a fraction on both sides of the equation. There are essentially two different methods of solving rational equations. First, if there is only one rational expression on each side of the equals sign, simply cross-multiply and solve. Cross-multiplying is done by setting the product of one numerator and one denominator equal to the opposite numerator-denominator product. It appear as

$$\dfrac{a}{b}=\dfrac{c}{d}\rightarrow ad=cb$$

In order to get the equation so that there is only one expression on each side of the equation, you may need to combine rational expressions.

Example 7.11: Solve $\dfrac{2x+1}{4x}+\dfrac{x}{x+1}=\dfrac{-7}{5}$ using cross-multiplication

Solution: Because we want to solve using cross-multiplication, we need to get a single expression on each side of the equation. Therefore, the left hand side of the equation must be simplified to a single expression.

$$\frac{2x+1}{4x} + \frac{x}{x+1} = \frac{(2x+1)(x+1)}{(4x)(x+1)} + \frac{x(4x)}{(x+1)(4x)} = \frac{6x^2+3x+1}{4x(x+1)}$$

Therefore, the equation simplifies to

$$\frac{6x^2+3x+1}{4x(x+1)} = \frac{-7}{5}$$

Next, cross multiply and solve the equation. In this example the equation is solved using the quadratic formula because it simplifies to a quadratic equation

$$5(6x^2+3x+1) = -7(4x)(x+1)$$
$$30x^2+15x+5 = -28x^2-28x$$
$$58x^2+43x+5 = 0$$

$$x = \frac{-(43) \pm \sqrt{(43)^2 - 4(58)(5)}}{2(58)} = \frac{-43 \pm \sqrt{689}}{116} \approx -.14, \ -.6$$

Example 7.12: Solve $\dfrac{1}{4-x} = \dfrac{5x}{x+1} + \dfrac{3}{4}$ using cross-multiplication

Solution: First, combine the rational expressions on the right side of the equation to get a single expression on each side of the equation.

$$\frac{5x}{x+1} + \frac{3}{4} = \frac{5x(4)}{4(x+1)} + \frac{3(x+1)}{4(x+1)} = \frac{20x+3x+1}{4(x+1)} = \frac{23x+1}{4x+4}$$

Therefore, the equation simplifies to

$$\frac{1}{4-x} = \frac{23x+1}{4x+4}$$

Next, cross multiply and solve the equation

$$\frac{1}{4-x} = \frac{23x+1}{4x+4}$$

$$(23x+1)(4-x) = 4x+4$$

$$92x - 23x^2 + 4 - x = 4x + 4$$

$$-23x^2 + 87x = 0$$

$$x(87 - 23x) = 0$$

Therefore,

$$98 - 23x = 0$$

$$98 = 23x$$

$$x = \frac{98}{23}$$

OR

$$x = 0$$

Note: Factoring was used to solve the equation. The quadratic formula could also have been used by setting $c = 0$ if you did not think to factor the equation.

TRY IT YOURSELF:

Question: Solve $\dfrac{3}{x-1} = \dfrac{2}{2x+5}$

Answer: $x = -\dfrac{13}{4}$

Question: Solve $\dfrac{(2x+3)}{x} + \dfrac{3x}{4} = \dfrac{x}{5}$

Answer: No real solutions. The equation simplifies to $11x^2 + 40x + 60 = 0$ which when solved using the quadratic formula yields no real solutions.

Question: Solve $\dfrac{x-4}{4} + \dfrac{x}{3} = 6$

Answer: $x = 12$

How do you solve a rational equation by using common denominators? The second way to solve a rational equation is by getting all elements of the equation to have the same denominator. Once all elements have the same denominator, simply multiply by that denominator and eliminate the problem of fractions altogether. To solve using this method

1. Find the common denominator
2. Convert all terms to have the common denominator
3. Multiply by the common denominator
4. Solve

Example 7.13: Solve $\dfrac{x+1}{4} = \dfrac{2x}{x+1}$ by finding common denominators

Solution: First, the least common denominator must be determined. The simplest way to find a common denominator when working with rational expressions is by multiplying the denominators together. In this case the common denominator is

$$4 \cdot (x+1) = 4(x+1)$$

Next, convert all fractions to have this same common denominator. The expression on the right side of the equation must be multiplied by 4/4, and the expression on the left side of the equation must be multiplied by $(x + 1)/(x + 1)$.

$$\frac{x+1}{4} \cdot \frac{x+1}{x+1} = \frac{2x}{x+1} \cdot \frac{4}{4}$$

$$\frac{(x+1)^2}{4(x+1)} = \frac{8x}{4(x+1)}$$

Third, multiply by the common denominator, which is $4(x + 1)$ in this problem.

$$\frac{(x+1)^2}{4(x+1)} \cdot 4(x+1) = \frac{8x}{4(x+1)} \cdot 4(x+1)$$

$$(x+1)^2 = 8x$$

Finally, simply solve for x, remembering to check for extraneous solutions

$$(x+1)^2 = 8x$$
$$x^2 + 2x + 1 = 8x$$
$$x^2 - 6x + 1 = 0$$

Quadratic Formula:

$$x = \frac{6 \pm \sqrt{(-6)^2 - 4(1)(1)}}{2(1)} = 3 \pm \frac{\sqrt{32}}{2} = 3 \pm 2\sqrt{2}$$

Check for extraneous solutions:

$$x = 3 + \sqrt{2} \qquad \frac{(3+2\sqrt{2})+1}{4} = \frac{2(3+2\sqrt{2})}{(3+2\sqrt{2})+1} \rightarrow TRUE$$

$$x = 3 - \sqrt{2} \qquad \frac{(3-2\sqrt{2})+1}{4} = \frac{2(3-2\sqrt{2})}{(3-2\sqrt{2})+1} \rightarrow TRUE$$

Example 7.14: Solve $\frac{x}{x+1} + \frac{2}{x+2} = \frac{4x+1}{3(x+1)}$ by finding common denominators.

Solution: In this example there are three terms to get into a common denominator. To solve this we can either combine two so that there is only one term on each side of the equation, or we can simply get all three to a common denominator. This is the faster method. To find the common denominator, we simply multiply the denominators of all three terms together.

$$(x+1) \cdot (x+2) \cdot (3) = 3(x+1)(x+2)$$

Next, convert all terms to have the same common denominator by multiplying by the two denominators the term doesn't have.

$$\frac{x}{x+1} \cdot \frac{3(x+2)}{3(x+2)} + \frac{2}{x+2} \cdot \frac{3(x+1)}{3(x+1)} = \frac{4x+1}{3(x+1)} \cdot \frac{(x+2)}{(x+2)}$$

$$\frac{3x(x+2)}{3(x+1)(x+2)} + \frac{6(x+1)}{3(x+1)(x+2)} = \frac{(4x+1)(x+2)}{3(x+1)(x+2)}$$

Third, multiply each side of the equation by the common denominator, eliminating the denominators of all three terms.

$$\left(\frac{3x(x+2)}{3(x+1)(x+2)} + \frac{6(x+1)}{3(x+1)(x+2)}\right)3(x+1)(x+2) = \left(\frac{(4x+1)(x+2)}{3(x+1)(x+2)}\right)3(x+1)(x+2)$$

$$3x(x+2) + 6(x+1) = (4x+1)(x+2)$$

Finally, solve for x

$$3x(x+2) + 6(x+1) = (4x+1)(x+2)$$
$$3x^2 + 6x + 6x + 6 = 4x^2 + x + 8x + 2$$
$$x^2 - 3x - 4 = 0$$
$$(x+1)(x-4) = 0$$
$$x = -1, 4$$

TRY IT YOURSELF:

Question: What common denominator should be used when solving the equation $\frac{m+4}{4} + \frac{m-1}{4} = \frac{m+4}{4m}$?

Answer: $4m$.

Usually to find the common denominator you would multiply all of the terms together, which would give $(4)(4)(4m) = 64m$. While this is a common denominator of the equation and could be used to solve it, the LEAST common denominator (which requires the least extra algebra to be used when solving) is clearly $4m$, because each of the terms can easily be converted to this denominator. It is useful to look for situations when multiple denominators use the same term to make sure the least common denominator is used, instead of a more difficult denominator.

Question: What common denominator should be used to solve $\frac{1}{2a^2} + \frac{1}{a} = -\frac{1}{2}$?

Answer: $2a^2$.

Question: Solve $\frac{5}{5-w} + \frac{w^2}{5-w} = -2$ by finding a common denominator

Answer: $w = -5, 3$

2-8: EQUATIONS OF LINES

What is slope-intercept form of a line? The most common form of equation for a line to be written in is the slope-intercept form, which is $y = mx + b$. The "m" in the equation represents the slope of the line, and is always just before the variable x. The "b" in the equation indicates the y-intercept of the equation. In other words, the "b" indicates where the line crosses the y axis. This form is the most common because it is the simplest form to graph from. Simply follow the steps:

1. Move the equation into slope-intercept form.
2. Determine the y-intercept.
3. Determine the slope to continue graphing around the y-intercept.

Example 8.1: Graph the line $y = 2x - 1$. Note: Each tick mark represents one unit of measurement in each of the following graphs..

Answer: Because the line is in slope-intercept form (the y is alone with a coefficient of 1, and the x has an exponent of 1), we can see that the slope of the line is 2 ($m = 2$) and the y-intercept equals 1 ($b = -1$). Based on this we can plot the graph:

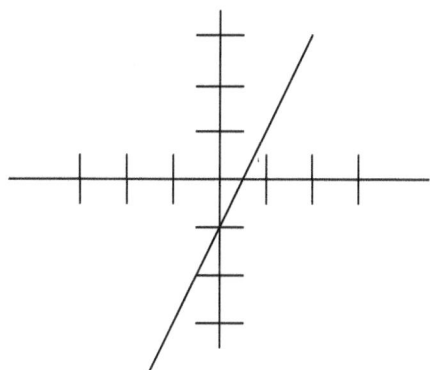

Example 8.2: Use the following graph to write the equation of the line in slope-intercept form.

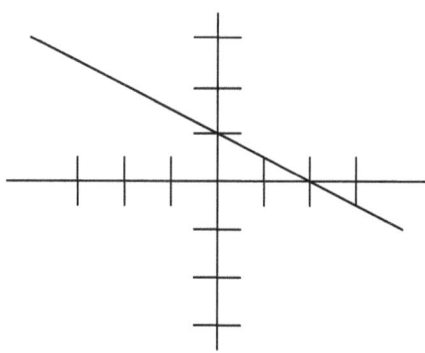

Solution: Two pieces of information are needed to write the equation of a line in slope-intercept form. Slope-intercept form is $y = mx + b$, so we need to determine the slope "m" and the y-intercept "b". By looking at the graph we can clearly see that the graph intersects the y axis where $y = 1$. Therefore the y-intercept, or "b" is 1. Therefore

$y = mx + 1$

To find the slope we take two arbitrary points which lie on the graph, such as (0,1) and (2,0), and use them to find slope as follows:

$m = \dfrac{y_2 - y_1}{x_2 - x_1}$ where "point 1" is (0,1) and "point 2" is (2,0)

$m = \dfrac{0 - 1}{2 - 0} = -\dfrac{1}{2}$

Therefore, the equation of the line is $y = -\dfrac{1}{2}x + 1$

TRY IT YOURSELF:

Question: Rewrite the following equation in slope-intercept form $3x + 2y = 1$

Answer: $y = -\dfrac{3}{2}x + \dfrac{1}{2}$

Question: Graph the line described by $y = -3x + 2$

Answer:

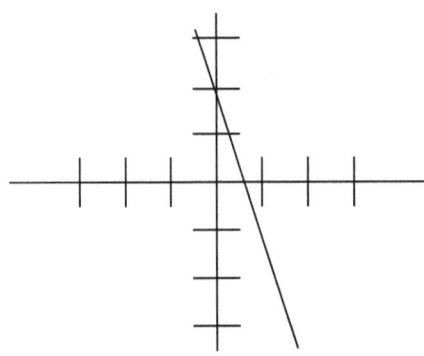

Question: Write the equation of the line described by the following graph in slope-intercept form.

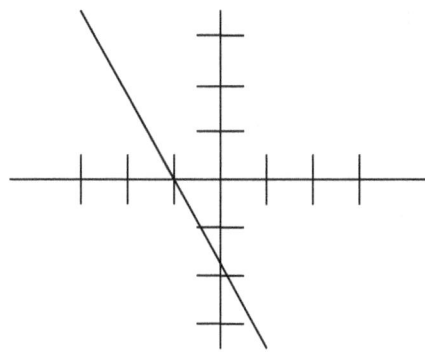

Answer: $y = -2x - 2$

Question: Identify the slope and y-intercept of the line $y = 4x - 2$

Answer: The line has a slope of 4 and a y-intercept of -2.

What is point-slope form of a line? While the slope-intercept equation of a line uses the slope and y-intercept to graph the line, the point-slope form of a line utilizes the slope and one of the points that the graph of the line passes through. The general formula of the point-slope form of a line is

$$(y - y_1) = m(x - x_1)$$

Where the line has a slope of "m" and passes through the point (x_1, y_1)
Note: An equation of a line in point-slope form can be written for ANY point that is on the given line.

Typically when you are asked to graph an equation in point-slope form you will be given either the slope and a point on the line, or two points on the line. In some cases you will be given a single point, and the equation of a parallel line. In cases such as these recall that parallel lines have the same slope. To write the equation of a line using two points (or the slope and a point) simply

1. Determine the slope, either because it has been given or using the two points and the formula $m = \dfrac{y_2 - y_1}{x_2 - x_1}$
2. Choose one of the points to use in the formula (it doesn't matter which)
3. Plug the point and slope into the point-slope equation $(y - y_1) = m(x - x_1)$

Example 8.3: Write the equation of the line that passes through the points (0,1) and (2,6) in point-slope form.

Solution: First we will find the slope using the two points. In this example we will designate (0,1) and point 1 and (2,6) as point two. Therefore, the slope is

$$m = \frac{y_2 - y_1}{x_2 - x_1} = \frac{6-1}{2-0} = \frac{5}{2}$$

Next, we arbitrarily choose one of the two points to use to write the equation. We will write equations for each of the points here.

(0,1): $y - 1 = \frac{5}{2}(x - 0)$

(2,6): $y - 6 = \frac{5}{2}(x - 2)$

Note: Although the two equations look different initially, they actually describe the SAME line. In fact, notice that when they are simplified, they result in the same equation, which is the equation of the line in slope-intercept form.

(0,1):
$$y - 1 = \frac{5}{2}(x - 0)$$
$$y - 1 = \frac{5}{2}x - 0$$
$$y = \frac{5}{2}x + 1$$

(2,6):
$$y - 6 = \frac{5}{2}(x - 2)$$
$$y - 6 = \frac{5}{2}x - 5$$
$$y = \frac{5}{2}x + 1$$

Example 8.4: Write the equation of the line that has a slope of 8 and passes through the point (2,7).

Solution: Although the question doesn't specifically instruct that the equation should be written in point-slope form, the information that we have been given is the slope and a point on the line, so this will be the easiest form to work with. All that needs to be done is inserting the information into the equation as follows.

$$y - 7 = 8(x - 2)$$

If the slope-intercept form of the line were needed, all that would need to be done is some basic simplification to get the equation

$y - 7 = 8(x - 2)$
$y - 7 = 8x - 16$
$y = 8x - 9$

Example 8.5: Determine the *y*-intercept of a line with a slope of 5 which passes through the point (4,1).

Solution: First, write the equation of the line. Based on the information provided in the problem, point-slope form should be used:

$y - 1 = 5(x - 4)$

From here, simply simplify to find the slope-intercept form of the equation and determine the *y*-intercept.

$y - 1 = 5(x - 4)$
$y - 1 = 5x - 20$
$y = 5x - 19$

Therefore, the *y*-intercept is –19

TRY IT YOURSELF:

Question: Write the equation of a line that passes through the point (4,7) and runs perpendicular to the line $y = \frac{1}{2}x + 8$ in point-slope form.

Answer: $y - 7 = -2(x - 4)$

Question: Determine the slope of the line described by the equation $y - \frac{1}{2} = -3(x + 4)$

Answer: $m = -3$

Question: Determine a point through which the line $y - 2 = -5(x + 4)$ passes

Answer: (–4, 2)

2-9: ABSOLUTE VALUE

What is an absolute value? Absolute value refers to the distance between a number and 0 on the number line. Because distance cannot be negative, absolute values are always positive.

What is the notation for absolute value and how do we find it? The notation for absolute value is two vertical lines with the terms you wish to find the absolute value of in between them. For example, $|x-5|$ indicates that you should find the absolute value of "$x-5$". An absolute value is found by making sure that whatever is inside the absolute value becomes positive. If it is negative, change it to a positive. If it is positive, leave it as it is.

Examples of finding absolute values:

$|-2| = 2 \qquad |4| = 4 \qquad |5-10| = 5 \qquad -|1| = -1$

Solving single-variable equations with absolute values: To solve an equation with an absolute value in it use the following steps:

1. Get the absolute value on one side of the equals sign, with everything else opposite.
2. Solve the inside of the absolute value for both the positive and negative form of whatever is on the other side of the equals sign.

Absolute values will always have two solutions. The positive form of what it is equal to, and the negative form of what it is equal to. This is because the absolute value will turn any negatives positive.

Example 9.1: Solve $|x+5| - 4 = -3$

Solution: First isolate the absolute value on one side of the equation, in this case by adding 4 to each side of the equation

$|x+5| - 4 = -3$
$|x+5| = 1$

Second, solve for the positive and negative forms of the answer, in this case 1 and −1

$$x + 5 = 1$$
$$x = -4$$

$$x + 5 = -1$$
$$x = -6$$

Therefore, $x = -4, -6$. This can be verified by substituting them into the original equation.

Example 9.2: Solve $|2x - 4| + 1 = 3x + 1$

Solution: First isolate the absolute value on one side of the equation, in this case by subtracting "–1" from each side of the equation.

$$|2x - 4| + 1 = 3x + 1$$
$$|2x - 4| = 3x$$

Second, solve for the positive and negative forms of the answer, in this case $3x$ and $-3x$

$$2x - 4 = 3x$$
$$x = -4$$

$$2x - 4 = -3x$$
$$5x = 4$$
$$x = \frac{4}{5}$$

Inequalities and absolute values: When there is an absolute value in an inequality equation, the resulting answer will actually be a range of numbers rather than specific answers. Solve absolute value inequalities in the following steps:

1. Isolate the absolute value on one side of the inequality (as you would if it were a regular absolute value equation).
2. Remove the absolute value and solve for *x* normally (also as you would normally).
3. Remove the absolute value, flip the inequality symbol, and solve for the negative portion of the answer.

Example 9.3: Solve $|x-1|+3>5$

Solution: First, isolate the absolute value on one side of the inequality, in this example this is done by subtracting three from both sides of the equation

$|x-1|+3>5$

$|x-1|>2$

Next we solve normally, removing the absolute values

$x-1>2$

$x>3$

Finally, we solve for the negative portion of the answer by flipping the inequality and solving for -2 instead of 2

$x-1<-2$

$x<-1$

Therefore, $x>3$ and $x<-1$

TRY IT YOURSELF:

Question: Solve $|3x+2|-4=0$

Answer: $x=\dfrac{2}{3},-2$

Question: Solve $|x-1|\geq 2$

Answer: $x\leq -1$
$x\geq 3$

Question: Solve $|3x-7|+1=2x+2$

Answer: $x=8,\dfrac{6}{5}$

2-10: DIRECT AND INVERSE VARIATION

What is direct variation? Variation refers to the way that an equation or variable changes. Essentially, every two variable equation describes the way that one variable changes in relation to another. When one variable increases as another increases, and decreases as it decreases, this is referred to as direct variation. This is because the two variables will change in direct proportion to one another. The direct variation relationship is described with the general equation

$$y = kx$$

In this equation k, any unspecified constant, is called the constant of proportionality. If an equation or problem can be put into this form, then that equation is considered to be an example of direct variation.

Example 10.1: The area of a circle varies with the radius according to the formula $A = 2\pi r$. Is this relationship directly proportional? What is the constant of proportionality?

Solution: Yes, the relationship is an example of direct variation. This is true because it can be put into the form (or is in the form) $y = kx$. In the case of the circumference of a circle, the constant of proportionality, or the number according to which the variable varies, is 2π.

Example 10.2: The height of a rectangle varies directly with its width. If the height is 20 when the width is 10, what is the constant of proportionality?

Solution: If the height of the rectangle varies with its length, and we know that the relationship is directly proportional, we can determine that the equation describing the height fits into the form $y = kx$. By substituting y with h (for the height of the rectangle) and x with w (to represent the width of the rectangle, the following equation is determined:

$h = kw$

Next, simply substitute the known values of 10 and 20 into the correct variables and solve for the unknown constant k.

$20 = k(10)$
$k = 2$

Example 10.3: The number of rooms in an apartment varies directly with the square feet. If the number of rooms is 2 when the square feet in the apartment is 360, determine the number of rooms in a 900 square foot apartment.

Solution: Knowing that the relationship between rooms (r) and square feet (f) varies directly, the equation can be written:

$r = kf$

Solving the equation with the known values of $r = 2$ and $f = 360$ gives the constant of proportionality and completes the equation

$2 = k(360)$

$k = \dfrac{1}{180}$ (or 1 room per 180 square feet)

$r = \dfrac{1}{180} f$

This completed equation can be used to determine that a 900 square foot apartment would have

$r = \dfrac{1}{180} f$

$r = \dfrac{1}{180}(900) = 5$ rooms

TRY IT YOURSELF:

Question: The variable y varies directly with the variable x such that $y = 15$ when $x = 3$. What is y when x is 7?

Answer: 35

Question: The variable m varies directly according to a. If when $a = (\dfrac{1}{2})$ $m = 20$, find m when a is 60.

Answer: 2400

What is inverse variation? While direct variation describes equations in which one variable is directly proportional to another, inverse variation describes equations that are inversely proportional to each other. This means that as one variable increases, the other decreases and vice versa. The general formula for an inverse variation equation is

$$y = \frac{k}{x} \text{ or } xy = k$$

where k is the constant of proportionality, and can be any constant. Any equation or problem which can be described by this formula is considered an example of inverse variation.

> Example 10.4: As the speed with which a car travels increases, the time it will take to reach the destination decreases. Is this an example of direct variation or inverse variation?
>
> Solution: Inverse variation. If speed increasing results in a decrease in travel time, the two must be inversely proportional. Therefore, it is an example of inverse variation.
>
> Example 10.5: The time (h) it takes a block of ice from the store to melt varies inversely with the temperature (t). If a block melts in 2 hours when it is 50 degrees outside, how long will it take to melt when the temperature is 85?
>
> Solution: Because we know the problem is an inverse variation problem, the formula initially be set up as
>
> $$h = \frac{k}{t}$$
>
> Next, find k by substituting the values of $h = 2$ and $t = 50$ and solving.
>
> $$2 = \frac{k}{50}$$
> $$k = 100$$
>
> Finally, substitute $t = 85$ into the completed equation to find the melting time
>
> $$h = \frac{100}{t}$$
> $$h = \frac{100}{85} = 1.18 \text{ hours}$$

TRY IT YOURSELF:

Question: The force needed to break a board varies inversely with the length of the board. If the force required to break a 10-inch board is 45 pounds, what force is required for a 6-inch board?

Answer: 75 pounds

Question: M varies inversely with the variable O. If $M = 150$ when $O = 20$, what is the constant of variation?

Answer: 3000

Question: The pressure of a certain amount of gas in a tube varies inversely with the volume of the tube. If the pressure is 440 psi when the volume of the tube is 100 square centimeters, what is the pressure when the volume is 120 square centimeters?

Answer: 366.7 pounds

2-11: CONCEPTS OF ALGEBRAIC FUNCTIONS

FUNCTIONS AND THEIR GRAPHS

What is a function? A mathematical function represents a systematic manner in which to find a *value*. In other words, when you input information into a function you will generate a specific "unique" output. A function is usually written as $f(x)$.

For example, let's look at the function: $f(x) = x + 2$ and the value of $x = 3$

The input is the value $x = 3$ while the output will be what you find when you plug "3" in for x in the equation $f(x) = x + 2$.

$$f(x) = x + 2$$
$$f(3) = 3 + 2$$
Therefore, $f(3) = 5$

Can you figure out what the value of $f(10)$ given $f(x) = x + 2$?

$$f(x) = x + 2$$
$$f(10) = 10 + 2$$
Therefore, $f(10) = 12$

How do functions relate to graphing? Functions pair up x values with y values. Functions must have only one y (or output) value for each x (or input).

What are domain and range? Once it has been determined if a graph can be defined as a function, then domain and range can be used to further define the graph. Domain refers to the set of x values that can be input into an equation, and range refers to the set of y values to which the graph can be equal.

What is the domain of a function? The domain of a function refers to all the possible values you can use for "x" in the function $f(x)$ otherwise known as the first number in each ordered pair. The function $f(x) = 2x$ produced the following ordered pairs: (**−1**, −2), (**0**,0), (**1**,2), (**2**,4), (**3**,6). The domain represents the bolded numbers which are {−1, 0, 1, 2, and 3}.

What is the range of a function? The range of a function refers to all the possible values you can determine for the output $f(x)$ or "y". The range from the previous $f(x) = 2x$ is the second number in each ordered pair. (−1,−2), (0,0), (1,2), (2,4), (3,6). Therefore, the range is {−2, 0, 2, 4, 6}.

How are domain and range expressed? Domain and range are generally expressed using brackets and parenthesis. For example if the range for a particular function includes 0 and goes to infinity, it would be expressed as $[0, \infty)$. The bracket indicates that the 0 is included in the range. A parentheses indicates that a number is not included in the range, and is always used in the case of infinity because it is cannot be reached. Domain and range can also be expressed as an equation or inequality. For example if the domain of the function includes all real numbers, but excludes the number two, the domain could be written as $x \neq 2$. Generally, however, this sort of notation is avoided and instead the union sign is used. In the case of the domain being all real numbers except 2, it would be expressed $(-\infty, 2) \cup (2, \infty)$.

Example 11.1: Consider the equation $y = \dfrac{1}{x}$.

The domain of the equation is $(-\infty, 0) \cup (0, \infty)$, because $x \neq 0$. Dividing by 0 is undefined.

The range of this equation is $(-\infty, \infty)$, because the graph continues to both positive and negative infinity in the y direction.

Example 11.2: Consider the equation $y = x^2$.

The domain of the equation is $(-\infty, \infty)$.

The range of the equation is [0, ∞) because *y* will always be greater than 0, but goes to infinity as *x* does.

How can you tell if a graph represents a function? Use the "vertical line test" to determine if a graph represents a function. The vertical line test states that if you draw a vertical line through a piece of the graph and it intersects the graph at one more than one point then it is NOT a function. (Remember for every "*x*" value you can have only ONE "*y*" value in order for the relationship to be a function.)

Following is a visual representation to explain the vertical line test.

$f(x) = x^2$ is a function as the red vertical line passes through the graph at only one *y* value.

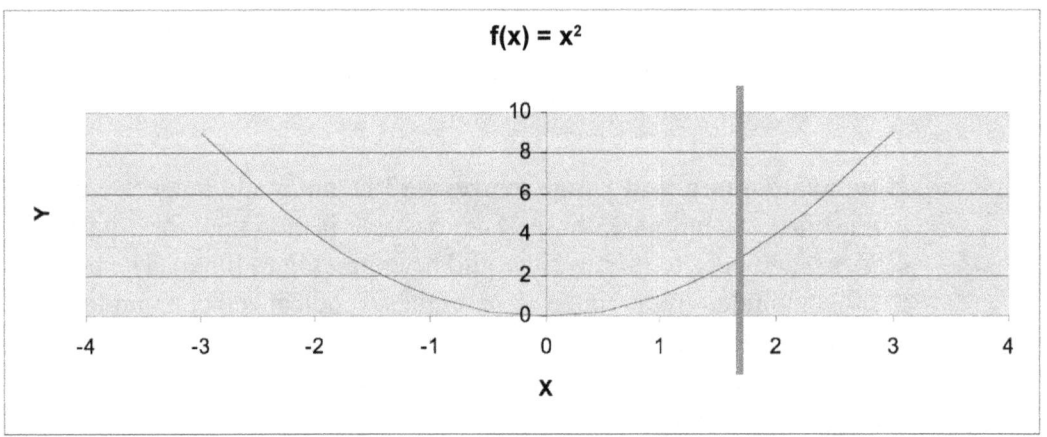

The following graph is NOT a function because the red vertical line passes through more than one *y* value.

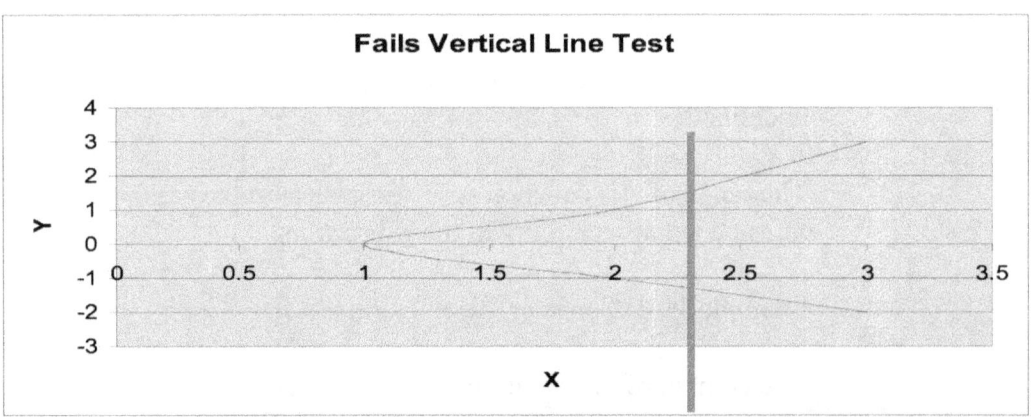

How do you find the composition of two functions? The composition of two functions takes the terms of one function and substitutes them into the other function. The composition of two functions is denoted as $f(g(x))$.

For example, find $f(g(x))$
When $f(x) = x^2 + 10$ and $g(x) = 3x$
$f(g(x)) = f(3x) = (3x)^2 + 10 = 9x^2 + 10$
Therefore, $f(g(x)) = 9x^2 + 10$

TRY IT YOURSELF:

Question: Find the domain and range of the function $y = \dfrac{1}{\sqrt{6-x}}$

Answer: $D: (-\infty, 6)$
$R: (0, \infty)$

Question: Find the domain and range of the function $y = \sqrt{x+3}$

Answer: $D: [-3, \infty)$
$R: [0, \infty)$

Question: Evaluate $f(x) = 12x^2 + 1$, $x = 3$

Answer: $f(3) = 109$

FINDING THE INVERSE OF FUNCTIONS

Inverse functions are pairs of functions that can reverse the effect of each other. To find an inverse function, you must interchange the domain and range. In other words, switch the x and y values.

If the original function is $f(x)$ then the inverse is denoted as $f^{-1}(x)$.

Example 11.3: Find the inverse of $f(x) = 3x + 5$.

Solution:
Step #1: Set $y = 3x + 5$
Step #2: Interchange x and y to get $x = 3y + 5$
Step #3: Solve for y to get $f^{-1}(x)$.

$x = 3y + 5$

$$3y = x - 5$$
$$y = \frac{x-5}{3}$$
$$f^{-1}(x) = \frac{x-5}{3}$$

Example 11.4: Find the inverse of $f(x) = 2 - x^2$.

Solution:
Step #1: Set $y = 2 - x^2$
Step #2: Interchange x and y to get $x = 2 - y^2$
Step #3: Solve for y to get $f^{-1}(x)$.
$$x = 2 - y^2$$
$$y^2 = -x + 2$$
$$y = \sqrt{-x + 2}$$
$$f^{-1}(x) = \sqrt{-x + 2} \text{ OR } f^{-1}(x) = \sqrt{2 - x}$$

Example 11.5: Find the inverse of $f(x) = \frac{1}{2}x^3$.

Solution:
Step #1: Set $y = \frac{1}{2}x^3$
Step #2: Interchange x and y to get $x = \frac{1}{2}y^3$
Step #3: Solve for y to get $f^{-1}(x)$.

$$x = \frac{1}{2}y^3$$
$$y^3 = 2x$$
$$y = \sqrt[3]{2x}$$
$$f^{-1}(x) = \sqrt[3]{2x}$$

Example 11.6: Find the inverse of the function $f(x) = \sqrt{x} - 15$.

Solution:
Step #1: Set $y = \sqrt{x} - 15$
Step #2: Interchange x and y to get $x = \sqrt{y} - 15$
Step #3: Solve for y to get $f^{-1}(x)$.

$$x = \sqrt{y} - 15$$
$$\sqrt{y} = x + 15$$
$$y = (x + 15)^2$$
$$f^{-1}(x) = (x + 15)^2 \text{ OR } f^{-1}(x) = x^2 + 30x + 225$$

TRY IT YOURSELF:

Question: Find the inverse of $f(x) = \dfrac{1}{x+2}$

    Answer: $f^{-1}(x) = \dfrac{1-2x}{x}$

Question: Find the inverse of $f(x) = \dfrac{1+\sqrt{2x}}{4}$

    Answer: $f^{-1}(x) = \dfrac{(4x-1)^2}{2}$

COMPOSITION OF TWO FUNCTIONS

To find the composition of two functions means you take the function of a function. The composition of two functions takes the terms of one function and substitutes them into the other function. The composition of two functions is denoted as $f(g(x))$.

Let's say the two functions are $f(x)$ and $g(x)$. The composition of the two functions is $h(x)$.

This means $h(x) = g(f(x))$.
In other words, the composite function $h(x)$ is the function $g(x)$ of the function $f(x)$.

Note: The order of the composition matters.

$g(f(x)) \neq f(g(x))$

For example, find $g(f(x))$ and $f(g(x))$ if the functions are $f(x) = x + 4$ and $g(x) = x^2$ where $x = 6$.

Follow these steps to find $g(f(x))$:
Step #1: Find $f(x)$ where $x = 6$.

$f(6) = 6 + 4 = 10$

Step #2: Plug this answer in for $f(x)$ in $g(f(x))$.

$g(10) = 10^2 = 100$

So $g(f(x)) = 100$

Follow these steps to find $f(g(x))$:
Step #1: Find $g(x)$ where $x = 6$

$g(6) = 6^2 = 36$

Step #3: Plug this answer in for $g(x)$ in $f(g(x))$.

$f(36) = 36 + 4 = 40$
$f(g(x)) = 40$

As you can see $g(f(x)) \neq f(g(x))$ because $100 \neq 40$.

Finding the composition of two functions does not always involve a specific value for x. Typically you will simply be given the equations for two functions and told to find their composition. When this is the case, simply substitute the entire equation into the other in place of x.

Example 11.7: Find $f(g(x))$ when $f(x) = x^2 + 1$ and $g(x) = 2x$

Solution:
$f(g(x)) = x^2 + 1$
$f(2x) = (2x)^2 + 1$
$f(2x) = 4x^2 + 1 = f(g(x))$

Example 11.8: Find $g(f(x))$ and $f(g(x))$ if the functions are $f(x) = 2x + 3$ and $g(x) = 3x + 2$ where $x = -1$.

Solution:
Find $g(f(x))$:

$f(-1) = 2(-1) + 3 = 1$
$g(1) = 3(1) + 2 = 5$
$g(f(x)) = 5$

Find $f(g(x))$:

$g(-1) = 3(-1) + 2 = -1$
$f(-1) = 2(-1) + 3 = 1$
$f(g(x)) = 1$

COMBINING FUNCTIONS

You can add, subtract, multiply and divide functions. To solve these types of problems, evaluate each function and then add, subtract, multiply, or divide based on the question.

Example 11.9: Add functions.
Given functions $f(x) = 3x$ and $g(x) = x + 5$.

Find $f(2) + g(5)$.

Solution:
Step #1: Evaluate each function.

$f(x) = 3x$
$f(2) = 3(2)$
$f(2) = 6$

$g(x) = x + 5$
$g(5) = 5 + 5$
$g(5) = 10$

Step #2: Plug in the values.

$f(2) + g(5) = 6 + 10 = 16$

So the answer is 16.

Example 11.10: Subtract functions.
Given functions $f(x) = 4x + 10$ and $g(x) = x - 4$.

Find $f(3) - g(7)$.

Solution:
Step #1: Evaluate each function.

$f(x) = 4x + 10$
$f(3) = 4(3) + 10$
$f(3) = 22$

$$g(x) = x - 4$$
$$g(7) = 7 - 4$$
$$g(7) = 3$$

Step #2: Plug in the values.

$$f(3) - g(7) = 22 - 3 = 19$$

So the answer is 19.

TRY IT YOURSELF:

Question: Find $f(g(x))$ if $f(x) = \sqrt{x}$ and $g(x) = 4x^2$

Answer: $f(g(x)) = 2x$

Question: Find $f(g(x))$ if $f(x) = 10x + 3$ and $g(x) = \dfrac{x}{2}$ for $x = \dfrac{1}{2}$

Answer: $f(g(.5)) = 5.5$

Question: Find $f(x) + g(x)$ if $f(x) = 10x + 3$ and $g(x) = (x+1)^2$

Answer: $f(x) + g(x) = x^2 + 12x + 4$

Sample Test Questions

ALGEBRA AND FUNCTIONS QUESTIONS

1. $(4x^2 + x - 7) + (3x^2 - 2x + 1)$

   A. $7x^2 - x + 6$
   B. $7x^2 + x + 6$
   C. $x^2 - x + 6$
   D. $7x^2 + 3x - 6$
   E. $7x^2 + 3x - 8$

2. $2(3x^2 + 2x - 3) - 3(x^2 - 5x - 2)$

    A. $3x^2 + 17x$
    B. $3x^2 - 11x$
    C. $3x^2 + 19x + 1$
    D. $9x^2 + 19x$
    E. $3x^2 + 19x$

3. Which of the following terms is not "like" the others?

    A. $3x^2$
    B. $4x^2$
    C. $2y^2$
    D. x^2
    E. All of the above are like terms

4. $2(x + 2) + 4(3x + 1) + 2x$

    A. $16x + 6$
    B. $16x + 8$
    C. $14x + 10$
    D. $12x + 16$
    E. $8x + 6$

5. Which of the following represents the MOST factored form of $2x^2 + 4x - 6$?

    A. $(2x - 2)(x + 3)$
    B. $(x - 1)(2x + 6)$
    C. $(x - 1)(2x + 6)$
    D. $(2x + 2)(x - 3)$
    E. $2(x - 1)(x + 3)$

6. Factor $6x^2 + x - 1$

    A. $(2x + 1)(3x - 1)$
    B. $(2x - 1)(3x + 1)$
    C. $(6x - 1)(x + 1)$
    D. $(x - 1)(6x + 1)$
    E. $(2x - 6)(3x + 1)$

7. Factor $x^2 + 6x - 16$

   A. $(x-8)(x+2)$
   B. $(x+8)(x-2)$
   C. $(x-8)(x-2)$
   D. $(x+8)(x+2)$
   E. None of the above

8. Completely factor $8x^2 + 36x + 28$

   A. $(2x+7)(4x-4)$
   B. $(2x-7)(4x+4)$
   C. $4(2x+7)(x+1)$
   D. $(2x+7)(4x+1)$
   E. $4(x+7)(2x+1)$

9. Which of the following is the simplest form of $\dfrac{(2x^2y)^3}{8xy}$?

   A. $\dfrac{8x^6y^3}{8xy}$
   B. $\dfrac{(2x^2y)^3}{8xy} = \dfrac{x^3}{64}$
   C. $\dfrac{(2x^2y)^3}{8xy} = \dfrac{xy^2}{4}$
   D. x^5y^2
   E. $\dfrac{(2x^2y)^3}{8xy} = \dfrac{x^5y^2}{4}$

10. Which of the following is the simplest form of $\dfrac{(xwz)^2(2xz)}{4xyz}$?

    A. $\dfrac{(xwz)^2}{2y}$
    B. $\dfrac{x^3w^2z^3}{2}$
    C. $\dfrac{x^2wz^2}{2}$
    D. $\dfrac{2(xwz)^2}{y}$
    E. $\dfrac{2x^3w^2z^3}{4xyz}$

11. Simplify $(x^2yz)(z^3y)(2x^0y)$

    A. $2y^3z^4$
    B. $2x^3y^3z^4$
    C. $2x^2y^3z^4$
    D. $2(xyz)^3$
    E. None of the above

12. Which rule would be used to simplify the following term: $x^5 \cdot x^3y^2$?

    A. Exponential rule
    B. Multiplication rule
    C. Power rule
    D. Quotient rule
    E. Product rule

13. Simplify $(x^2)(x^3)^2$

    A. x^9
    B. x^{10}
    C. x^7
    D. x^8
    E. x^{6^2}

14. Rewrite $x\sqrt[3]{x^2}$

    A. $x^{\frac{5}{3}}$
    B. $x^{\frac{3}{5}}$
    C. $x^{\frac{3}{2}}$
    D. $x^{\frac{5}{2}}$
    E. $x^{\frac{2}{5}}$

15. Simplify using polynomial long division $\dfrac{3x^3 + 2x^2 + 4x + 400}{x+6}$

    A. $3x^2 + 16x + 68 + \dfrac{408}{x+6}$

    B. $3x^2 - 16x + 68 + \dfrac{8}{x+6}$

    C. $3x^2 + 16x - 68 - \dfrac{8}{x+6}$

    D. $x^2 - 16x + 68 - \dfrac{x+6}{8}$

    E. $3x^2 - 16x + 68 - \dfrac{x+6}{8}$

16. Simplify $\dfrac{2x^2 + 11x + 12}{2x+3}$

    A. $x + 4$
    B. $x + 2$
    C. $2x + 3$
    D. $x + 4 + \dfrac{1}{2x+3}$
    E. $x - 4 + \dfrac{1}{2x+3}$

17. Divide $\dfrac{4x^2 + 18x + 1}{2x}$

    A. $2x + 9 + \dfrac{x}{2}$
    B. $2x^2 + 9x + \dfrac{x+1}{2}$
    C. $2x - 9$
    D. $x + 9 + \dfrac{1}{2x}$
    E. $2x + 9 + \dfrac{1}{2x}$

18. Divide $\dfrac{x^2+5x-14}{3x+1}$

    A. $\dfrac{x}{3}+\dfrac{14}{3}-\dfrac{112}{(3x+1)}$

    B. $3x+\dfrac{14}{3}-\dfrac{112}{(3x+1)}$

    C. $\dfrac{x}{3}+\dfrac{14}{9}-\dfrac{112}{9(3x+1)}$

    D. $\dfrac{x}{3}-\dfrac{14}{9}+\dfrac{112}{9(3x+1)}$

    E. $\dfrac{x}{3}-\dfrac{14}{9}+\dfrac{9}{(3x+1)}$

19. Solve $\dfrac{2}{3}x+1=\dfrac{1}{6}x-6$

    A. $x=14$
    B. $x=5$
    C. $x=-14$
    D. $x=-5$
    E. $x=-\dfrac{3}{2}$

20. Solve $\dfrac{3}{7}x-4=1$

    A. $x=\dfrac{35}{3}$

    B. $x=\dfrac{3}{35}$

    C. $x=\dfrac{3}{12}$

    D. $x=\dfrac{1}{4}$

    E. $x=12$

21. Solve $\dfrac{x}{12}+\dfrac{3}{4}=\dfrac{x}{6}-\dfrac{1}{2}$

    A. $x=\dfrac{15}{4}$

    B. $x=\dfrac{4}{15}$

    C. $x=\dfrac{5}{12}$

    D. $x=\dfrac{12}{5}$

    E. $x=15$

22. Solve for a: $5a+11b-1=2(a+2)-b$

    A. $a=-4b+2$

    B. $a=4b+\dfrac{3}{5}$

    C. $a=-\dfrac{10}{3}b+\dfrac{5}{3}$

    D. $a=-4b+1$

    E. $a=-4b+\dfrac{5}{3}$

23. Solve for x: $3x+1=4(x+y)-3$

    A. $x=4y-4$
    B. $x=2-4y$
    C. $x=4y-2$
    D. $x=4-4y$
    E. $x=2y-4$

24. Solve the inequality $-\dfrac{3}{2}x + 5 > 1 + x$

    A. $x < -\dfrac{8}{5}$

    B. $x < \dfrac{8}{5}$

    C. $x < \dfrac{5}{8}$

    D. $x < -\dfrac{5}{8}$

    E. $x > -\dfrac{8}{5}$

25. Solve the inequality $-10x - 3x - 4 > 9$

    A. $x < 1$
    B. $x < -1$
    C. $x < 1$
    D. $x > -1$
    E. $x > 1$

26. Find the simultaneous solution to $\begin{array}{l}2x + 2y = 10 \\ -8x + 3y = -1\end{array}$

    A. (4, 1)
    B. (2, 4)
    C. (1, 4)
    D. (1, 8)
    E. None of the above

27. Solve the system $\begin{array}{l} 2y-7=3x \\ 4x+y=1 \end{array}$

A. $\left(-\dfrac{5}{11}, \dfrac{31}{11}\right)$

B. $\left(\dfrac{5}{11}, -\dfrac{31}{11}\right)$

C. $\left(\dfrac{31}{11}, -\dfrac{5}{11}\right)$

D. $(-1, 5)$

E. $(-1, 2)$

28. Which of the following systems has the simultaneous solution $\left(\dfrac{3}{2}, -\dfrac{1}{2}\right)$?

A. $\begin{array}{l} x+y=1 \\ y+2=x \end{array}$

B. $\begin{array}{l} x+3y=13 \\ x+4y=18 \end{array}$

C. $\begin{array}{l} x+2y=1 \\ 2y+2=3x \end{array}$

D. $\begin{array}{l} 2y-3=x \\ 4x+y=1 \end{array}$

E. $\begin{array}{l} x+y=1 \\ x-y=2 \end{array}$

29. Solve $2x^2 - 5x + 4$

   A. $x = 1, -\frac{3}{2}$

   B. $x = 1, \frac{3}{2}$

   C. $x = -1, \frac{3}{2}$

   D. $x = -1, \frac{2}{3}$

   E. $x = 1, \frac{2}{3}$

30. Which of the following equations is quadratic?

   A. $3xy + 2x = 1$
   B. $4x + 2x$
   C. $2(\frac{x}{y}) = 7 + x$
   D. $3x^2 + 2x = -1$
   E. $4x + 2 = 2x + 1$

31. Which of the following equations is linear?

   A. $3xy + 2x = 1$
   B. $4x + 2x$
   C. $2(\frac{x}{y}) = 7 + x$
   D. $3x^2 + 2x = -1$
   E. $4x + 2 = 2x + 1$

32. Solve $x^2 + 4x + 3$

    A. $x = 1, 3$
    B. $x = -1, -3$
    C. $x = -1, 3$
    D. $x = 1, -3$
    E. None of the above

33. Complete the square of the quadratic equation $x^2 - 4x - 3$

    A. $(x-2)^2 - 7$
    B. $(x-2)^2 + 7$
    C. $(x+2)^2 + 7$
    D. $(x+4)^2 + 7$
    E. $(x-4)^2 + 7$

34. Complete the square: $2x^2 - x - 1$

    A. $\left(x + \dfrac{1}{4}\right)^2 + \dfrac{9}{16}$
    B. $\left(x - \dfrac{1}{4}\right)^2 - \dfrac{9}{16}$
    C. $\left(x + \dfrac{1}{2}\right)^2 + \dfrac{3}{2}$
    D. $\left(x - \dfrac{1}{2}\right)^2 - \dfrac{3}{2}$
    E. None of the above

35. Which of the following is NOT a method for solving a quadratic equation?

    A. Completing the square
    B. Factoring
    C. Addition method
    D. Square root property
    E. Quadratic formula

36. Solve using the quadratic equation $2x^2 + 4x - 9$

   A. $1 \pm \dfrac{\sqrt{22}}{2}$

   B. $1 \pm \dfrac{\sqrt{22}}{4}$

   C. $-1 \pm \dfrac{\sqrt{88}}{2}$

   D. $\dfrac{-4 \pm \sqrt{88}}{2}$

   E. $-1 \pm \dfrac{\sqrt{22}}{2}$

37. Which of the following properly identifies the quantities "a," "b," and "c" for the equation $x^2 + 3x - 1 = 2x^2 + 3$?

   A. $a = -1$
   $b = -3$
   $c = 4$

   B. $a = -1$
   $b = -3$
   $c = -4$

   C. $a = 1$
   $b = 3$
   $c = -1$

   D. $a = 1$
   $b = -3$
   $c = 4$

   E. $a = 3$
   $b = 3$
   $c = 2$

38. How many real roots does the equation $x^2 + 5x - 4$ have?

   A. 2
   B. 1
   C. 0
   D. 3
   E. 5

39. Solve $\sqrt[3]{12x + 9} = 2$

   A. $x = \dfrac{1}{12}$
   B. $x = \dfrac{5}{6}$
   C. $x = -\dfrac{1}{12}$
   D. $x = -\dfrac{5}{6}$
   E. None of the above

40. Which of the following expressions is NOT a radical expression?

   A. $\sqrt{x^2 + 3x}$
   B. $\sqrt{4x + 1} - 3x$
   C. $3 + \sqrt[7]{2x}$
   D. $2x^2 + \sqrt[3]{8}$
   E. All of the above are radical expressions

41. Solve the radical equation $\dfrac{\sqrt{17x - 1}}{3x} = 2$

   A. $x = \dfrac{1}{19}$
   B. $x = 2.16$
   C. $x = \dfrac{35x}{17}$
   D. $x = \dfrac{1}{6}$
   E. No solution

42. Solve $x = \sqrt{42 - x}$

   A. $x = -7$
   B. $x = 6$
   C. $x = 6, -7$
   D. $x = 4, 6$
   E. No solution

43. Solve $\sqrt{-30x - 9} = 3x$

   A. $x = -3$
   B. $x = -(1/3)$
   C. $x = -3, -(1/3)$
   D. $x = 3, 4$
   E. No solutions

44. Solve $\frac{3}{4}x = \sqrt{18x - 135}$

   A. $x = 12$
   B. $x = 20$
   C. $x = 12, 20$
   D. $x = 14$
   E. No solutions

45. Solve $\frac{6}{x} - \frac{9}{x-1} = \frac{1}{4}$

   A. $x = 3, 8$
   B. $x = 4, -6$
   C. $x = -3, -8$
   D. $x = 4$
   E. $x = -3$

46. Solve $\frac{1}{x^2 - 3x} + \frac{1}{x - 3} = \frac{3}{x^2 - 3x}$

   A. 2
   B. −3
   C. 4
   D. −2
   E. 0

47. Solve $\dfrac{1}{3x^2} = \dfrac{x+3}{2x^2} - \dfrac{1}{6x^2}$

   A. –3
   B. 1
   C. 0
   D. 4
   E. –2

48. Solve $\dfrac{4}{x^2 - 8x + 12} = \dfrac{x}{x-2} + \dfrac{1}{x-6}$ using common denominators

   A. $x = 4, -1$
   B. $x = -1$
   C. $x = 6$
   D. $x = 6, -1$
   E. $x = 4, 6$

49. What common denominator should be used when solving $\dfrac{2h-3}{h-3} - 2 = \dfrac{12}{h+3}$ using common denominators?

   A. $-2(h+3)(h-3)$
   B. $(h+3)2$
   C. $(h+3)(h-3)$
   D. $2h + 7$
   E. None of the above

50. Solve $\dfrac{2b}{b-1} + \dfrac{b-5}{b^2-1} = 1$

   A. $b = -4, 1$
   B. $b = 2, -1$
   C. $b = 4$
   D. $b = 6, 4$
   E. $b = 1, -6$

51. Rewrite the following equation in slope-intercept form $2y - 8x = -4$

   A. $(y-1) = 4(x+1) - 2$
   B. $y - x = 4x$
   C. $y = 4x - 2$
   D. $y = 4(x-1) + 2$
   E. $y - 4x = 2$

52. Identify the y-intercept of the line $y = 2.5x - 1$

   A. -2.5
   B. 2.5
   C. 1
   D. 0
   E. -1

53. What is the equation of the line describing the following graph in slope-intercept form?

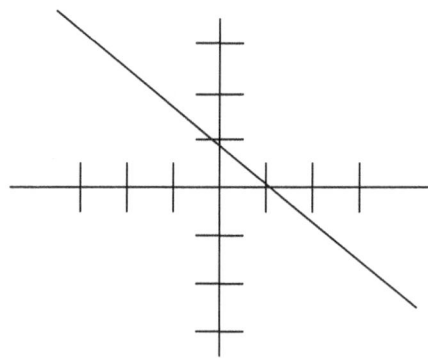

   A. $y = -x + 1$
   B. $y = x - 1$
   C. $y = 2x + 1$
   D. $y = -1 - x$
   E. $x + y = 1$

54. Which of the following is the correct point-slope formula for the line perpendicular to $y = -\frac{1}{3}x - 5$ which passes through the point (1,2)?

A. $y - 2 = -\frac{1}{3}(x - 1)$

B. $y - 1 = -\frac{1}{3}(x - 2)$

C. $y - 1 = 3(x - 2)$
D. $y + 1 = 3(x + 2)$
E. $y - 2 = 3(x - 1)$

55. What is the slope of the line $y - 2 = 6(x - 4)$?

A. 0
B. 2
C. –2
D. –4
E. 6

56. What is the *y*-intercept of the line which passes through the points (5,1) and (7, 5)?

A. 9
B. –9
C. 4
D. –4
E. 7

57. Solve $2|x + 1| - 4 = 1$

A. $x = -11, 9$
B. $x = -9, 11$
C. $x = 7, 6$
D. $x = 4, -3$
E. $x = 3, -4$

58. Which of the following is NOT a solution to $3|x - 1| - 2 \geq 4$?

A. –4
B. –2
C. 10
D. 2
E. 4

59. Solve $4|6x-2|=8$

   A. $x = \dfrac{2}{3}$

   B. $x = \dfrac{3}{2}, 1$

   C. $x = 0, \dfrac{2}{3}$

   D. $x = \dfrac{2}{3}, 1$

   E. $x = 0, 4$

60. Simplify $3\left|\dfrac{1}{3}(2+1)-(3+1)^3\right|$

   A. 143
   B. −18
   C. 37
   D. 154
   E. 189

61. Linear equations are an example of

   A. Exponentiality
   B. Direct variation
   C. Rational expressions
   D. Arithmetic medians
   E. Inverse variation

62. The area of a circle varies directly with the square of the radius. If the area (A) is 16π when the radius (r) is 4, what is the area of a circle with radius 5?

   A. 18π
   B. 20π
   C. 25π
   D. 28π
   E. 32π

63. The variable d varies in direct proportion to the variable p such that when $d = 33$, $p = 1.5$. What is the constant of proportionality?

    A. 6
    B. 18
    C. 27
    D. 13
    E. 22

64. The height and width of a rectangle vary such that the area of the rectangle is always equal to 1. This is an example of

    A. Exponential proportionality
    B. Direct variation
    C. Simple proportionality
    D. Rational variation
    E. Inverse variation

65. Which of the following is NOT an example of inverse variation?

    A. $y = \dfrac{3}{x}$

    B. $x = \dfrac{2}{y}$

    C. $y = \dfrac{x}{15}$

    D. $xy = 14$

    E. All of the above are examples of inverse variation

66. The average life expectancy of a giraffe varies inversely with the number of spots on the bottom of its feet. If a giraffe with 20 spots is expected to live 15 years, how long will a giraffe with 8 spots live?

    A. 38 years
    B. 45 years
    C. 20 years
    D. 18 years
    E. 9 years

67. What is the vertical line test used to determine?

   A. Whether or not the graph has a defined slope
   B. If a graph is a vertical line with slope 0
   C. Whether or not a graph represents a function
   D. If the graph has a defined range
   E. None of the above

68. Which of the following is NOT a function?

   A. $y^2 = 5 + x$
   B. $y = 12x - 17 + x^2$
   C. $\frac{1}{2}y = 6x + 1$
   D. $y = 5$
   E. All of the above are functions

69. What is the domain of the function $y = \frac{1}{x}$?

   A. All real numbers
   B. $x > 3$
   C. $x < 0$
   D. $(-\infty, 0) \cup (0, \infty)$
   E. None of the above

70. Evaluate $f(x) = \frac{1}{2\sqrt{x+1}}$ for $x = 3$

   A. 0
   B. 1/4
   C. 2
   D. 3/4
   E. Undefined

71. Evaluate $f(x) = \dfrac{3\sqrt{x^2 - 1}}{4}$ for $x = 1$

    A. 0
    B. 1/4
    C. 2
    D. 3/4
    E. Undefined

72. What is the inverse of $f(x) = \dfrac{x+1}{x-2}$?

    A. $f^{-1}(x) = \dfrac{x+1}{2x-1}$

    B. $f^{-1}(x) = \dfrac{2x+1}{x-1}$

    C. $f^{-1}(x) = \dfrac{x-1}{2x+1}$

    D. $f^{-1}(x) = \dfrac{2x-1}{x+1}$

    E. None of the above

73. What is the inverse of $f(x) = \dfrac{2x+1}{3-x}$?

    A. $f^{-1}(x) = \dfrac{3x+1}{x-2}$

    B. $f^{-1}(x) = \dfrac{x-2}{3x+1}$

    C. $f^{-1}(x) = \dfrac{x+2}{3x-1}$

    D. $f^{-1}(x) = \dfrac{2x-1}{3+x}$

    E. $f^{-1}(x) = \dfrac{3x-1}{x+2}$

For questions 74 and 75 use

$f(x) = 2x + 7$
$g(x) = 15 - x + x^2$

74. Find $f(f(x))$

    A. $x + 14$
    B. $2x + 14$
    C. $4x + 14$
    D. $4x + 21$
    E. $2x + 21$

75. Find $2g(x) + f(x)$

    A. $2x^2 + 2x + 37$
    B. $2x^2 - 2x + 37$
    C. $2x^2 + 37$
    D. $2x^2 - 37$
    E. $x^2 - 2x + 23$

ALGEBRA AND FUNCTIONS KEY

1. A
2. E
3. C
4. B
5. E
6. A
7. B
8. C
9. D
10. A
11. C
12. E
13. D
14. A
15. C
16. A
17. E
18. C
19. C
20. A
21. E
22. E
23. D
24. B
25. B
26. C
27. A
28. A
29. B
30. D
31. E
32. B
33. A
34. B
35. C
36. E
37. D
38. A
39. C
40. D
41. A
42. B
43. E
44. C
45. C
46. A
47. E
48. D
49. C
50. A
51. C
52. E
53. A
54. E
55. E
56. B
57. A
58. D
59. C
60. E
61. B
62. C
63. E
64. E
65. C
66. A
67. C
68. A
69. D
70. B
71. A
72. B
73. E
74. D
75. C

Section 3: Geometry and Measurement

3-1: AREA AND PERIMETER OF A POLYGON AND A CIRCLE

PERIMETER AND AREA OF PLANE FIGURES

How do you find the perimeter of a figure? The perimeter is the SUM of the length of each side of the figure.

Following are the perimeter formulas for a square, rectangle, triangle, and circle.

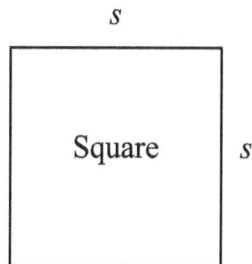

Perimeter of a square = $s + s + s + s = 4s$

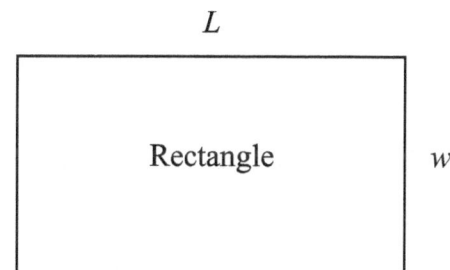

Perimeter of a rectangle = $L + w + L + w = 2L + 2w$

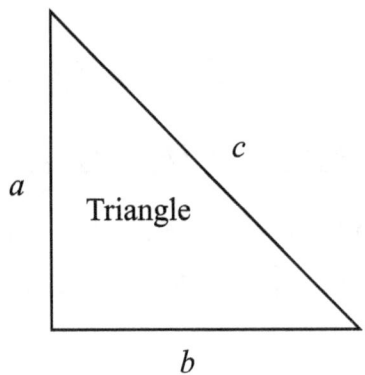

Perimeter of a triangle = a + b + c

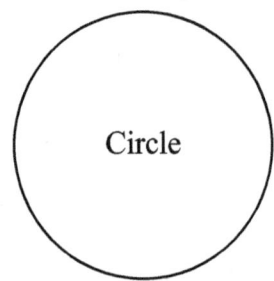

Note: The perimeter of a circle is referred to as the "circumference"
Circumference = $2\pi r$
Where r = radius of the circle

How do you find the area of a figure? Area represents the entire region within the perimeter of the figure.

Following are area formulas for a square, rectangle, and triangle. The colored region represents the "area" of the figure.

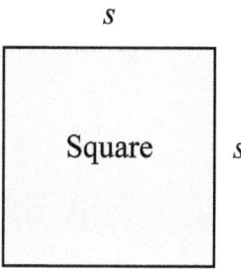

Area of a square = $s * s = s^2$

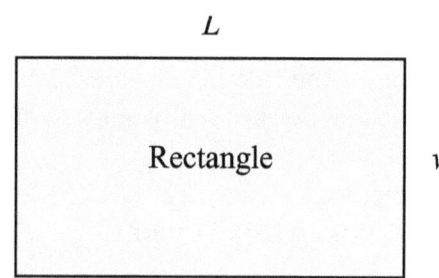

Area of a rectangle = $L * w$

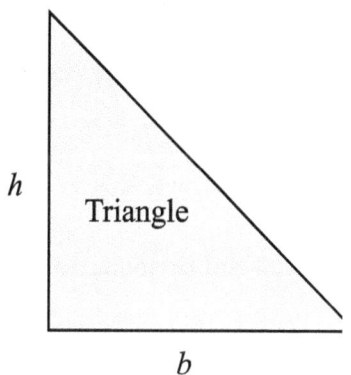

Area of a triangle = $½ bh$

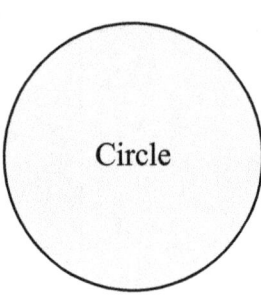

Area of a circle = πr^2

Example 1.1: Find the area and perimeter of a rectangle with side lengths 20 and 5

Solution: If the side lengths are 20 and 5, this means that $l = 20$ and $w = 5$ (or vice versa, it doesn't really matter which way you define it). Therefore,

Perimeter = $2l + 2w = 2(20) + 2(5) = 50$
Area = $(l)(w) = (20)(5) = 100$

Example 1.2: Find the area and circumference of a circle with diameter of 10.

Solution: The radius of a circle is half the diameter. Therefore the radius of a circle with a diameter of 10 is 5. This can be used to determine that

Circumference = $2\pi r = 2\pi(5) = 10\pi$
Area = $\pi r^2 = 25\pi$

TRY IT YOURSELF:

Question: Find the area and perimeter of a square with side length 3

Answer: Perimeter = 12 and Area = 9

Question: Find the area of the triangle

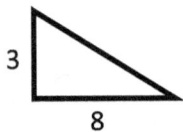

Answer: 12

Question: Which has a greater area, a square with side length 10 or a rectangle with side lengths of 9 and 11?

Answer: A square with side length 10

What is a polygon? A polygon is any figure with "many" sides (poly is Latin for many). In other words, a polygon is a closed figure (a shape without any holes in the edges) composed of all straight lines, which has at least three sides. Certain polygons can be identified by the number of sides that they have, the most common of which are:

Number of Sides	Name
3	Triangle
4	Quadrilateral
5	Pentagon
6	Hexagon
7	Heptagon
8	Octagon
9	Nonagon
10	Decagon
11	Undecagon
12	Dodecagon

Within each classification of polygon, there are other, more specific classifications which can be used. For example, squares, trapezoids, rhombuses, and rectangles are all considered quadrilaterals.

Example 1.3:

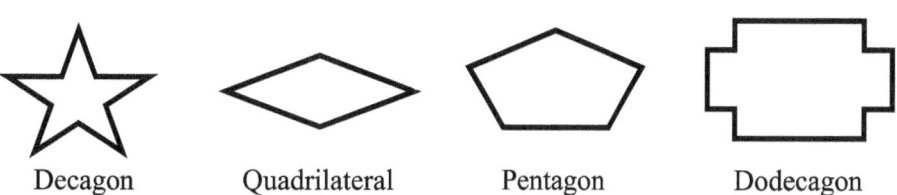

Decagon   Quadrilateral   Pentagon   Dodecagon

3-2: VOLUME OF A BOX, CUBE, AND CYLINDER

What is volume? The volume of a solid is the amount of three-dimensional space that it takes up. You should be familiar with the volume of a box, and cube, and a cylinder.

Volume of a box: A "box" is essentially the three-dimensional version of a rectangle. A box has three different measurements: length, width, and height. To find the volume of a box, simply multiply these three quantities.

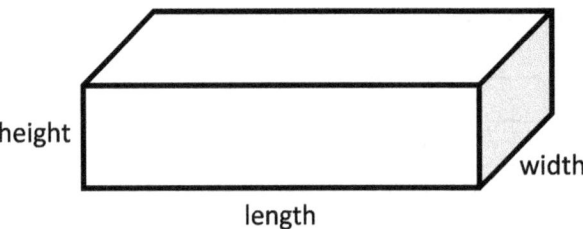

Volume = (length)(width)(height)

Volume of a cube: While a box is the three dimensional representation of a rectangle, a cube is the three dimensional representation of a square. This means that all of the side lengths are the same, like a dice. In other words, length = width = height, and the formula can be shortened to s^3, where s represents any of the three quantities.

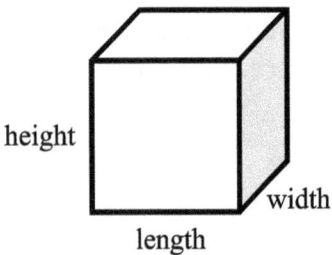

length = width = height
Volume = length^3 = width^3 = height^3

Volume of a cylinder: The cylinder is a three dimensional figure which is shaped like a soup can. You can also picture it like a big stack of circles. Much like the volume of any other figure, to find the volume of a cylinder, simply multiply the area of the base and the height. In the case of a cylinder, the area of the base is simply a circle. Therefore the formula for a cylinder is:

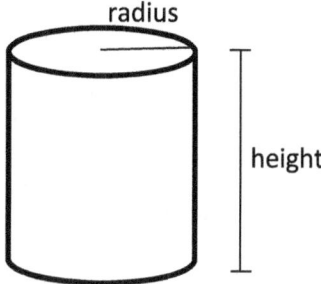

Volume = $\pi r^2 h$

Note: The cylinder pictured above is referred to as a right cylinder because the top is centered perfectly over the bottom, so that the height is equal to the side length. Some cylinders will be leaning and off centered. This results in two different heights, the "perpendicular" height (how far above the bottom of the cylinder the top cylinder is), and the "slant" height. When this is the case, the perpendicular height must be used to calculate volume.

Example 2.1: A box is built which perfectly fits 60 cubic inches of a particular chemical. If the box is 2 inches tall and 6 inches wide, how long must it be to perfectly fit the chemical?

Solution: The formula for the volume of a box is (base)(width)(height). According to the problem, this product should yield 60. Therefore, simply substitute the known values into the equation and solve for the length.

Volume = (*length*)(*width*)(*height*)
60 = (*length*)(6)(2)
length = 5 *inches*

Example 2.2: A construction worker needs to build a column at the front of a building. The column will be shaped like a perfect cylinder with a radius of 3 feet and a height of 12 feet. To the worker's surprise, when the cement that he will use arrives, it is a different amount than he ordered. If 296.9 cubic feet of cement arrives, will the column be too tall or too short? How much taller/shorter will it be?

Solution: The equation for the volume of the column will be $\pi r^2 h$. Because we know how much cement arrived, we can calculate the height of the column that will result as

$$Volume = \pi r^2 h$$
$$296.9 = \pi(3)^2(h)$$
$$h = 10.5 \text{ feet}$$

Because the column was meant to be 12 feet tall, it will be 1.5 feet (18 inches) too short.

TRY IT YOURSELF:

Question: Thomas is constructing a case that will perfectly hold his stack of CD's. Each CD is a circle with a radius of 2 inches and a height of 1/16 inch. If Thomas has 33 CD's, what will the volume of the case he constructs be if he stacks the CD's one on top of the other perfectly in the case?

Answer: Approximately 25.9 cubic inches

Question: What is the volume of a dice block with a side length of $\frac{1}{2}$ inch?

Answer: $\frac{1}{8}$ cubic inches

Question: Jennika is trying to figure out how much extra she will be charged if she packs her suitcase full of sand and flies it home with her from vacation. Assume that sand weighs 12 pounds per cubic foot. If the dimensions of her suitcase are 2 feet × 3 feet × .75 feet, and she is charged $5.00 for every pound above 30, what will the extra charge be?

Answer: $120.00

3-3: PYTHAGOREAN THEOREM AND SPECIAL PROPERTIES OF ISOSCELES, EQUILATERAL AND RIGHT TRIANGLES

What are the properties of a triangle? A triangle is a polygon with three sides. Some of the properties of triangles are

1. The sum of the angles in any triangle will always equal 180 degrees.

Example 3.1: Find the magnitude of the third angle

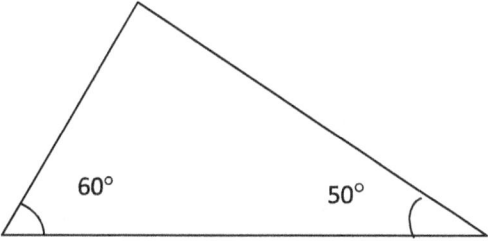

Solution: The sum of the three angles must be 180. Therefore
$60 + 50 + x = 180$, and the final angle "x" must be equal to 70 degrees.

2. The sum of any two sides of a triangle will always be greater than the third side

Example 3.2:

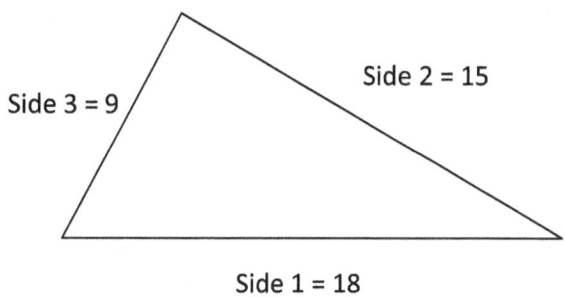

According to this property:

Side 1 + Side 2 > Side 3
Side 2 + Side 3 > Side 1
Side 1 + Side 3 > Side 2

All of which are true, so it is a legitimate triangle.

3. The longest side of the triangle will always be opposite the greatest angle

There are many different classifications of triangles based on side lengths, angle properties, and orientations. The three most important types of triangles are isosceles, equilateral and right triangles, and each is associated with a certain set of unique properties and classifications.

What is an isosceles triangle? An isosceles triangle is any triangle which has two side lengths that are the same, and one which is different. Because two of the side lengths are the same, two of the corresponding angle measures will also be the same. The following is an isosceles triangle:

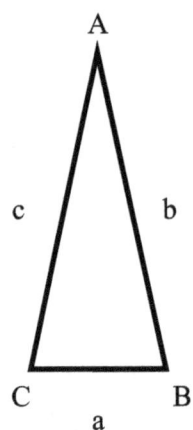

Because the triangle is isosceles, we know that

$\bar{c} = \bar{b} \neq \bar{a}$

and

$\angle B = \angle C \neq \angle A$

Also, note that the two congruent (or equal) sides of an isosceles triangle are referred to as the legs. The third side is then referred to as the base.

What is an equilateral triangle? An equilateral triangle is a triangle for which all three sides have the same length. An equilateral triangle will also always be equiangular – meaning that all of the angles will be the same as well. Although the side lengths of an equilateral triangle can be anything, every equilateral triangle will have the same angle measures. This is because every triangle has angle measures which add to 180 degrees. Therefore, if all angles are equal they will be (180 degrees)/(3 angles) = 60 degrees. The following is an equilateral triangle:

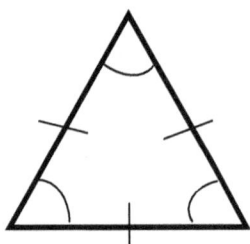

Note: The dashes going through each of the sides indicates that they are congruent (the same). Similarly, the single arc without any actual angle label is used to indicate that the angles are all congruent with each other. This is a standard notation to be familiar with.

What is a right triangle? A right triangle is a triangle with a "right" angle. A right angle is a 90 degree angle. Right triangles are triangles, therefore, where one of the sides makes a perfect corner. There are many special properties associated with right triangles, including the Pythagorean Theorem. The following is an example of a right triangle:

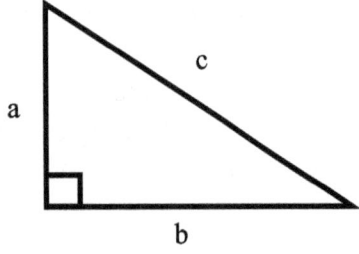

The right angle of a right triangle (and nearly every other time you see a right angle) will always be denoted with a little square corner symbol on the right angle. The side which is opposite the right angle will always be the greatest side, and is referred to as the hypotenuse. The hypotenuse is always labeled as "c" on a right triangle. The remaining two side lengths are referred to as the legs, and are denoted "a" and "b."

What is the Pythagorean Theorem? The Pythagorean Theorem is used to find the side lengths of a right triangle. Remember that the Pythagorean Theorem can ONLY be used to solve RIGHT triangles. The Pythagorean Theorem states that the length of the hypotenuse square is equal to the sum of the square of the lengths of the legs. Stated mathematically, the Pythagorean Theorem states that:

$$a^2 + b^2 = c^2$$

Example 3.3: The legs of a triangle are 3 inches and 4 inches respectively. Find the length of the hypotenuse.

Solution: The triangle described above would appear

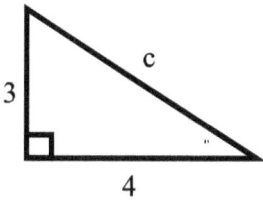

With $a = 3$, $b = 4$, and c is unknown. Using the Pythagorean Theorem

$$a^2 + b^2 = c^2$$
$$(3)^2 + (4)^2 = c^2$$
$$9 + 16 = c^2$$
$$c = \sqrt{25} = 5$$

Example 3.4: The hypotenuse of a right triangle is 13, and one of the legs has a length of 5. What is the length of the remaining leg?

Solution: Based on the information in the problem, we can determine that $c = 13$ and $a = 5$. Substituting this information into the Pythagorean Theorem yields the following solution:

$$a^2 + b^2 = c^2$$
$$(5)^2 + b^2 = (13)^2$$
$$b^2 = 169 - 25 = 144$$
$$b = \sqrt{144} = 12$$

What are the special right triangles? There are two "special" right triangles which appear often and are useful to work with. These triangles are the 30-60-90 triangle and the 45-45-90 triangle.

30-60-90 triangle: This triangle is a special case in which the three angles of the right triangle are 30 degrees, 60 degrees, and the right angle 90 degrees. When the triangle has these angle measures the side lengths will have certain proportions with each other. The side opposite the 30 degree angle will have side length x, the hypotenuse will have side length $2x$ (it will be twice the leg), and the longer side, the side opposite the 60 degree angle, will be $x\sqrt{3}$:

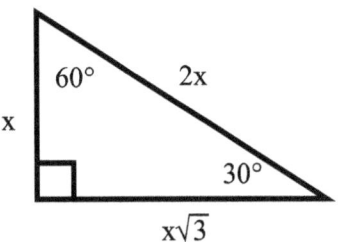

45-45-90 triangle: This triangle is a special case in which the three angles of the right triangle are 45 degrees, 45 degrees, and 90 degrees. In other words, it is an "isosceles right" triangle, because two of the angles have the same measure. As a result, the side lengths of a 45-45-90 triangle will have the following proportions:

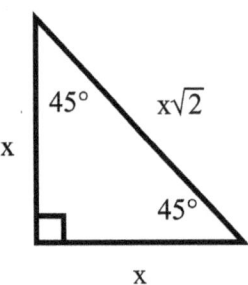

Example 3.5: Find the length of the hypotenuse of the triangle pictured below

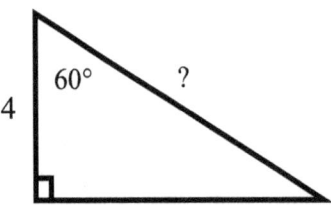

Solution: The triangle is a 30-60-90 triangle. Therefore, the hypotenuse will have a length that is twice the length of the shorter leg. The shorter leg is 4. Therefore, the length of the hypotenuse is 8.

Example 3.6: A square of side length 4 is cut diagonally into two triangles. What is the length of the cut that must be made to do this?

Solution: A square has four right angles. In order to cut it diagonally into two triangles, the resulting triangles will therefore be 45-45-90 triangles. If the side lengths of the 45-45-90 triangles are 4, then the hypotenuse is $4\sqrt{2}$.

TRY IT YOURSELF:

Question: An isosceles triangle has a base of length 7. The angle opposite the base has a measure of 40 degrees. What is the magnitude of the remaining two angles?

Answer: Both angles have a measure of 70.

Question: Determine x

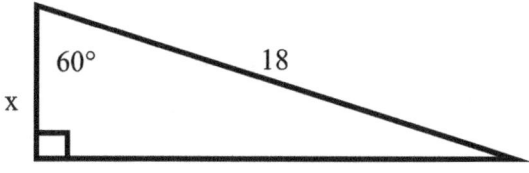

Answer: 9

Question: Determine x

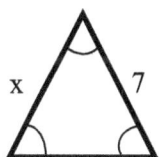

Answer: 7

Question: Determine x

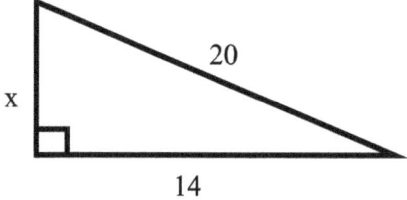

Answer: 14.3

3-4: PROPERTIES OF PARALLEL AND PERPENDICULAR LINES

What is a point? A point is a single, definable unit in space. Points have no dimension or mass, meaning they have no length, width or height. Rather, a point simply a description of a location. For example, the point below has been labeled "*A*."

What is a ray? A ray is simply an extension of a point that extends indefinitely in any one direction. In other words, a ray is like a line that starts at a point and continues on forever. Lines exist only in one dimension, with no width or height. Rather they simply have infinite length.

What is a line? A line, like a ray, exists in only two dimensions, with an infinite length but no width or height. However, instead of starting a point, like a ray, lines extend indefinitely in both directions. Therefore, lines have no starting point and no ending point. Lines may be broken down into line segments, which have both a defined starting point and ending point. Lines can be labeled either as a single element, such as line a below, or according to the farthest out identifiable endpoints, with a line drawn across the top. Segments are always identified according to their endpoints with a horizontal line drawn across the top.

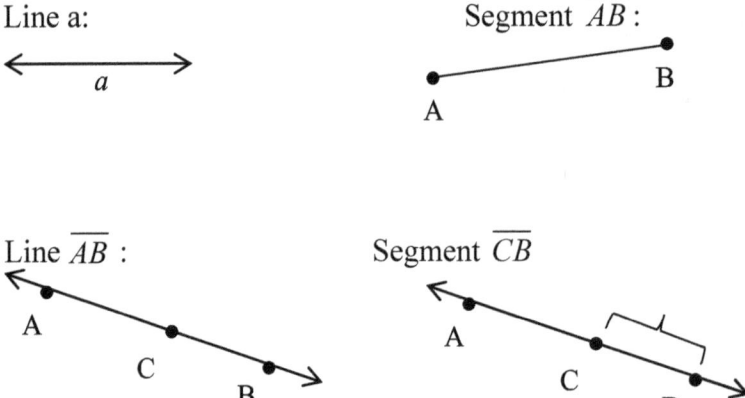

What is an angle? An angle is created when two rays or lines originate at the same point. The point from which the elements diverge (or where they come together depending on what you prefer) is referred to as the vertex. Angles can be labeled based on the line segments that join them, or the point from which they diverge as follows:

Angle K or ∠K :   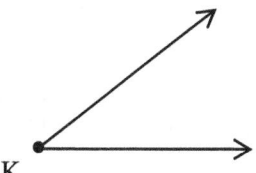   ∠JKL :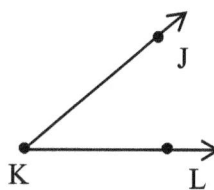

Angles are measured in degrees, with 360 degrees being a complete circle. Since 360 degrees are a circle, a 180 degree angle is a straight line, and a 90 degree angle is a perfect corner. 90 degree angles are also referred to as right angles. The following is a right angle:

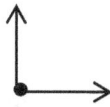

Angles which measure less than 90 degrees are called acute angles. The following are acute angles:

   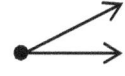

Angles which measure more than 90 degrees are called obtuse angles. The following are obtuse angles:

What are complementary angles? Two angles whose measure adds to exactly 90 degrees are referred to as complementary angles.

Example 4.1: 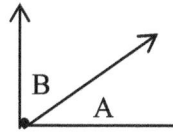   Angle *A* and Angle *B* are COMPLEMENTARY

Example 4.2: What is the complement of a 20 degree angle?

Solution: Complementary angles sum to 90 degrees, so the complement of 20 degrees is 70 degrees.

What are supplementary angles? Two angles whose measure adds to exactly 180 degrees are referred to as supplementary angles.

Example 4.3: 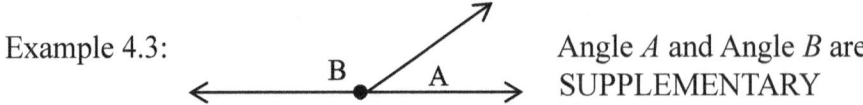 Angle *A* and Angle *B* are SUPPLEMENTARY

Example 4.4: What is the supplement of 45 degrees?

Solution: Supplementary angles sum to 180 degrees, so the supplement of 45 degrees must be (180 degrees − 45 degrees) or 135 degrees.

PARALLEL AND PERPENDICULAR LINES

What are parallel lines? Two lines are parallel if they lie in the same plane and never intersect. Parallel lines are denoted by the $||$ symbol.

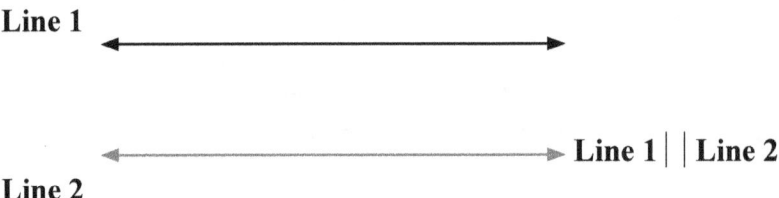

What are perpendicular lines? Two lines are perpendicular if their intersection forms a right angle. Perpendicular lines are denoted by the $\perp$.

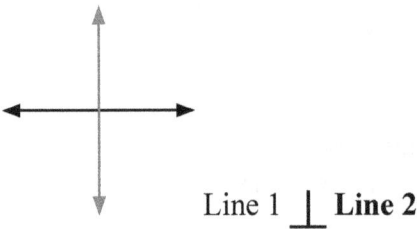

Line 1 $\perp$ Line 2

What are some properties of parallel lines? When two parallel lines exist that are both intersected by the same third line, a set of interesting angle relationships emerges. Consider the parallel lines pictured below. Note that line *n* is parallel to line *o*, or $n \perp o$. Line *m* would be called the **transversal**.

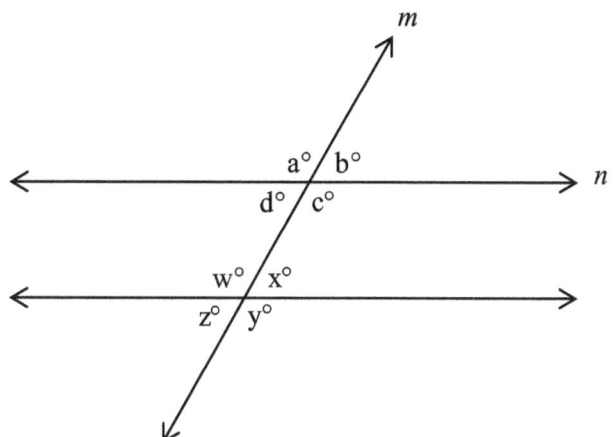

Interior Angles are the angles that are between the two lines or in the middle of them. The interior angles are angles d, c, w, and x.

Alternate Interior Angles are the angles that are interior angles on opposite sides of line m. There are two sets of alternate interior angles: d and x, and c and w. Alternate interior angles are **congruent**. In other words, they have the same measure. Therefore $c = w$ and $d = x$.

Exterior Angles are angles that are on the side of the two lines. The exterior angles are angles a, b, z, and y.

Alternate Exterior Angles are the angles that are exterior angles on opposite sides of line m. There are two sets of alternate exterior angles: a and y, and b and z. Alternate exterior angles are also congruent. Therefore $a = y$ and $z = b$.

Corresponding Angles are the angles that occupy the same position relative to the transversal (line m), on the parallel lines. There are four sets of corresponding angles: a and w, b and x, c and y, and d and z. Corresponding angles will always be congruent. Therefore, $a = w$, $b = x$, $c = y$, and $d = z$.

Consecutive Interior Angles are the interior angles on the same side of the transversal (line m). There are two sets of consecutive interior angles: d and w, and c and x. Consecutive interior angles will be supplementary.

Consecutive Exterior Angles are the exterior angles that are on the same side of the transversal line. There are two sets of consecutive exterior angles: a and z, and b and y. Consecutive exterior angles will be supplementary.

Vertical Angles do not only appear on parallel lines, but any time two lines intersect. Vertical angles are angles that are across from each other when two lines intersect. In the example above there are four sets of vertical angles. Vertical angles are always congruent. Therefore, $a = c$, $b = d$, $w = y$, and $x = z$.

Example 4.5: Using the diagram, identify the alternate exterior and interior, and the consecutive interior and exterior angles.

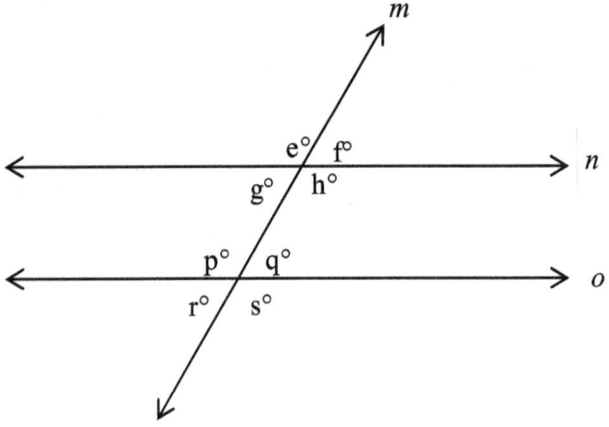

Solution:
Alternate interior: $\angle g, \angle q$ and $\angle p, \angle h$
Alternate exterior: $\angle e, \angle s$ and $\angle r, \angle f$
Consecutive interior: $\angle g, \angle p$ and $\angle h, \angle q$
Consecutive exterior: $\angle e, \angle r$ and $\angle f, \angle s$

Example 4.6: Using the diagram in the previous example, determine the measure of angle *e* if angle *r* is 75 degrees.

Solution: There are a number of ways to go about this. One example is to note that angle *r* and angle *e* are consecutive exterior angles, making them supplementary.

Another method is to note that angle *r* and *g* are congruent because they are corresponding angles. From there, note that *g* and *e* are supplementary because they lie on the same straight angle. Note: "Straight angle" is another term for a 180 degree angle, or line.

The answer is angle *e* is 180 − 75 = 105 degrees.

TRY IT YOURSELF:
Use the following diagram for the four "Try It Yourself" questions:

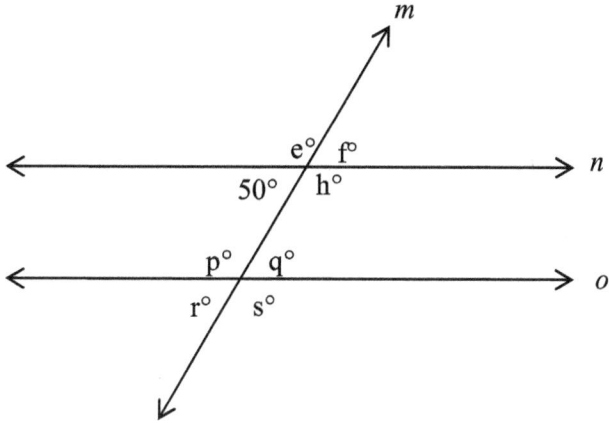

Question: Find the measure of angle *f*

Answer: 50°

Question: Find the measure of angle *s*

Answer: 130°

Question: Find the measure of angle *r*

Answer: 50°

Question: Identify the transversal

Answer: line *m*

3-5: COORDINATE GEOMETRY

What is the coordinate grid? The coordinate grid is a visual method of displaying and representing points. Essentially a coordinate grid is an intersection of two number lines which intersect at right angles. The intersection point represents zero on each of the number lines, and it is referred to as the origin. The horizontal line is referred to as the *x*-axis, and the vertical line is referred to as the *y*-axis. Points are described by their location relative to the two grids. A coordinate takes the form (*x*,*y*). For example:

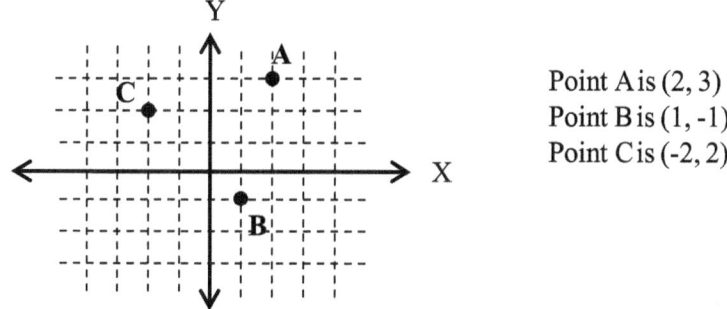

Point A is (2, 3)
Point B is (1, -1)
Point C is (-2, 2)

TRY IT YOURSELF:

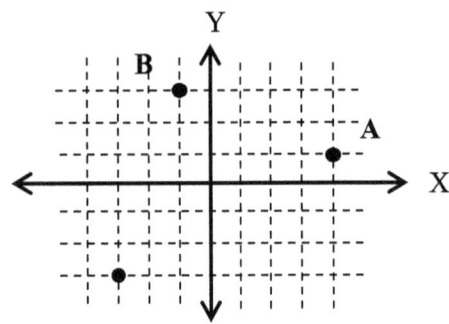

Question: Point *A* is located where on the coordinate grid?

Answer: (4,1)

Question: Point *B* is located where on the coordinate grid?

Answer: (–1, 3)

Question: Point *C* is located where on the coordinate grid?

Answer: (–3, –3)

3-6: SLOPE

FINDING SLOPES

The slope of a line is the ratio of change along the vertical to the change along the horizontal. In other words, the steepness of the line.

The Slope Formula states: The slope, *m*, of the line that contains the points (x_1, y_1) and (x_2, y_2) is given by: $m = \dfrac{y_2 - y_1}{x_2 - x_1} = \dfrac{rise}{run}$

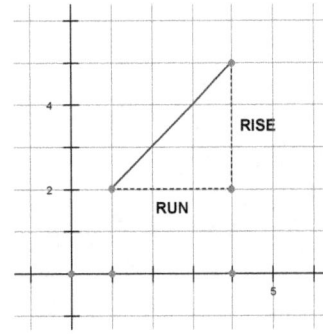

Example 6.1: Find the slope of a line that contains points (2,5) and (6,11).

Solution:

$$m = \frac{11-5}{6-2} = \frac{6}{4} = \frac{3}{2}$$

Example 6.2: Find the slope of a line that contains points (18,4) and (3,14).

Solution:

$$m = \frac{14-4}{3-18} = \frac{10}{-15} = \frac{-2}{3}$$

5 Tips about Slope:

Tip #1: Notice that the slope of example 1, $\frac{3}{2}$ and the slope of example 2, $\frac{-2}{3}$, are the negative reciprocal of each other. This means the lines are perpendicular to each other.

Tip #2: In contrast, parallel lines have the same slope.

Tip #3: A horizontal line has a slope of zero. (It remains flat.)

Tip #4: A vertical line has an undefined slope. (The difference between the *x*-values is zero and a fraction with a zero denominator is undefined.)

Tip #5: Always write slope in its simplest form. For example, $\frac{4}{8}$ should be written as $\frac{1}{2}$.

TRY IT YOURSELF:

Question: Find the slope of a line with points (15,6) and (21,6)

Answer: The slope is zero. This is a horizontal line.

Question: Find the slope of a line with points (3, 7) and (21, 15)

Answer: $\frac{4}{9}$

How do you graph quadratic functions? A quadratic function is better recognized graphically as a parabola. This means that it will essentially look like a "u." The lowest point on the graph is referred to as the vertex, and can be located either based on the equation or the graph. The most basic parabola is $y = x^2$. This parabola has a vertex at (0,0).

For a quadratic function $y = a(x-b)^2 + c$ the vertex will be (b, c). This is because numbers which are "inside" the square with the x will result in a horizontal translation. If "b" is positive the translation will be to the left, and if "b" is negative the translation will be to the right. Numbers which are "outside" the square (such as c in the prior example) will result in vertical translations. A positive value for c will result in an upward translation, and a negative value will result in a downward translation. The "a" in the equation will stretch the graph so that it is taller and thinner (if $a > 1$) or so that it is flatter and wider (if $0 < a < 1$).

Furthermore, if "a" is positive, the graph will appear as a parabola (curve) which opens upward. If it is negative, it will appear as a parabola which opens downward.

Example 6.3: Determine the vertex of and graph the function $y = (x + 2)^2 - 1$.

Solution: The vertex can be determined from the equation as (−2, −1). Because the "x^2" is positive it opens upward. Therefore, the approximate graph is

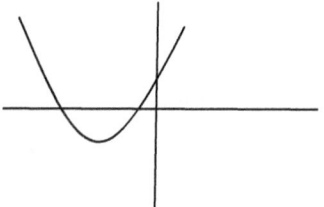

Example 6.4: Determine the vertex of $y = x^2 + 16x + 3$

Solution: One very useful trick when an equation is not in the form described above is completing the square because it translates the equation into this form. This would yield the equation:

$y = x^2 + 16x + 3$
$y + (64) = x^2 + 3x + 3 + (64)$
$y + 64 = (x + 8)^2 + 3$
$y = (x + 8)^2 + (3 - 64)$
$y = (x + 8)^2 - 61$

Therefore, the vertex of the equation is (–8, –61)

How do you graph other functions? If you cannot remember how to graph a particular type of equation, or if you are given an equation to graph that you do not recognize, one of the easiest ways to graph an equation is by substituting numbers for "x" into the equation, and solving for their corresponding "y" coordinates. This way you can determine the coordinate points that the graph passes through, and simply connect them.

Example 6.5: Draw the graph of the equation $2x + 4y = 16$

Solution: You could simply reorder this equation to find a form that is easier to graph; however, in this example we will solve by determining 3 points that the line passes through. We chose the x-intercept, the y-intercept, and a third arbitrary point.

Find the x-intercept and y-intercept.

x-intercept:

$2x + 4y = 16$
$2x + 4(0) = 16$
$2x = 16$
$x = 8$

So the x-intercept is (8,0).

y-intercept:

$2x + 4y = 16$
$2(0) + 4y = 16$
$4y = 16$
$y = 4$

So the y-intercept is (0,4).

An easy way to find a third point on the graph is to write the equation in terms of y.

$$2x + 4y = 16$$
$$4y = 16 - 2x$$
$$y = 4 - \frac{1}{2}x$$

Then pick an arbitrary value for x. Then solve for y. Let's say $x = 4$, then solve for y.

$$y = 4 - \frac{1}{2}x$$
$$y = 4 - \frac{1}{2}(4)$$
$$y = 4 - 2 = 2$$

So (4,2)

Create a table to organize the three points (x, y) that satisfy the equation.

x	y	(x,y)
0	4	(0, 4)
8	0	(8, 0)
4	2	(4, 2)

Graph the three points and draw a line through the points.

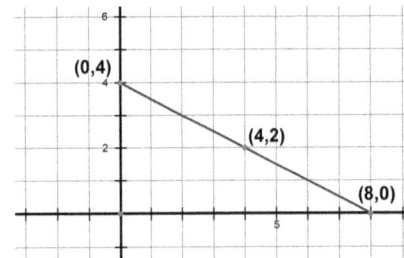

Example 6.6: Draw the graph of the equation

Solution: Begin by selecting a series of arbitrary *x*-values to substitute into the equation, and graphing the resulting coordinates:

X	Y
−1	−1
$-\dfrac{1}{2}$	$-\dfrac{1}{8}$
0	0
1/2	1/8
1	1

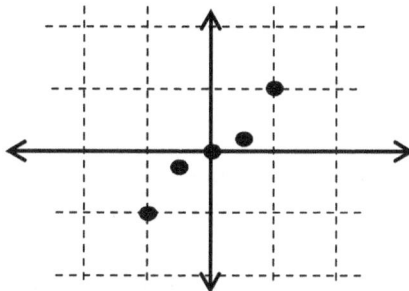

Next, simply draw a line through the graphed points

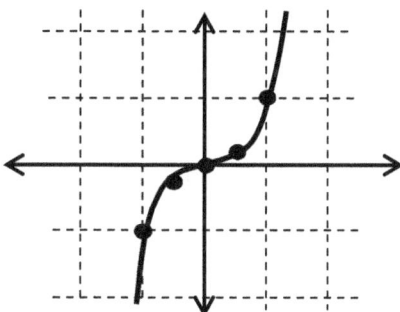

3-7: GEOMETRIC VISUALIZATION

What is meant by geometric visualization? Geometric visualization is the ability to understanding how different alterations to a shape will affect the shape or change it. There is really no methodical way to learn how to do this except by practicing. One thing that can be helpful is drawing a sketch, or comparing the problem to something in real life.

Example 7.1: A square is folded lengthwise twice, and two holes are punched in the center. When the paper is unfolded, how many holes will be in the paper?

Solution: If the paper is folded twice lengthwise, this means it must have been divided into four sections:

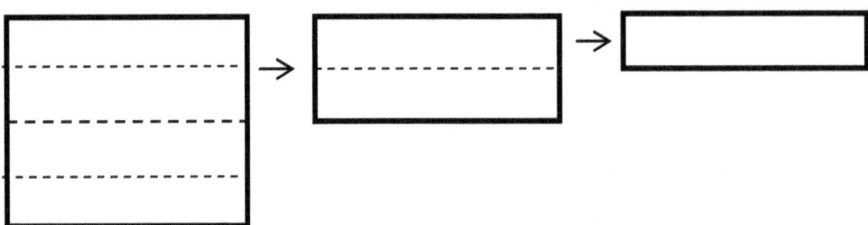

Therefore, if the final square has 2 holes punched in it, the whole sheet will have four times as many holes in it, so it will have

2(4) = 8 holes

Example 7.2: A circle is folded in half twice and the end is cut out of it. What shape will be in the center of the circle once it is unfolded?

Solution: The following sketch describes the situation described above:

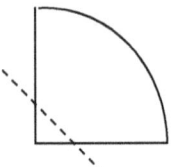

Therefore, when it is unfolded, the circle will appear:

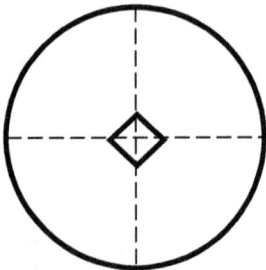

And the shape at the center is a square.

How do you determine the degrees in a convex polygon? A convex polygon is any polygon that has all angles less than 180 degrees. In other words, it doesn't cave "inwards" in any places. Typically you will deal with convex polygons.

Example 7.3: Convex polygon: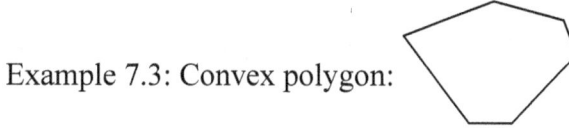

NOT convex polygon:

To determine the number of angles in a convex polygon, you can draw triangles going to each of the corners, and count the number of triangles. Because all triangles have 180 as the sum of their angles, you can multiply 180 by the number of triangles to find the sum of the angles of any convex polygon.

Example 7.4: Determine the sum of the angles in the following polygon:

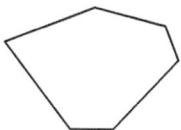

Solution: First, divide the area within the polygon into triangles:

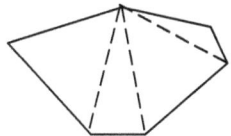

Then, count the number of triangles. In this case there are 4 triangles.

Third, multiply the number of triangles by 180 to determine the total.

4(180) = 720 degrees

Example 7.5: Determine the measure of the final angle

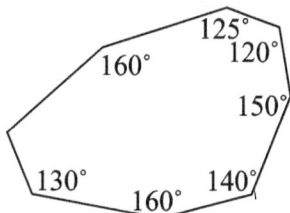

Solution: First, determine the total degrees in the polygon by dividing into triangles, and multiplying the number of triangles by 180.

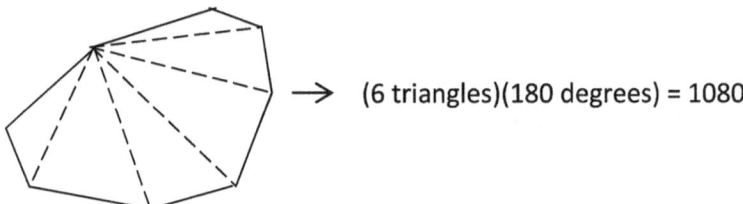

→ (6 triangles)(180 degrees) = 1080

Next, simply subtract all of the known angles from 1080 to determine the measure of the final angle.

1080 – (160 – 125 – 120 – 150 – 140 – 160 – 130) = 95 degrees

TRY IT YOURSELF:

Question: If the following shape is folded to form a block, which number will be opposite the 5? Opposite the 1?

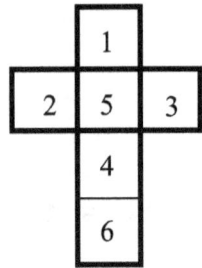

Answer: Opposite the 5 will be the 6, and opposite the 1 will be the 4.

Question: What is the cross section of a sphere?

Answer: A cross section is the shape that you would get if you cut a sheet out of a shape. For sphere, the cross section is a circle.

Question: A 45-45-90 triangle is cut from the midpoint of each of its legs, to the midpoint of the hypotenuse. What shape remains?

Answer: Simply sketch out the situation and it becomes clear that the remaining shape is a square.

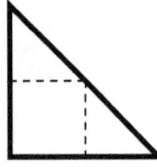

3-8: SIMILARITY

What is a regular polygon? A regular polygon is a polygon which has all of its sides with the same length, and all of its angles the same measure. Regular polygons are typically the most basic form a particular polygon can take. For example, a "regular" triangle would be an equilateral triangle. This is because equilateral triangles have all the same angles (60 degrees) and all their sides will be congruent. As another example, consider a regular quadrilateral. This will be the shape which has four sides of equal length, with four corners of equal degree measures. In other words, a regular quadrilateral is a square.

Example 8.1: Determine the measure of each of the angles of a regular pentagon.

Solution: First, remember that a pentagon is a five-sided polygon. Because it is regular we know that all of the sides and all of the angles will be congruent. The total sum of all of the angles will be 180 times the number of triangles that can be drawn in the pentagon. And is

The pentagon has five different angles, so because they are all the same measure we can simply divide the total by five to find that each angle measures

540 ÷ 5 = 108 degrees

What are similar polygons? Two polygons are considered similar if they have congruent angle measures, and their sides of proportional lengths. For example, consider polygons *ABCDE* and *VWXYZ* below.

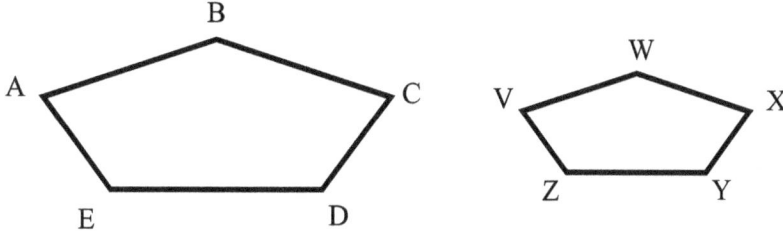

Although the two pentagons are different sizes, if we are told that they are similar, we can determine that

∠A ∠V
∠B ∠W
∠C ∠X
∠D ∠Y
∠E ∠Z

And that

$$\frac{AB}{VW} = \frac{BC}{WX} = \frac{CD}{XY} = \frac{DE}{YZ} = \frac{AE}{VZ}$$

Note: In terms of terminology, the endpoints of the line segment are used to signify the length of the segment, and the endpoints with a line drawn over top of them will be used to signify the segment itself.

Example 8.2: If triangle *ABC* is similar to triangle *XYZ*, find *YZ*

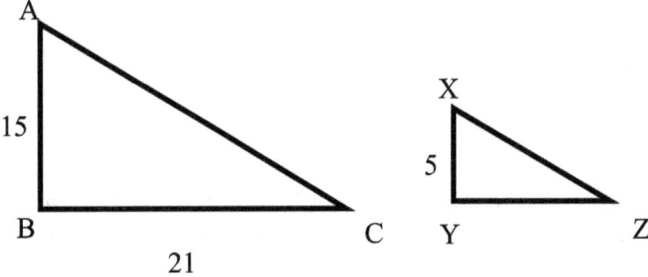

Solution: Because the triangles are known to be similar, their sides must be proportional. Therefore, the following ratio can be set up, and then we simply solve for *YZ*.

$$\frac{\overline{AB}}{\overline{XY}} = \frac{\overline{BC}}{\overline{YZ}}$$

$$\frac{15}{5} = \frac{21}{YZ}$$

$$15(YZ) = 105$$

$$YZ = 7$$

Example 8.3: Assume you are given the following information about the figure below: $\overline{CD} \parallel \overline{AE}$, $\triangle BCD \sim \triangle BEA$, $\angle BEA = 50°$, $\angle CBA = 110°$. Determine the measure of angle *CDB*.

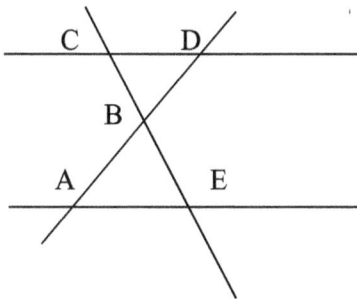

Solution: If the two triangles are similar, then we know that angle *BEA* is equal to angle *BCD*. Therefore angle *BCD* = 50 degrees. Because angle *CBA* and angle *CBD* must be supplementary (they are on a straight angle), 180-angle *CBA* = angle *CBD* = 70 degrees. The sum of the three angles in triangle *BCD* is 180. Therefore,

180 – (angle *BCD*) – (angle *CBD*) = angle *CDB*
180 – 50 – 70 = angle *CDB* = 60 degrees

How are congruence and similarity different? If two triangles are similar it means that the corresponding sides are all proportional to one another. If they are congruent then the corresponding sides are all exactly equal to each other. Congruence is indicated with the symbol ≅ and similarity with the symbol ~.

TRY IT YOURSELF:

Question: Determine the measure of each of the angles in a regular decagon.

Answer: 144 degrees

Question: Find *x* if the two rectangles are similar

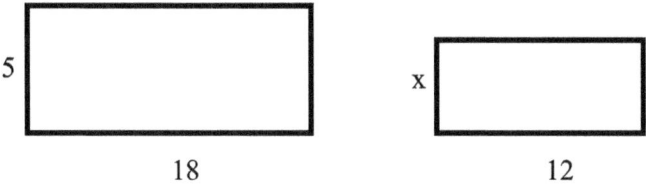

Answer: 3.33

Question: Find the length of segment *AB*

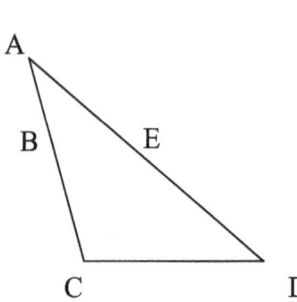

$\overline{BE}$ $\overline{CD}$
AE = 4
AD = 10
AC = 75

Answer: 3

3-9: TRANSFORMATIONS

SIMPLE TRANSFORMATIONS OF FUNCTIONS

What is symmetry? Many graphs can be described as symmetric. A graph can be symmetric about the *y* axis, the *x* axis, and the origin. A graph which is symmetric about the *y* axis will have the same *y* coordinate when evaluating $f(x)$ as when evaluating $f(-x)$ (See example a). A graph which is symmetric about the *x* axis would have points appearing at both (x, y) and $(x, -y)$ (see example b). Therefore the graph which is symmetric about the *x* axis is not a function. A graph which is symmetric about the origin will have opposite values of *y* coordinates when evaluating $f(x)$ and $f(-x)$ (see example c).

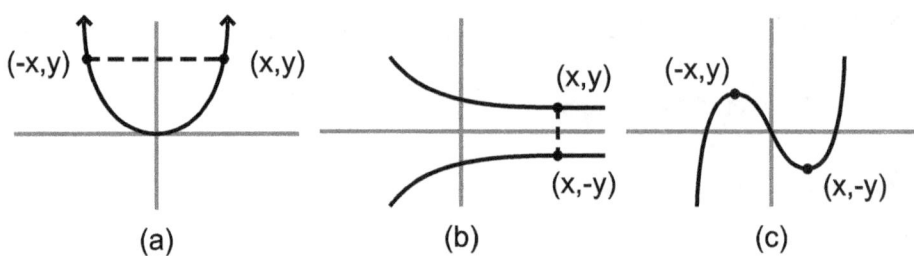

What are translations? A translation is when the shape of the function is kept the same, but it is shifted to a different place on the coordinate graph.

A vertical translation is when the graph shifts up or down on the *y* axis. Vertical translations occur when a number is added to the end of the function.

For example:

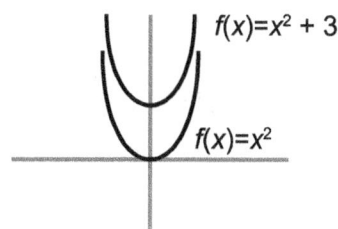

A horizontal translation is when the graph shifts right or left along the *x* axis. Horizontal transformations occur when a number is added after the *x*, but still inside the square.

For example, the graphs of $y = x^2$ and $y = (x+3)^2$

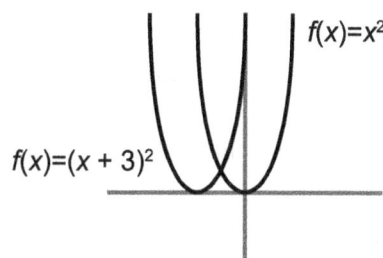

What are reflections? A reflection is when the graph of a function is mirrored onto another part of the graph. Generally reflections occur across either the *x* or *y* axis. A graph will be symmetric across the line it is reflected over.

The graph of $y = -f(x)$ is the same as the graph of $y = f(x)$ reflected across the *x* axis. For example, $y = x^2$ and $y = -x^2$

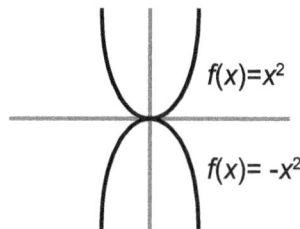

Example 9.1: How does the graph of $y = 2(x - 1)^2 + 1$ differ from that of $y = x^2$?

Solution: The graph will be affected by the "2" in front of the parenthesis by being stretched to be taller and thinner than the original graph. In addition, it has undergone a horizontal translation of one to the right, and a vertical translation of one upward.

Example 9.2: Write the equation of the graph of $y = x^2$ that has been reflected across the *y*-axis, and shifted two to the right and one down.

Solution: To achieve the reflection across the *y*-axis, put a negative in front of the x^2. To achieve the shift two right, subtract two directly from the *x* (this value will be within the parenthesis). To achieve the shift one down, subtract a 1 at the end of the equation.

$$y = -(x - 2)^2 - 1$$

TRY IT YOURSELF:

Question: A triangle is plotted on a graph such that its corners are at the coordinates (1, 1), (3, 1), and (1, 2). What will be its coordinates if it is reflected across the *y* axis?

Answer: (−1, 1), (−3, 1), and (−1, 2)

Question: What transformation has been performed the graph of $y = x^2$ if the equation becomes $y = (x + 1)^2$?

Answer: Horizontal translation (one to the left)

Sample Test Questions

GEOMETRY AND MEASUREMENT QUESTIONS

1. A triangle a perimeter of 49. Two of the side lengths are known to be 21 and 7. What is the length of the final side?

    A. 21
    B. 7
    C. 14
    D. 18
    E. 25

2. What is the perimeter of the triangle if the square has an area of 10?

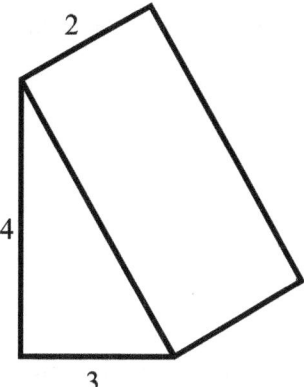

   A. 8
   B. 9
   C. 10
   D. 11
   E. 12

3. What is the area of a square with a perimeter of 20?

   A. 15
   B. 20
   C. 25
   D. 30
   E. 35

4. Which of the following is NOT a three-dimensional representation?

   A. Sphere
   B. Cube
   C. Cylinder
   D. Parallelogram
   E. Box

5. A cylinder is stacked on top of a cube. If the base of the cylinder is exactly the same as the face of the cube (i.e., it fits the top perfectly), and the two are the same height. If the cube has a volume of 27 cubic centimeters, what is the volume of the cylinder?

   A. 21.2 cubic centimeters
   B. 23.5 cubic centimeters
   C. 17.6 cubic centimeters
   D. 19.7 cubic centimeters
   E. 24.1 cubic centimeters

6. A trucking company is contracted to carry a load of sand from a beach, 20 miles to a customer's home. The customer wants as much sand as can possible fit in the back of the truck to be carried. The trucks dimensions are 20 ft x 8 ft x height. If the company charges $10.00 per pound, and 50 cents per mile to have the sand moved, and sand weighs .5 pounds per cubic foot, then how tall is the truck if they charge $8010.00 to ship the sand?

   A. 8 feet
   B. 9 feet
   C. 10 feet
   D. 11 feet
   E. 12 feet

7. Identify the type of polygon:

   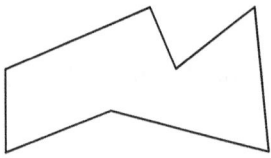

   A. Hexagon
   B. Heptagon
   C. Nonagon
   D. Dodecagon
   E. Octagon

8. Determine the volume (in cubic units) of the shape. Assume that the box is composed of two square ends joined by four rectangles.

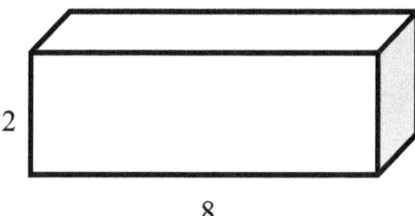

   A. 16
   B. 22
   C. 28
   D. 32
   E. 35

9. In a 30-60-90 triangle, the side length "x" is directly across from which angle measure?

   A. 30
   B. 60
   C. 45
   D. 90
   E. None of the above

10. Equilateral triangles are also

    A. Similar
    B. Equiangular
    C. Right
    D. Pythagorean
    E. None of the above

11. The Pythagorean Theorem is used to find side lengths of a _____ triangle

    A. Equilateral
    B. Similar
    C. Isosceles
    D. Right
    E. Equiangular

12. The sum of the angles of a triangle is always

   A. 45 degrees
   B. 60 degrees
   C. 90 degrees
   D. 180 degrees
   E. 360 degrees

13. Determine x

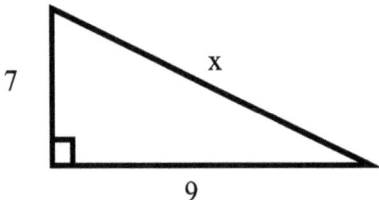

   A. 10
   B. 11.4
   C. 9.8
   D. 15
   E. 16

14. What can be determined about x?

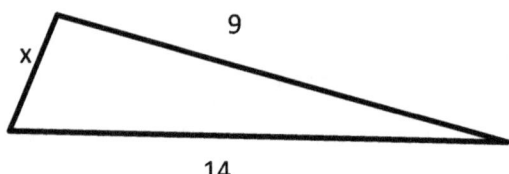

   A. $x > 14$
   B. $0 < x < 23$
   C. $x < 1$
   D. $x > 9$
   E. None of the above

15. Find the area of the triangle pictured below

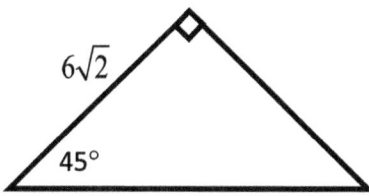

A. 28.4
B. 32.1
C. 34
D. 36
E. 39.56

For questions 16-20 refer to the diagram below:

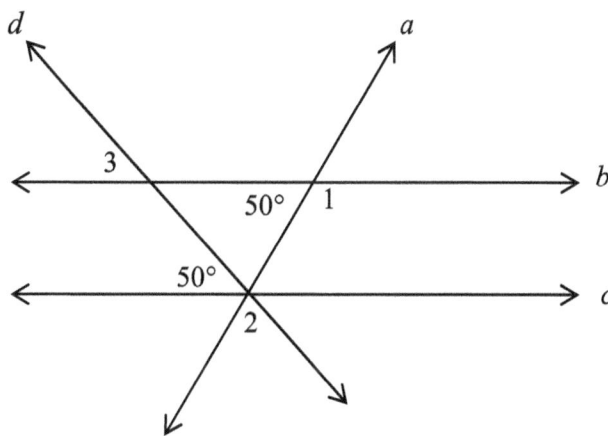

16. Which line is the transversal?

A. *a*
B. *b*
C. *c*
D. *d*
E. *a* and *d*

17. Which lines are parallel?

    A. *a* and *c*
    B. *a* and *b*
    C. *b* and *c*
    D. *b* and *d*
    E. *d* and *c*

18. Determine the measure of angle 1

    A. 30°
    B. 50°
    C. 80°
    D. 130°
    E. 150°

19. Determine the measure of angle 2

    A. 30°
    B. 50°
    C. 80°
    D. 130°
    E. 150°

20. Determine the measure of angle 3

    A. 30°
    B. 50°
    C. 80°
    D. 130°
    E. 150°

For questions 21-25 use the following diagram for which the measure of angle *a* is 120 degrees:

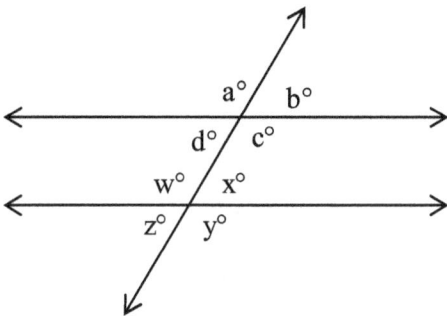

21. What is the measure of angle *y*?

    A. 30 degrees
    B. 60 degrees
    C. 90 degrees
    D. 120 degrees
    E. 150 degrees

22. Angle *b* and angle *z* are

    A. Alternate interior angles
    B. Consecutive exterior angles
    C. Corresponding angles
    D. Alternate exterior angles
    E. Consecutive interior angles

23. Angle *c* and angle *x* are

    A. Alternate interior angles
    B. Corresponding exterior angles
    C. Corresponding interior angles
    D. Alternate exterior angles
    E. Consecutive interior angles

24. Which of the following are alternate exterior angles with a measure of 60 degrees?

    A. *a* and *y*
    B. *b* and *z*
    C. *a* and *b*
    D. *a* and *z*
    E. *b* and *y*

25. Which of the following are alternate interior angles with a measure of 120 degrees

    A. *d* and *x*
    B. *c* and *x*
    C. *d* and *w*
    D. *a* and *c*
    E. *c* and *w*

26. Find the slope of the line with points (0, 7) and (9, 10)

    A. 0
    B. (1/3)
    C. 2
    D. 3
    E. (1/2)

27. The point (0,0) is called

    A. Origin
    B. Intersection
    C. Middle
    D. Institution point
    E. None of the above

28. A vertical line has a slope of

    A. 0
    B. 1
    C. –1
    D. A vertical line can have any slope
    E. A vertical line has an undefined slope

29. Line perpendicular to $y = \frac{1}{2}x + 5$ has a slope of

    A. –2
    B. 2
    C. $-\frac{1}{2}$
    D. $\frac{1}{2}$
    E. 5

30. How many of the following lines have positive slopes?

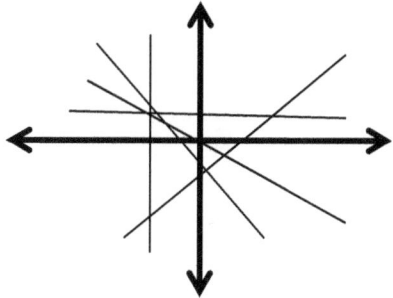

A. 0
B. 1
C. 2
D. 3
E. 4

31. Determine the vertex of $y = -3(x-5)^2 + 2$

A. (−5, 2)
B. (5, 2)
C. (2, −5)
D. (−2, −5)
E. (5, −2)

32. Which of the following is NOT true of the graph of $y = 2(x-1)^2 + 3$?

A. The graph opens upward
B. The graph is a parabola
C. The graph is taller and thinner than that of $y = x^2$
D. The vertex of the graph is (−1, 3)
E. All of the above are true

33. If the following shape is folded to make a cube, what will be the product of the four numbers adjacent to the 1?

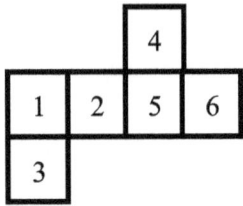

 A. 60
 B. 120
 C. 135
 D. 144
 E. 180

34. A circular paper is folded in half two times and cut as shown. The resulting circle when the paper is unfolded will have which polygon cut from the center?

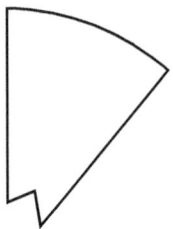

 A. Quadrilateral
 B. Hexagon
 C. Heptagon
 D. Dodecagon
 E. Octagon

35. Determine the sum of the angles in the following polygon

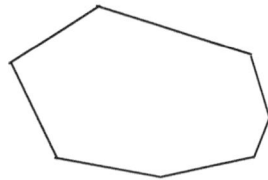

 A. 540
 B. 720
 C. 900
 D. 1080
 E. 1260

36. Determine *x*

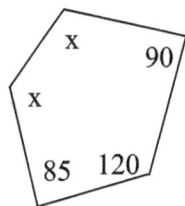

A. 122.5
B. 110
C. 130
D. 175
E. 132.5

37. All circles are

A. Congruent
B. Equilateral
C. Similar
D. Isosceles
E. Palladian

38. Two polygons are similar. Their corresponding angles are

A. Proportional
B. Regular
C. Bisecting
D. Right
E. Congruent

39. Consider the following two similar polygons. If $AB = 12$, $HI = 3$, and $JK = 2$ then $CD = ?$

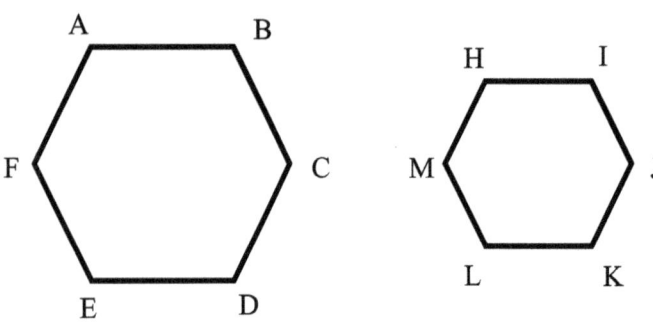

   A. 2
   B. 4
   C. 6
   D. 8
   E. 10

40. Given that $\overline{EB} \parallel \overline{DC}$, $AE = 3.5$, $AD = 10$, $DC = 5$, find EB.

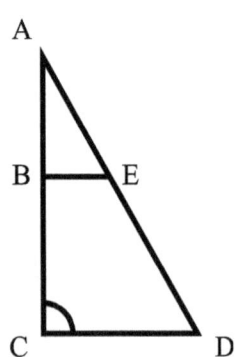

   A. 1.75
   B. 1.89
   C. 1.55
   D. 2.15
   E. 1.25

41. Determine the measure of each angle in a regular nonagon

   A. 30 degrees
   B. 60 degrees
   C. 72 degrees
   D. 140 degrees
   E. 144 degrees

42. Which of the following is the graph of $y = 2x$ that has undergone a horizontal translation?

A.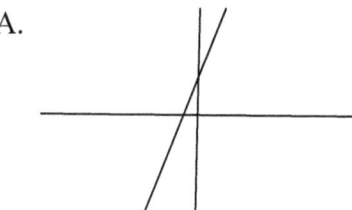
B.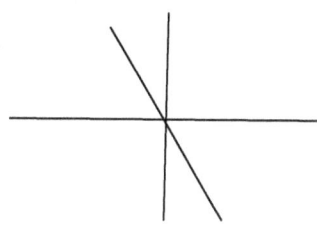

C.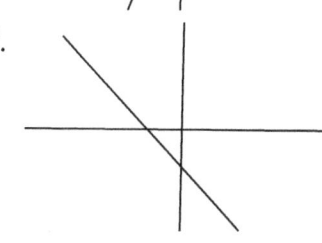
D.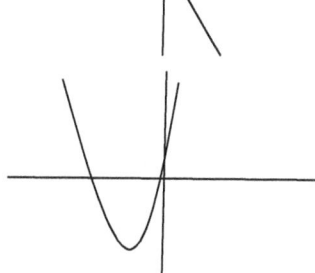

E. None of the above

43. Write the equation of the graph $y = \frac{1}{2}x$ that has been stretched to be twice as steep, and has undergone a vertical translation of positive 4.

A. $y = 2x - 14$
B. $y = \frac{1}{4}x - 4$
C. $y = x + 4$
D. $y = -\frac{1}{4}x + 4$
E. None of the above

44. Consider the location of the following triangle on a coordinate grid. If it is translated such that two of its corners are at (1, 1) and (3, 1), what type of transformation has occurred and what will the coordinate of the final corner be?

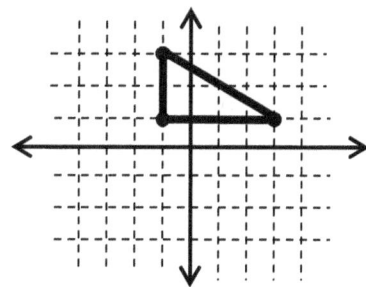

A. Vertical translation, (1, −1)
B. Horizontal translation, (1, 3)
C. Rotation, (−3, 1)

D. Vertical translation, (2, 3)
E. Rotation, (1, –3)

45. Consider the location of the following triangle on the coordinate grid. If it is rotated 90 degrees clockwise about the point (3, 1), which of the following points will NOT be one of its corners?

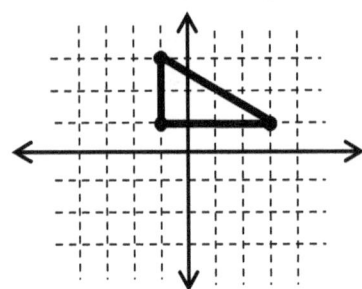

A. (3, 1)
B. (1, 3)
C. (3, 5)
D. (5, 5)
E. Neither A nor B

GEOMETRY AND MEASUREMENT KEY

1. A	16. E	31. B
2. E	17. C	32. D
3. C	18. D	33. D
4. D	19. C	34. E
5. A	20. B	35. C
6. C	21. D	36. A
7. B	22. D	37. C
8. D	23. E	38. E
9. A	24. B	39. D
10. B	25. E	40. A
11. D	26. B	41. D
12. D	27. A	42. A
13. B	28. E	43. C
14. B	29. A	44. E
15. D	30. B	45. B

Section 4: Data Analysis, Statistics, and Probability

4-1: DATA INTERPRETATION

DATA INTERPRETATION AND REPRESENTATION

What are quantitative and qualitative variables? There are two basic types of variables. Quantitative variables are numerical data. Temperature, time, and age are all quantitative variables because they can be represented by a number. Qualitative variables are variables that are represented by a category or label. Gender, political party, and hometown are all examples of qualitative variables.

Tables: Tables are generally the simplest way to organize numerical data, or two sets of quantitative variables. In math for example, x and y values are often organized into a table with one column representing x values, and a second column representing the corresponding y values.

The following table is an example of a table representing the values for $f(x) = x^2$ here.

X	Y
1	1
2	4
3	9
4	16

Scatterplots: Scatterplots are used to determine the relationship between two quantitative variables. The two variables are defined with one as dependent or explanatory, and the other as independent or response. The independent variable is plotted along the x axis, and the dependent variable is plotted along the y axis.

The following is an example of a scatterplot. The scatterplot shows the relation between height and age for a random group of students in an elementary school. Both of the variables (age and height) are quantitative, and each data point (meaning each set of age and height) are plotted appropriately.

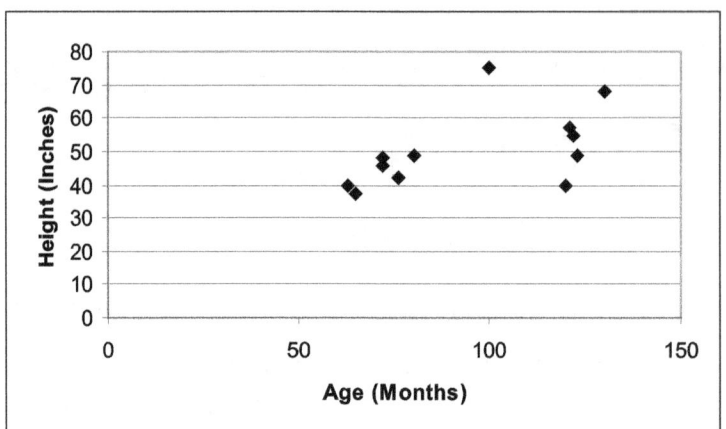

Line graphs: Like scatterplots, line graphs display the relation between two quantitative variables. Line graphs are the best type of graph to use to show a change in one variable over time (the second variable).

The following example shows a line graph representing the average price of gasoline per gallon in the U.S. The independent variable (time) is plotted against the dependent variable (price per gallon), and the relationship is shown by the graph.

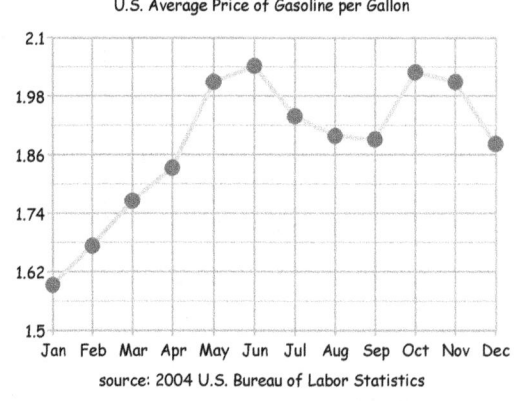

Pie charts: Pie charts are used when showing the relationship between categorical, or qualitative values. A pie chart is generally used when you want to show how one group of data relates to the whole. For example, if there are 21 boys and 15 girls in a class, the resulting pie chart would have two sections. The section representing boys will be larger, because proportional to the whole (the class) there are more boys.

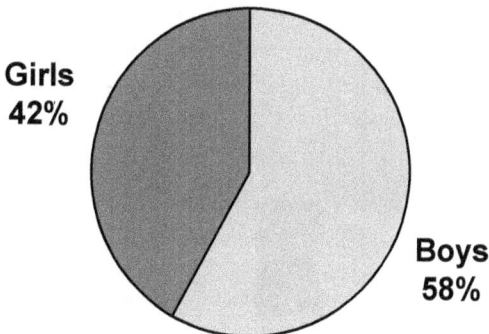

Histograms: Histograms are used with a single quantitative value. Mainly, histograms help show the distribution of data. The variable is listed along the x axis, however instead of using individual values, histograms use ranges. Along the y axis you use the number of data points that fall within the range, determining the height of the bar. Because of this, adjacent columns are placed next to each other with the sides touching. For example, the following histogram shows the distribution of ages of United States presidents at the time of their inauguration.

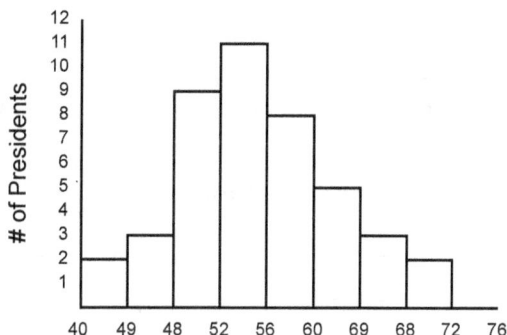

Bar graphs: Bar graphs are very similar to histograms. However they are used with a single qualitative variable, instead of a quantitative one. Bar graphs are also used to show distribution. The independent variable is listed along the x axis, and will be a category. The y axis, like with histograms, shows the number of data points that fit each respective category.

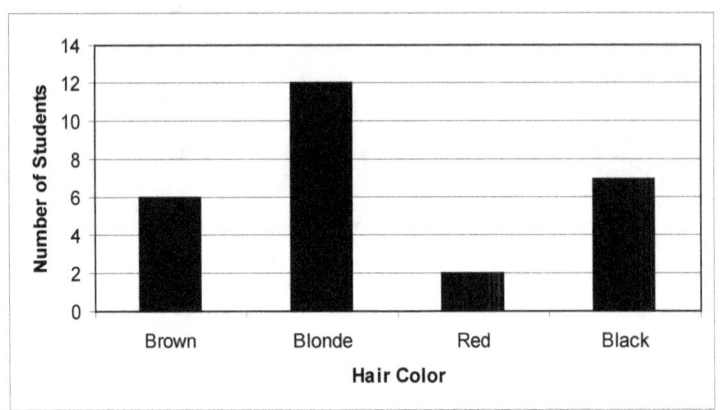

Interpreting tables and graphs: It is important that you are able to interpret and use the information presented in graphs and tables. First, attempt to understand the information that is being presented in the graph or table, and then consider how that information relates to the information the question is asking for.

Example 1.1: A polling of 1575 students at a local high school yields the following information about book preferences among students. Are any book genres preferred by greater than 12% of the student body?

	Fiction	Fantasy	Romance	Nonfiction	Poetry	Total
Sophomores	142	132	135	64	25	525
Juniors	140	347	105	21	37	525
Seniors	146	100	115	15	51	525
Total	428	579	355	100	113	1575

Solution: The information on the table gives the breakdown by both year in school, and by book genre. However, the question itself does not require/ask you to consider the differences in different classes, therefore, the column totals (the bottom row of the table) can be used.

To find the percentages simply divide each of the column/genre totals by the grand total of 1575 students, giving that

Genre	Fiction	Fantasy	Romance	Nonfiction	Poetry	Total
Total (%)	27.2	36.8	22.5	6.3	7.2	100

Therefore, there are three book genres which are the preferred genre of greater than twelve percent of the students – fiction, fantasy, and romance.

Example 1.2: Use the following data set to construct a pie chart which describes the breakdown of book preferences within each class (i.e., create one pie chart for each class).

	Fiction	Fantasy	Romance	Nonfiction	Poetry	Total
Sophomores	142	132	135	64	25	525
Juniors	140	347	105	21	37	525
Seniors	146	100	115	15	51	525
Total	428	579	355	100	113	1575

Solution: First, consider what information is needed. To construct the pie chart requires knowing the percentage of students which prefer each book choice, relative to the class totals. Because each class had 525 students polled, simply divide each total by 525, and ignore the column totals.

	Fiction	Fantasy	Romance	Nonfiction	Poetry	Total
Sophomores	27%	25%	26%	12%	5%	100%
Juniors	27%	66%	20%	4%	7%	100%
Seniors	28%	19%	22%	3%	10%	100%

Next, construct the pie charts. Because they are relative to class totals, create one pie chart for each ROW of data.

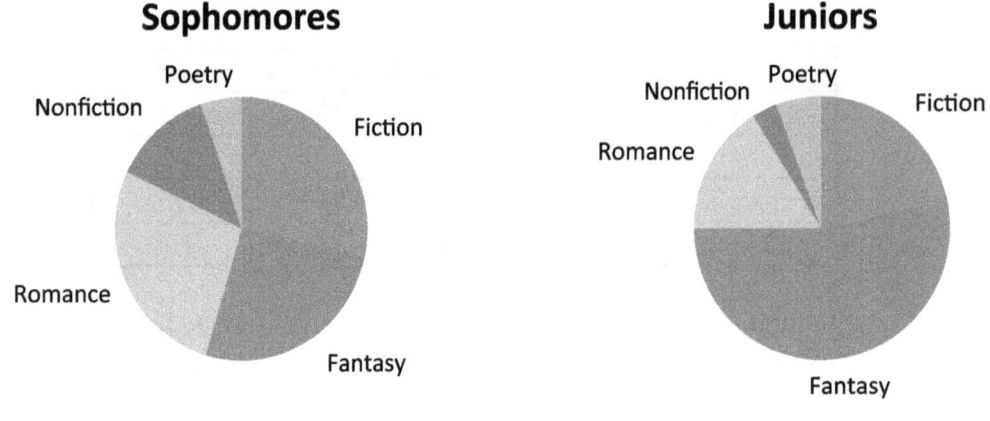

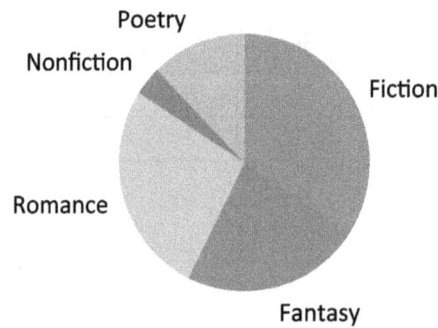

TRY IT YOURSELF:

Question: What type of graph should be used to show the distribution of time spent watching TV for a sample of 400 children?

Answer: Histogram

Question: A survey of 1000 teenagers yields the following data relating to favorite class. If 30% of the students surveyed were seniors, how many seniors consider math to be their favorite class?

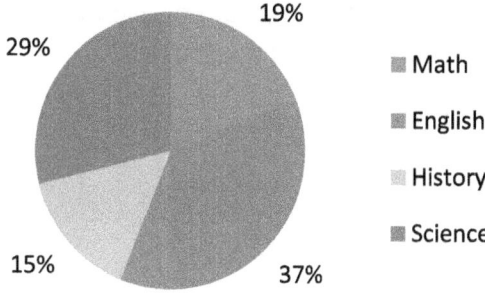

Answer: 57

Question: A line graph charts the change in temperature over the course of a year. Which variable is dependent, which variable is independent, and what type of variables are they?

    Answer: Independent = time = quantitative
                  Dependent = temperature = qualitative

4-2: DESCRIPTIVE STATISTICS

What is the "center" of a set of data? There are three different measures of center which are typically used in statistics. These measures are mean, median, and mode. Each is found differently, and has a slightly different meaning. However, depending on the circumstance, each can be considered the "center" of the data. Finding the center of a data set is a useful way to understand the data better. If there is a large amount of data, the center can be an easy way to describe it, or to make it more useful.

What is the "mean" of a set of data? The mean, which is also referred to as the arithmetic mean or the average, can be found using the following formula

$$Mean = \frac{\sum X}{n}$$

Where x is the value of each element in the data set, and n is the number of elements in the data set.

Example 2.1: Find the average of the following data set: 1, 3, 14, 7, 4, 54, 21, 32, 25

Solution: To find the average, simply find the sum of each element in the set, and divide by the total number of elements in the set.

Sum: 1 + 3 + 14 + 7 + 4 + 54 + 21 + 32 + 25 = 161
$n = 9$

161 ÷ 9 = 17.89

Example 1.4: A fourth grade class takes a math test. The following table lists the scores that each student in the class got on their test. What is the average score?

Student:	Score:	Student:	Score:	Student:	Score:
Andrew	85	Jennika	100	Erik	78
Justin	92	Kyle	95	Ashley	98
Jane	68	Dave	86	Karin	85
Kory	79	Derik	91	Sean	84
Sally	82	Sam	88	Aaron	86

Solution: To find the average score in the class, first determine the sum of all the scores, then divide by the total number of students:

Sum: 85 + 92 + 68 + 79 + 82 + 100 + 95 + 86 + 91 + 88 + 78 + 98 + 85 + 84 + 86 = 1297
# of students: 15

Therefore, the average score on the test was 1297 ÷ 15 = 86.5 percent

What is the median of a set of data? The median of a data set is the number that is in the "middle." In other words, when the numbers in the data are lined up from lowest to highest, it is the element that has as many numbers lower than it as it does higher than it. To find the median, order the numbers, and then determine which number is in the middle of the set.

Example 2.2: Find the median of the following set of numbers: 1, 3, 14, 7, 4, 54, 21, 32, 25

Solution: First the numbers must be ordered from lowest to highest:

1, 3, 4, 7, 14, 21, 25, 32, 54

From here there are two ways to determine which number is the median. First, cross of numbers one at a time from the beginning and end of the list until only one number is left, as shown below:

1, 3, 4, 7, 14, 21, 25, 32, 54

Second, you can determine the median term by counting the number of elements in the data set, adding 1, and dividing by two, as follows:

There are 9 terms in the data set. (9 + 1) ÷ 2 = 5, so it will be the fifth number in the data set, which is 14.

Example 2.3: Find the median of the following set of numbers: 4, 5, 1, 7, 12, 15, 4, 6, 2, 10

Solution: First, order the numbers from lowest to highest

1, 2, 4, 4, 5, 6, 7, 10, 12, 15

Next, determine which element is the median. Notice that this set has an even number of values. To find the median when this is the case, AVERAGE the two middle numbers. In this case

Median = (5 + 6) ÷ 2 = 5.5

What is the mode? The mode is the number that occurs most frequently in a set of data. A data set can have more than one mode if two different numbers appear equally frequently.

Example 2.4: Find the mode of the following set of numbers: 4, 5, 1, 7, 12, 15, 4, 6, 2, 10

Solution: The number 4 appears twice whereas each other number appears only once. Therefore the mode is 4.

What is the "range"? The range is simply the difference between the largest data value and the smallest data value. For example, the range in the set of {2, 4, 7, 8, 10, 12, 24} is 24 − 2 = 22.

What is "standard deviation"? Standard deviation relates data points to the mean of the sample data set. In other words, standard deviation is the mean of how far away the data points are from the actual mean. When s is large, the data is spread out. When s is small, the data is closer together.

Standard deviation (s) is calculated using: $s = \sqrt{\dfrac{\sum_{i=1}^{n}(X_i - \bar{X})^2}{N}}$

Where $\bar{X}$ = the arithmetic mean of the data set

X_i = the value of each number in the data set

N = Number of values in the data set

Example of standard deviation: Find the standard deviation of the following set of numbers: {12, 6, 7, 3, 15, 10, 18, 5}.

$$\bar{X} = \frac{12+6+7+3+15+10+18+5}{8} = \frac{76}{8} = 9.5$$

$$s = \sqrt{\frac{(12-9.5)^2 + (6-9.5)^2 + (7-9.5)^2 + (3-9.5)^2 + (15-9.5)^2 + (10-9.5)^2 + (18-9.5)^2 + (5-9.5)^2}{8}}$$

Therefore, $s = \sqrt{23.75} = 4.87$

What are the properties of standard deviation? The properties of standard deviation include:

1. $s = \sqrt{\dfrac{\sum_{i=1}^{n}(X_i - \bar{X})^2}{N}}$

2. You will often study "normal distribution." A normal distribution can be broken down into standard deviation from the mean. Following is the normal distribution curve.

The center of the normal distribution represents the mean value. You can go 1 standard deviation in either the left or right direction by calculating $\bar{X} - s$ or $\bar{X} + s$.

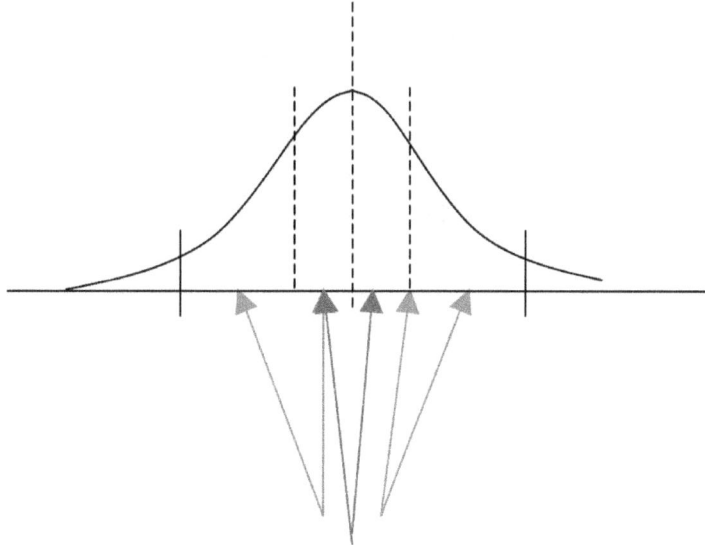

For a normal distribution:

– – – 68.27% of the numbers are within one standard deviation of the mean.

——— 95.45% of the numbers are within two standard deviations of the mean.

——— 98% of the numbers are within three standard deviations of the mean.

4-3: PROBABILITY

What is probability? Probability is defined as the likelihood that an event will occur expressed as the ratio of the number of favorable outcomes in the set of outcomes divided by the total number of possible outcomes.

What are outcomes and events? An outcome is the result of an experiment or other situation involving uncertainty. An event is a collection of outcomes.

Example 3.1: When flipping a standard coin, identify the event, outcomes, and probability of flipping a "heads."

Solution: The event would be the act of flipping the coin. The outcomes (or results of an event) are either a heads or tails.

The probability is the number of possible occurrences of a specific outcome, divided by the number of total possible outcomes. In other words,

$$\text{Probability of "heads"} = \frac{\text{\# of heads}}{\text{\# of possible outcomes}} = \frac{1}{2} \text{ or } .5$$

How is probability notated? The probability of an event is written as P(Event). Probabilities must be between 0 and 1, with 0 indicating that something will NEVER happen, and 1 indicating that something will ALWAYS happen (it has a perfect probability of happening).

Example 3.2: Determine the probability that flipping a coin will result in either a heads or a tails.

Solution: The probability will be written as P(Heads or Tails). Because the only two options when flipping a coin are heads and tails, the probability will be 1. Therefore, P(Heads or Tails) = 1.

What is the maximum a probability can be? The maximum amount that a probability can be is 1. The sum of the probabilities of all possible outcomes will always equal 1.

Example 3.3: Jonathan rolls a standard six-sided dice 50 times and tracks the results of each of his rolls. Determine the probability of each number rolling:

Event:	1	2	3	4	5	6
# Occurrences:	5	9	6	8	7	15

Solution:

P(1) = .1   P(2) = .18   P(3) = .12
P(4) = .16   P(5) = .14   P(6) = .3

Therefore, the sum of all possible outcomes is

$$P(1) + P(2) + P(3) + P(4) + P(5) + P(6)$$
$$= .1 + .18 + .12 + .16 + .14 + .3$$
$$= 1$$

And the maximum probability AND the sum of a possible probabilities is 1.

How do you find the probability of a simple event occurring or NOT occurring?
The probability of a simple event is simply the number of favorable outcomes over the number of total possible outcomes. To find the probability that a simple event will NOT occur, simply subtract the probability that it WILL occur from 1. This works because the probability of all possible outcomes that can occur will be 1 (we know that one of the outcomes has to occur). Therefore, if the outcome is NOT the one we are studying it must have been another outcome.

Example 3.4: 10 poker chips have been placed in a bag and mixed together. There are 4 blue chips, 3 red chips, 2 yellow chips, and 1 gold chip. If chips are pulled out of the bag at random, what is the probability that

(a) A gold chip will be selected?
(b) A red or blue chip will be selected?
(c) A yellow chip will NOT be selected?

Solution (a):
$$P(Gold) = \frac{\text{\# of gold chips}}{\text{\# of chips}} = \frac{1}{10} \text{ or } .1$$

Solution (b):
$$P(Red \text{ or } Blue) = \frac{\text{\# of blue chips + red chips}}{\text{\# of chips}} = \frac{4+3}{10} \text{ or } .7$$

Notice that P(Red or Blue) = P(Red)+P(Blue). This will always be the case when considering the probability that one event OR the other will happen.

Solution (c):
NOTE: P(NOT Yellow) = P(IS Blue or Red or Gold) = 1-P(Yellow)
P(NOT Yellow) = 1 − .8 = .2

Example 3.5: The probability that it will rain tomorrow is 35%. What is the probability that it will NOT rain?

Solution: P(NOT rain) = 1 − P(Rain) = 1 − .35 = .65 OR 65%

TRY IT YOURSELF:

Question: A standard six sided die is rolled. What is the probability that 7 rolls?

Answer: P(7) = 0

Question: A standard six sided die is rolled. What is the probability that an even number does NOT roll?

Answer: P(NOT Even) = .5

Question: There are 25 marbles in a bag. 5 are blue, 7 are green, 10 are yellow and 3 are red. What is the probability that a yellow marble is picked at random from the bag?

Answer: P(Yellow) = .4

What is compound probability and how is it found? Compound probability deals with probability when an event is occurring multiple times (or multiple events are occurring, etc.). For example, rolling a dice 3 times, flipping a coin 10 times, picking a card twice, or any other event. The idea is that it happens more than once, so the probabilities are compounded.

What are dependent and independent events? Two events are independent if one occurring does not affect the other. Alternately, two events are dependent if one occurring does affect the probability of the other. For example, the probability of getting a parking ticket is dependent upon parking. Therefore, parking and getting a parking ticket are dependent events. Another way to tell whether events are dependent or independent is if their order matters. If one event must happen before another then the events are dependent.

Example 3.6: Determine whether the following are dependent or independent events:

(a) Flipping a coin three times
(b) Picking two marbles out of a bag if you replace the marble in between picks
(c) Picking two marbles out of a bag if you do NOT replace the marbles between picks

Solution (a): The events are all independent of each other – no matter how many times you flip a coin it will always have a .5 probability of being heads and a .5 probability of being tales.

Solution (b): The events are independent. The same number of marbles and types of marbles will be in the bag after each pick, so the probabilities will all remain the same.

Solution (c): The events are dependent. After each pick the distribution of marbles changes, so the probabilities of picking certain marbles will all be altered accordingly.

How are independent and dependent events notated? An independent event is noted as a normal probability, in other words as P(Event). For example, the probability of event "A" is P(A). Dependent events, however, have to indicate what event has already happened. For example, if you are flipping a coin and want to know the probability that you will flip heads (event "H") given that you have already flipped tales (event "T") this would be signified as P(H|T). This is read as "the probability of H given T."

Example 3.7: A box has 3 different balls in it. One blue, one red, and one green. What is the probability that you pick out the green ball at random? How would you signify the probability of picking out a green ball at random if the red ball has already been chosen?

Solution: The original probability of picking out the green ball would be

$$P(Green) = \frac{1 \text{ green ball}}{3 \text{ total balls}} = .33$$

If the red ball has already been chosen it would be signified as P(Green|Red) or "the probability of green, given that red has already been chosen."

How do you compute compound probability for independent events? Compound probability is essentially the probability of one event AND another event (contrasted with the probability of one event OR another event, in which case the probabilities are simply added). When independent events are compounded, you multiply the probabilities together.

Example 3.8: P(A) = .2 and P(B) = .3. Determine P(A and B) if A and B are both independent events?

Solution: This is an example of compound probability. Simply multiply the two probabilities together:

P(A and B) = P(A)*P(B) = .2*.3 = .06

Example 3.9: What is the probability of flipping two heads in a row when flipping a regular coin?

Solution: This is an example of compound probability when two events are independent of each other. When flipping a coin P(H) = .5, where "H" is the outcome of heads. Because the flips of the coin are independent of each other, the probability of two heads is

P(H)*P(H) = .5*.5 = .25

Example 3.10: You randomly pick one card out of each of two standard decks of cards. What is the probability of picking the same card from each deck?

Solution: This is an example of compound probability. You can think of it as the probability of picking a specific card from one deck AND a specific card from the second deck. The probability of picking any specific card from a deck is (1 card)/(52 cards in a deck) = 1/52. Therefore, the probability is:

$$\frac{1}{52} \cdot \frac{1}{52} = \frac{1}{2704} = .00037$$

How do you compute compound probability for dependent events? Compound probability for dependent events is computed as follows:

P(A then B) OR P(A and B) where B occurs after A = P(A)*P(B|A)

In other words, it is calculated essentially the same way a regular compound probability, but taking into account the change in probabilities after the first event has occurred.

Example 3.11: A bag contains slips of paper with the numbers 0-9 written on them. Compute the probability of first picking out the slip that says 8, and then picking out the slip that says 3.

Solution: This is a compound probability problem with dependent events. If the first pick is event A and the second pick is event B, it probability would be calculated as:

$$P(A) = \frac{1 \text{ slip of } \#8}{10 \text{ slips of paper}} = .1$$

$$P(B|A) = \frac{1 \text{ slip of } \#3}{9 \text{ slips of paper remaining}} = .11$$

P(B then A) = P(A)·P(B|A) = (.1)(.11) = .011

Example 3.12: A bag is filled with 6 marbles. 2 marbles are white, 2 marbles are green, and 2 marbles are yellow. Note: The marbles will NOT be placed back in the bag at any point. What is the probability that first a green marble will be picked and then a white marble?

Solution: Total Number of outcomes = 6 marbles

First Pick (6 marbles):

$$P(W) = \frac{2}{6}$$
$$P(G) = \frac{2}{6}$$
$$P(Y) = \frac{2}{6}$$

Second Pick (5 marbles left):

$$P(W|G) = \frac{2}{5}$$
$$P(G|G) = \frac{1}{5}$$
$$P(Y|G) = \frac{2}{5}$$

Therefore, $P(G \text{ and } W) = P(W|G) \cdot P(G)$

$$P(G) = \frac{2}{6} \qquad P(W|G) = \frac{2}{5}$$

$$P(G \text{ and } W) = \frac{2}{6} \cdot \frac{2}{5} = \frac{4}{30} = \frac{2}{15}$$

Example 3.13: The probability of selecting a green marble and then a red marble out of a bag of marbles is .05. If there are 30 marbles in the bag and 3 of them are green, then what is the probability of picking a red marble, given that a green marble has already been selected?

Solution: We know that P(Green then Red) = P(G)*P(R|G). From the problem we are given that P(Green then Red) = .05. If 3 out of the original 30 marbles are green, then the probability of selecting a green marble initially, or P(G) is .1. Therefore, the equation can be reordered and solved to find the P(R|G)

P(Green then Red) = P(G) * P(R|G)

.05 = .1 * P(R|G)

P(R|G) = .5

TRY IT YOURSELF:

Question: There are 40 marbles in a bag. There are 10 each of yellow, green, blue, and purple marbles. What is the probability of drawing first a green, then a blue marble without replacing the first marble?

Answer: 6.4%

Question: Natalie is flipping a quarter. What is the probability that if she flips the quarter four times, she will get four heads in a row?

Answer: 6.25%

Question: Based on the following distribution, what is the probability of rolling a 4?

Roll:	1	2	3	4	5	6
Probability:	.1	.15	.35	?	.1	.2

Answer: P(4) = .1

Question: Sheryl is a contestant on a game show. In front of her are 5 different doors and behind each door is a prize. She knows that the five prizes are a candy bar, one hundred dollars, a new hair dryer, a car, and a cruise to Hawaii. What is the probability that she picks the cruise to Hawaii on her first attempt? Her second?

Answer: First attempt: .2   Second attempt: .25

Sample Test Questions

DATA ANALYSIS, STATISTICS AND PROBABILITY QUESTIONS

1. Which of the following is NOT a qualitative variable?

   A. Gender
   B. Height
   C. Hair color
   D. Eye color
   E. Skin tone

2. A certain class has 26 people in it. If each of the individuals in the class rolls a dice two times, and then the total number of heads and tails are counted, which of the following will most likely represent the resulting distribution?

   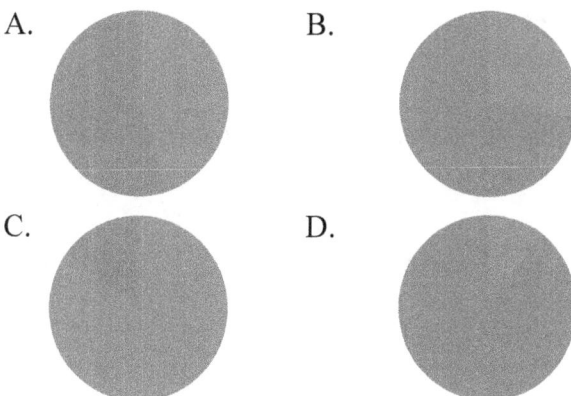

   A.
   B.
   C.
   D.
   E. None of the above

3. The bar graph below illustrates the number of a certain species of birds that are owned by a zoo in various years. What is the percentage change in the number of birds from 1998 to 2002?

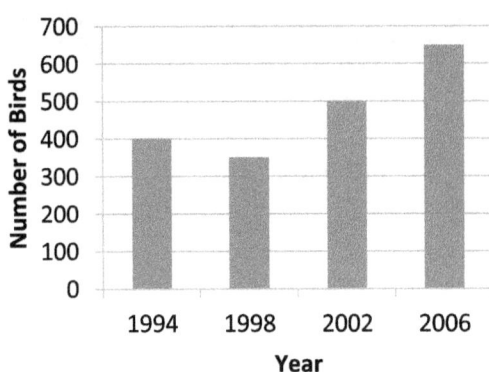

A. 30 percent increase
B. 13 percent decrease
C. 43 percent increase
D. 15 percent decrease
E. 85 percent increase

4. Based on the following scatterplot, the data most likely have a _____ relationship

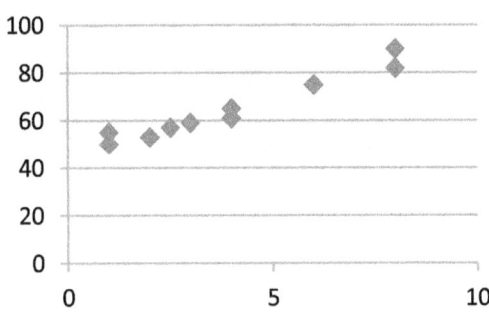

A. Linear
B. Quadratic
C. Exponential
D. Correlated
E. None of the above

For questions 5-10 use the following table. The table displays data relating to the number of three different models of cars (A, B, and C) bought in each of four different years (1995, 1998, 2001, 2004).

	1995	1998	2001	2004	Total
A	250	190	100	60	600
B	105	108	127	x	500
C	207	58	265	z	700
Total	562	y	492	w	1800

5. $x = ?$

   A. 160
   B. 170
   C. 239
   D. 356
   E. 390

6. $y = ?$

   A. 160
   B. 170
   C. 239
   D. 356
   E. 390

7. $z = ?$

   A. 160
   B. 170
   C. 239
   D. 356
   E. 390

8. $w = ?$

   A. 160
   B. 170
   C. 239
   D. 356
   E. 390

9. Which car, if any, had a consistent increase in sales?

    A. A
    B. B
    C. C
    D. B and C
    E. No car

10. What percentage of total car sales were 1995 model A's?

    A. 13.8
    B. 44.5
    C. 41.7
    D. 15.4
    E. None of the above

11. Sydney's math class receives their grades based on the average of four test scores. If Sydney has the following track record of scores, and wants to get at least a 93% in her class, what must she get on the final?

    | Test 1 | 85 |
    | Test 2 | 99 |
    | Test 3 | 89 |
    | Final | ? |

    A. 96
    B. 97
    C. 98
    D. 99
    E. 100

12. Find the mean and median of the following set of numbers: 14, 14, 16, 18, 17, 21, 22

    A. Mean = 17.4, Median = 17
    B. Mean = 18, Mean = 17.4
    C. Mean = 14, Median = 18
    D. Mean = 16.8, Median = 17.5
    E. Mean = 16.8, Median = 18

13. Find the standard deviation of the following set of numbers: 3, 5, 7

   A. 0
   B. 1
   C. 2
   D. 3
   E. 4

14. Samantha has received the following scores on her geometry quizzes. What is the range of her quiz scores?

Quiz 1	98
Quiz 2	72
Quiz 3	82
Quiz 4	91
Quiz 5	85
Quiz 6	89

   A. 72 – 98
   B. 26
   C. 24
   D. 98
   E. 18

15. Samantha has received the following scores on her geometry quizzes. If her grade is based on her average quiz score, with a 2% increase for good participation, on a standard scale (91 – 100 = A, 81 – 90 = B, etc.) what grade will she receive?

Quiz 1	98
Quiz 2	72
Quiz 3	82
Quiz 4	91
Quiz 5	85
Quiz 6	89

   A. A
   B. B
   C. C
   D. D
   E. F

16. There are seven blue socks, three green socks, ten striped socks and 10 polka-dotted socks in a drawer. What is the probability that a person picking one sock at random from the draw would pick a striped sock?

    A. .33
    B. .4
    C. .55
    D. .7
    E. .9

17. There are seven blue socks, three green socks, ten striped socks and 10 polka-dotted socks in a drawer. What is the probability that a person picking one sock at random from the drawer would NOT pick a green sock?

    A. .1
    B. .33
    C. .5
    D. .78
    E. .9

18. A spinner is labeled from one to ten, with an equal probability of landing on any of the numbers. If a person spins the spinner at random, what is the probability that the spinner will land on either a 3 or an 8?

    A. .1
    B. .2
    C. .3
    D. .4
    E. .5

19. A weighted, six-sided die has the following probabilities of rolling different numbers. P(6) = ?

Outcome	Probability
1	.2
2	.05
3	.3
4	.4
5	.01
6	?

    A. .17
    B. .4
    C. .05
    D. .04
    E. 0

20. Which of the following is NOT an example of independent events?

    A. Flipping a coin
    B. Picking cards out of a deck with replacement
    C. Picking marbles out of a bag with replacement
    D. Turning in a final project and getting an A in the class
    E. All of the above are independent events

21. There are six poker chips in a bag. Three red, two blue, and one yellow. What is the probability of drawing first a red and then a yellow chip (Note: the chips are NOT replaced between picks)?

    A. $\frac{1}{12}$
    B. $\frac{1}{10}$
    C. $\frac{1}{36}$
    D. $\frac{1}{2}$
    E. $\frac{1}{5}$

22. Consider the following distribution of probabilities when rolling a 5-sided die. What is the probability of rolling a 4 two times in a row?

Roll:	1	2	3	4	5
Probability	.2	.45	.1	.2	.05

A. .04
B. .1
C. .45
D. .2
E. .02

23. There are 40 marbles in a jar. There are striped marbles, spotted marbles, and solid marbles. If the probability of drawing a solid marble is 1/8 and the probability of drawing a spotted marble is 1/2, how many marbles are striped?

A. 10
B. 15
C. 20
D. 25
E. 30

24. What is the probability of drawing first a diamond, then a red card out of a standard deck of cards (without replacing the cards between picks)?

A. 12.3%
B. 15%
C. 17.2%
D. 18.9%
E. 21%

25. What is the probability of drawing first an ace, then a diamond from a standard deck of cards (the cards ARE replaced between picks)?

A. 17.8%
B. 15%
C. 12.3%
D. 3%
E. 1.8%

26. What is the probability of drawing a spade or an ace from a standard deck of cards?

   A. $\dfrac{21}{51}$

   B. $\dfrac{17}{51}$

   C. $\dfrac{16}{51}$

   D. $\dfrac{13}{51}$

   E. $\dfrac{10}{51}$

27. A local potato chip factory purchases potatoes by the truckload. Each truck has 60 bags of potatoes in it. If approximately 10% of the potatoes in any random truck are rotten, how many total bags of potatoes are suitable to be made into potato chips?

   A. 6
   B. 25
   C. 35
   D. 46
   E. 54

28. 1/3 of the students in a kindergarten class have red hair and 1/2 have brown hair. In addition, every third child has blue eyes. What is the probability that a child selected at random will have brown hair, but will NOT have blue eyes?

   A. $\dfrac{1}{3}$

   B. $\dfrac{1}{6}$

   C. $\dfrac{1}{2}$

   D. $\dfrac{2}{3}$

   E. $\dfrac{4}{3}$

29. Which of the following should be used to display the distribution of a single quantitative variable?

   A. Bar graph
   B. Histogram
   C. Pie chart
   D. Table
   E. None of the above

30. A bag is filled with seven poker chips: four blue chips, two red chips, and one gold chip. What is the probability that a gold chip will NOT be drawn?

   A. $\dfrac{2}{7}$
   B. $\dfrac{4}{7}$
   C. $\dfrac{5}{7}$
   D. $\dfrac{6}{7}$
   E. None of the above

DATA ANALYSIS, STATISTICS, AND PROBABILITY KEY

1. B
2. A
3. C
4. A
5. A
6. D
7. B
8. E
9. B
10. A
11. D
12. A
13. C
14. B
15. B
16. A
17. E
18. B
19. D
20. D
21. B
22. A
23. B
24. A
25. E
26. C
27. E
28. A
29. B
30. D

Section 5: Logic, Logarithms and Exponents, Unit Conversions and Interest

5-1: LOGIC

What is logic based upon? Logic is related to given *statements*. A statement can be true or false. When a statement is true, its truth value is T. When a statement is false, its truth value is F. For example, 1 + 4 = 5 has a truth value of T.

Statements may include connective statements including: "and", "or", "not", "if…then", and "…if and only if…" Each connective has a symbol and formal name associated with it. Study the following table regarding this information.

Connective	Formal Name	Symbol
and	Conjunction	$\wedge$
or	Disjunction	$\vee$
not	Negation	$\neg$
If…then	Conditional	$\rightarrow$
…if and only if…	Biconditional	$\leftrightarrow$

What are Truth Tables?
Elementary truth tables represent those truth values of two statements with a specific connective. Let's use Statement 1 = S1 and Statement 2 = S2 to create truth tables.

Examine the truth table below.

S1	S2	S1$\vee$S2	S1$\wedge$S2	S1$\rightarrow$S2	S1$\leftrightarrow$S2
T	T	T	T	T	T
T	F	T	F	F	F
F	T	T	F	T	F
F	F	F	F	T	T

How do you read a Truth Table? Notice the first column and second row has "T" for both S1 and S2. This means that Statement 1 and Statement 2 were found to be true. Read across the second row to see how the "connectives" affect the truth value of the statement.

What are conditional statements? Conditional statements are written as "If…then" statements which include a hypothesis and conclusion. The hypothesis is what is given and the conclusion is what is to be proved.

For example, the statement you are given is "If a triangle has a right angle then it is a right triangle." The hypothesis is "If a triangle has a right angle" and the conclusion is "then it is a right triangle."

What is a counterexample? A counterexample is a statement which proves a rule false by presenting an exception to it.

For example, if your rule was "all boys are tall", then a counterexample could be if Tom was a boy who was short. Because Tom was an exception to the rule, or counter-example, the rule was proven false.

What is the Converse of a statement? The converse of a statement is the statement that is formed by switching the hypothesis with the conclusion.

For example, if your statement was "cats are tigers" then the converse of the statement would be "tigers are cats."

What is the Negative of a statement? The negative of a statement is the denial of a statement.

For example, if your statement was "a boy is tall" then the negative of the statement would be "a boy is not tall."

What is the Inverse of a statement? The inverse of a statement is formed by denying both the hypothesis and the conclusion.

For example, if your statement was "a boy is tall" then the inverse statement would be "a person who is not a boy is not tall."

What is the Contrapositive of a statement? The Contrapositive of a statement is created by switching the negative of the hypothesis with the negative of the conclusion.

What are necessary and sufficient conditions? Necessary and sufficient conditions are utilized to ascertain if the conditions in the hypothesis are "necessary or sufficient" to verify its conclusion.

How do you determine if you have necessary and sufficient conditions?

    1. First you need to determine whether you statement is true or false.
    2. Second determine if the converse of the statement is true or false.
    3. Apply the following four principles:

Principle 1: If a statement and its converse are both true, then the conditions in the hypothesis of the statement are necessary and sufficient for its conclusion.

Principle 2: If a statement is true and its converse is false, then the conditions in the hypothesis of the statement are sufficient but not necessary for its conclusion.

Principle 3: If a statement is false and its converse is true, then the conditions in the hypothesis are necessary but not sufficient for its conclusion.

Principle 4: If a statement and its converse are both false, then the conditions in the hypothesis are neither necessary nor sufficient for its conclusion.

TRY IT YOURSELF

Question: What is the converse of the statement "squares are rectangles"?

    Answer: "rectangles are squares"

    Explanation: The hypothesis of the original statement is "squares" and the conclusion is "rectangles." The converse of a statement switches the order of the hypothesis and conclusion.

Question: What is the negative of the statement "squares are rectangles"?

    Answer: "squares are not rectangles"

Question: What is the Inverse of the statement "squares are rectangles"?

    Answer "shapes that are not squares are not rectangles"

    Explanation: The Inverse of the statement denies both the hypothesis and the conclusion.

Question: What is the Contrapositive of the statement "squares are rectangles"?

    Answer: "shapes that are not rectangles are not squares"

Explanation: The Contrapositive of a statement is when you switch the negative of the hypothesis with the negative of the conclusion.

Question: Determine whether the conditions in the hypothesis are necessary or sufficient to justify the conclusion for the statement, "squares are rectangles."

Answer: The conditions in the hypothesis of the statement are sufficient, but not necessary for its conclusion.

Explanation: When determining necessary and sufficient conditions answer these two questions:

1) Is the statement true or false? Squares are rectangles so the statement is true.

2) Is the converse of the statement true or false? The converse is false because rectangles are not squares.

Principle 2 says that if the statement is true and the converse is false, then the conditions in the hypothesis of the statement are sufficient, but not necessary for its conclusion.

Question: Determine whether the conditions in the hypothesis are necessary or sufficient to justify the conclusion for the statement, "rectangles are squares."

Answer: The conditions in the hypothesis are necessary, but not sufficient for its conclusion.

Explanation: The statement is false. The converse of the statement is true. This follows Principle 3 which says the conditions in the hypothesis are necessary, but not sufficient for its conclusion.

Question: What is the difference between the Negative of a statement and Inverse of a statement?

Answer: A negative of a statement is a denial of the hypothesis. An Inverse of a statement is a denial of the hypothesis and a denial of the conclusion.

Question: Is the following statement true or false? Explain your answer. "If a triangle has three different side lengths then it is a scalene triangle."

Answer: False. A scalene triangle does have three different side lengths, but a right triangle has three different side lengths as well.

Question: Give the formal names for each connective in the following statements.
"An angle is acute if and only if it is less than 90°" _____
"Triangles and squares are geometric shapes." _____
"If a number can be written as a fraction then it is a rational number." _____
"Squares are rectangles, but rectangles are not squares." _____
"The number 2 can be referred to as an Integer, Whole number, Natural number, or Rational number." _____

Answer:
"An angle is acute if and only if it is less than 90°": **biconditional**
"Triangles and squares are geometric shapes." **conjunction**
"If a number can be written as a fraction then it is a rational number." **conditional**
"Squares are rectangles, but rectangles are not squares." **negation**
"The number 2 can be referred to as an Integer, Whole number, Natural number, or Rational number." **disjunction**

5-2: LOGARITHMS AND EXPONENTS

What are logarithms? Logarithms represent the exponent of a positive number. For example, if $b^x = N$ where "N" is a positive number and "b" is a positive number besides 1, then the exponent "x" is the logarithm of N to the base b.

This relationship can be written as $x = \log_b N$

This would be said "x equals log base "b" of "N."

Following are examples that will help demonstrate this relationship:

Example 2-1: Write $4^2 = 16$ using logarithmic notation.

Solution: 2 is the logarithm of 16 to the base 4 therefore logarithmic notation is $2 = \log_4 16$

Example 2-2: Evaluate $\log_4 64$.

Solution: $\log_4 64$ says that you have a base = 4 and you have to figure out what x value to use in order to satisfy $4^x = 64$. Therefore, x = 3 and $\log_4 64 = 3$.

LAWS OF LOGARITHMS: There are 3 basic laws of logarithms which include:

1. The logarithm of the product of two positive numbers M and N is equal to the sum of the logarithms of the numbers

$$\log_b MN = \log_b M + \log_b N$$

For example, $\log_2 3(5) = \log_2 3 + \log_2 5$

2. The logarithm of the quotient of two positive numbers M and N is equal to the difference of the logarithms of the numbers

$$\log_b \frac{M}{N} = \log_b M - \log_b N$$

For example, $\log_{10} \frac{17}{24} = \log_{10} 17 - \log_{10} 24$

3. The logarithm of the "pth" power of a positive number M is equal to "p" multiplied by the logarithm of the number

$$\log_b M^p = p \log_b M$$

For example, $\log_8 6^4 = 4 \log_8 6$

What are Natural Logarithms? Natural logarithms are logs with a base "e" which is a constant. Natural logarithms are denoted by ln.

You can find "e" on your scientific calculator. e = 2.718281828…

When would you use logarithms and exponents? Logarithms and exponents can be used when you calculate simple & compound interest and exponential growth.

Example of Simple Interest:
The formula for Simple Interest is $I = Prt$ where I = simple interest, P = principal, r = annual interest rate, and t = time.

If you borrow $400 at 10% interest for 1 year, how much interest will you end up paying on the loan?

$I = Prt$
$I = (\$400)(0.10)(1)$
$I = \$40$ in interest

Example of Compound Interest:
Compound interest is paid periodically over the term of a loan. This gives a new principal amount at the end of <u>each</u> interval of time.

Use $A = Pe^{rt}$ when interest in compounded continuously where A = Total amount owed (principal plus interest), P = Principal, r = annual interest rate, t = years

Find the amount of an investment if $10,000 is invested at 8% compounded continuously for 2 years.

$A = Pe^{rt}$
$A = 10,000e^{(0.08)(2)}$
$A = \$11,730$

5-3: UNIT CONVERSIONS

U.S. UNIT SYSTEM

U.S. Units of Length

In the United States, length is commonly measured in inches, feet, yards and miles. You are probably familiar with a ruler which is used to measure the length of smaller objects like a pen, sheet of paper, which you would typically measure in **inches**. But if you drive to the store, you would probably measure that distance in **miles**. The size of your kitchen would be measured in **feet**, and certain things like fabric are bought by the **yard.**

If an item is 12 inches long, you may also say it is 1 foot long, and that would be correct. So, what do you do when you need to know the length of something in a particular unit, but you only know the measurement in a different unit?

First, you need to know the equivalent measures. The table below shows the conversion factors between inches, feet, yards and miles.

> 12 inches (in) = 1 foot (ft)
> 3 feet (ft) = 1 yard (yd)
> 5,280 feet (ft) = 1 mile (mi)

To convert between different units, we need to use these conversion factors. If 12 inches equals 1 foot, then you can write the equation:

$$12 \text{ inches} = 1 \text{ foot}$$

Using Algebra, you can divide both sides of the equation by the same value and the equation will remain true. So, dividing both side by '1 foot' results in:

$$\frac{12 \text{ inches}}{1 \text{ foot}} = \frac{1 \text{ foot}}{1 \text{ foot}} = 1$$

From the **Identity Property of Multiplication,** you know that any number multiplied by 1 equals itself. Therefore, multiplying a number by a unit conversion factor allows us to change the units on a number without changing its actual measure.

Note that while you can write $\frac{12 \text{ inches}}{1 \text{ foot}} = 1$, the reciprocal is also true: $\frac{1 \text{ foot}}{12 \text{ inches}} = 1$
Using the table above, you can generate conversion factors in fraction form for each of the units you need to convert.

Example 3-1: Convert 9 inches to feet.

Solution: To convert inches to feet, we will need to use the conversion factor that relates inches to feet. This will be $\frac{1 \text{ foot}}{12 \text{ inches}}$. Since we want our final answer to be in 'feet', we want to choose a conversion factor with 'feet' in the numerator.

$$9 \text{ inches} = \frac{9 \text{ in}}{1}$$

Write 9 inches as a fraction. Dividing any number by 1 is equal to itself.

$$= \frac{9 \text{ in}}{1} \cdot \frac{1 \text{ ft}}{12 \text{ in}}$$

Multiply by the conversion factor that relates inches to feet. All conversion factors = 1 and multiplying any number by 1 does not change the value of that number.

$$= \frac{9 \cancel{\text{ in}}}{1} \cdot \frac{1 \text{ ft}}{12 \cancel{\text{ in}}}$$

Cancel out the units "inches".

$$= \frac{9 \text{ ft}}{12}$$

Simplify. Notice the units "feet" is what is remaining.

$$= .75 \text{ ft}$$

Simplify.

Remember to always include the units as you do the multiplication to make sure you are multiplying by the correct conversion factor. A common mistake is to use a reciprocal conversion factor. This can easily be avoided by *always* writing the units on your paper when doing the conversions.

Example 3-2: Convert 15 feet to inches.

Solution: In this example, we are converting from feet to inches so we will need to choose the proper conversion factor. Since we want to end up with 'inches' in the final answer, we will need to use 'inches' in the numerator of the conversion factor. Another way to look at it is that since we are starting with 'feet', we need a conversion factor with 'feet' in the denominator so that we can cancel out the units of 'feet'.

$$15 \text{ feet} = \frac{15 \text{ ft}}{1}$$

Write 15 feet as a fraction.

$$= \frac{15 \text{ ft}}{1} \cdot \frac{12 \text{ in}}{1 \text{ ft}}$$

Multiply by the conversion factor that relates inches to feet. Remember to use the proper units in the numerator and the denominator so that you may cancel units.

$$= \frac{15 \cancel{\text{ft}}}{1} \cdot \frac{12 \text{ in}}{1 \cancel{\text{ft}}}$$

Cancel out the units "feet".

$$= 180 \text{ in}$$

Multiply.

Example 3-3: Convert the length of a football field (120 yards) into miles. Round to the nearest thousandth.

Solution: For this example, there is no single entry in the conversion table that relates yards to miles. However, we know that 3 feet = 1 yard and 5,280 feet = 1 mile. Thus, we can convert from yards to miles by using feet as an intermediate step.

$120 \text{ yards} = \dfrac{120 \text{ yds}}{1}$ Write 120 yards as a fraction.

$= \dfrac{120 \text{ yds}}{1} \cdot \dfrac{3 \text{ ft}}{1 \text{ yd}} \cdot \dfrac{1 \text{ mi}}{5280 \text{ ft}}$ Multiply by both the conversion factor that relates feet to yards and the one that relates miles to feet. Keep track of the proper values in numerators and denominators by keeping track of where you want the units to end up.

Since we don't need to know the value of 120 yds in feet, we can combine both conversion factors in 1 step, saving time.

$= \dfrac{120 \cancel{\text{yds}}}{1} \cdot \dfrac{3 \cancel{\text{ft}}}{1 \cancel{\text{yd}}} \cdot \dfrac{1 \text{ mi}}{5280 \cancel{\text{ft}}}$ Cancel out the units "yd" and "ft". Note you are left with miles.

$= .068 \text{ mi}$ Multiply & divide.

U.S. Units of Weight

Converting units of weights is done the same way as units of length. Use the conversion factors in the table below. Ounces and pounds are units we typically measure food in, and tons would be used for the weight of a car or other very heavy item.

16 ounces (oz) = 1 pound (lb)
2000 pounds (lb) = 1 ton

Example 3-4: Convert 25 pounds into ounces.

Solution: Approach this problem the same way as when converting units of length. Use the weight conversions in the table above.

$$25 \text{ pounds} = \frac{25 \text{ lbs}}{1} \qquad \text{Write 25 pounds as a fraction.}$$

$$= \frac{25 \text{ lbs}}{1} \cdot \frac{16 \text{ oz}}{1 \text{ lb}} \qquad \text{Multiply by the conversion factor that relates ounces to pounds.}$$

$$= \frac{25 \cancel{\text{ lbs}}}{1} \cdot \frac{16 \text{ oz}}{1 \cancel{\text{ lb}}} \qquad \text{Cancel out the units "lb".}$$

$$= 400 \text{ oz} \qquad \text{Multiply.}$$

Example 3-5: Convert 224,000 ounces into tons.

Solution: Since you need to convert ounces into tons, you will need to use 2 conversion factors.

$$224{,}000 \text{ ounces} = \frac{224{,}000 \text{ oz}}{1} \qquad \text{Write 224,000 ounces as a fraction.}$$

$$= \frac{224{,}000 \text{ oz}}{1} \cdot \frac{1 \text{ lb}}{16 \text{ oz}} \cdot \frac{1 \text{ ton}}{2000 \text{ lbs}} \qquad \text{Multiply by both the conversion factors.}$$

$$= \frac{224{,}000 \cancel{\text{ oz}}}{1} \cdot \frac{1 \cancel{\text{ lb}}}{16 \cancel{\text{ oz}}} \cdot \frac{1 \text{ ton}}{2000 \cancel{\text{ lbs}}} \qquad \text{Cancel out the units "oz" and "lb".}$$

$$= 7 \text{ tons} \qquad \text{Multiply \& divide.}$$

U.S. Units of Volume

Converting units of weights is done using the conversion factors in the table below. Note that fluid ounces used as a measure of volume is different than ounces used as a measure of weight.

8 fluid ounces (fl oz) = 1 cup (c)
2 cups (c) = 1 pint (pt)
2 pints (pt) = 1 quart (qt)
4 quarts (qt) = 1 gallon (gal)

Example 3-6: Convert 10 cups to quarts.

Solution: You will need to use the conversion factors of $\frac{1\ pint}{2\ cups}$ and $\frac{1\ quart}{2\ pints}$ to convert cups to quarts.

$10\ cups$	$= \dfrac{10\ c}{1}$	Write 10 cups as a fraction.
	$= \dfrac{10\ c}{1} \cdot \dfrac{1\ pt}{2\ c} \cdot \dfrac{1\ qt}{2\ pt}$	Multiply by both the conversion factors.
	$= \dfrac{10\ \cancel{c}}{1} \cdot \dfrac{1\ \cancel{pt}}{2\ \cancel{c}} \cdot \dfrac{1\ qt}{2\ \cancel{pt}}$	Cancel out the units.
	$= \dfrac{5}{2}\ qts$	Multiply & divide.
	$= 2.5\ qts$	Or the result can be written as a decimal number.

Example 3-7: How many fluid ounces are in 1 gallon?

Solution: This problem requires you to convert gallons to fluid ounces. You can either just go ahead and use all 4 conversion factors and multiply them out, as in previous examples, or you create some intermediate conversion factors from the ones above. As you get more familiar with conversions, you will start to remember different equivalencies.

	$\dfrac{8\ fl\ oz}{1\ c} \cdot \dfrac{2\ c}{1\ pt} = \dfrac{16\ fl\ oz}{1\ pt}$	Multiplying the number of fluid ounces per cup by the number of cups per pint results in a new conversion factor of 16 fluid ounces per pint.
	$\dfrac{2\ pt}{1\ qt} \cdot \dfrac{4\ qt}{1\ gal} = \dfrac{8\ pt}{1\ gal}$	Likewise, we can determine the number of pints per gallon.
$1\ gallon$	$= \dfrac{1\ gal}{1} \cdot \dfrac{8\ pt}{1\ gal} \cdot \dfrac{16\ fl\ oz}{1\ pt}$	Use the new conversion factors from above to convert gallons into fluid ounces.
	$= \dfrac{1\ \cancel{gal}}{1} \cdot \dfrac{8\ \cancel{pt}}{1\ \cancel{gal}} \cdot \dfrac{16\ fl\ oz}{1\ \cancel{pt}}$	Multiply and cancel out the units.
	$= 128\ fl\ oz$	

Note that you do not need to create intermediate conversion factors. You can also just go ahead and use all the individual conversion factors in 1 step:

$$1 \text{ gallon} = \frac{1 \text{ gal}}{1} \cdot \frac{4 \text{ qt}}{1 \text{ gal}} \cdot \frac{2 \text{ pt}}{1 \text{ qt}} \cdot \frac{2 \text{ c}}{1 \text{ pt}} \cdot \frac{8 \text{ fl oz}}{1 \text{ c}}$$

$$= 128 \text{ fl oz}$$

METRIC UNIT SYSTEM

Most countries in the world use the metric system as the system of measurement. This system is actually a bit easier to learn because it is based on the number 10. You will just need to remember the basic unit of length, weight and volume as well as the prefixes that are used to scale each basic unit to larger or smaller quantities.
The following tables lists the definition of each of these prefixes:

Kilo- means thousands	*Milli-* means thousandths
Hecto- means hundreds	*Centi-* means hundredths
Deka- means tens	*Deci-* means tenths

Metric Units of Length

The basic metric unit of length is a meter. Using the prefixes, we can then build the following table with relationships between the units of metric length:

1 kilometer (km) = 1000 meters	1000 millimeters (mm) = 1 meter
1 hectometer (hm) = 100 meters	100 centimeters (cm) = 1 meter
1 dekameter (dam) = 10 meters	10 decimeter (dm) = 1 meter

Converting between different metric units of length is done the same way as converting between U.S. units of measurement, however, because it is based on always multiplying and dividing by 10, it is easier to do the conversions because you can just move the decimal point right or left the proper number of places.

Example 3-8: Convert 15 kilometer into meters.

Solution: Use the table above to find the conversion factor between kilometers into meters.

$$15\ km = \frac{15\ km}{1}$$ Write 15 kilometers as a fraction.

$$= \frac{15\ km}{1} \cdot \frac{1000\ m}{1\ km}$$ Multiply by the conversion factor.

$$= \frac{15\ \cancel{km}}{1} \cdot \frac{1000\ m}{1\ \cancel{km}}$$ Cancel out the units.

$$= 15{,}000\ m$$ Multiply.

Example 3-9: How many hectometers is equivalent to 2,317 centimeters?

Solution: Because the conversion factors are all multiples of 10, an alternative method to converting metric units is to just move the decimal point the correct number of places to the right or the left.

First, make a list of the units from **largest** to **smallest**:

km	hm	dam	m	dm	cm	mm

Then find the starting units (cm in this example) and the ending units (hm) on the table. You will see that to move from cm to hm on the chart, you will have to move 4 places left.

km	hm	dam	m	dm	cm	mm

So, move the decimal point in 2,317 cm a total of 4 places to the left, resulting in **0.2317 hm**.

You can see this is equivalent to the previous method you learned, but is much faster.

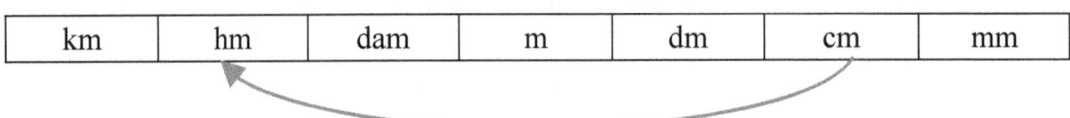

$$2317\ cm = \frac{2317\ \cancel{cm}}{1} \cdot \frac{1\ \cancel{m}}{100\ \cancel{cm}} \cdot \frac{1\ hm}{100\ \cancel{m}}$$ Multiply by the conversion factors, cancel out the units and divide.

$$= 0.2317\ hm$$

Metric Units of Weight

The basic metric unit of weight is the gram and the prefixes for smaller or larger units of weights are the same as those used for length. Apply the same relationships to generate the following table for metric units of weight:

1 kilogram (kg) = 1000 grams	1000 milligrams (mg) = 1 gram
1 hectogram (hg) = 100 grams	100 centigrams (cg) = 1 gram
1 dekagram (dag) = 10 grams	10 decigrams (dg) = 1 gram

Example 3-10: Convert 7.5 kg to mg.

Solution: First, make a list of the units from **largest** to **smallest**:

kg	hg	dag	g	dg	cg	mg

To convert from kg to mg you will need to move 6 places to the right.

kg	hg	dag	g	dg	cg	mg

Move the decimal point in 7.5kg a corresponding total of 6 places to the right, resulting in 7,500,000 mg.

Using conversion factors results in the same value.

$7.5 \, kg = \dfrac{7.5 \, kg}{1} \cdot \dfrac{1000 \, g}{1 \, kg} \cdot \dfrac{1000 \, mg}{1 \, g}$ Multiply by the conversion factors, cancelling out the units.

$= 7,500,000 \, mg$ Multiply.

Metric Units of Volume

The basic metric unit of volume is the liter (L) and the metric prefixes are the same as those for length and weight.

242 Math for Liberal Arts

1 kiloliter (kL) = 1000 liters	1000 milliliters (mL) = 1 liter
1 hectoliter (hL) = 100 liters	100 centiliters (cL) = 1 liter
1 dekaliter (daL) = 10 liters	10 deciliters (dL) = 1 liter

Example 3-11: How many deciliters are in 0.35 dekaliters?

Solution: List the units from **largest** to **smallest** and find the correct direction and number of places to move the decimal point.

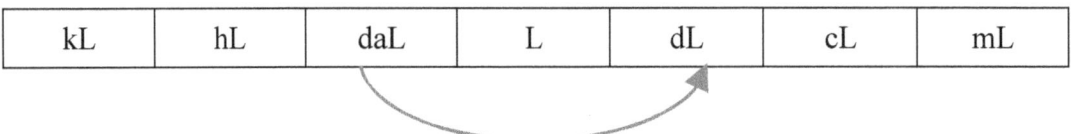

To convert from daL to dL you will need to move 2 places to the right. **0.35 daL = 35 dL**.

The conversion factor method will yield the same result:

$$.35\ daL = \frac{.35\ daL}{100} \qquad \text{Write .35 daL as a fraction.}$$

$$= \frac{.35\ daL}{100} \cdot \frac{10\ L}{1\ daL} \cdot \frac{10\ dL}{1\ L} \qquad \text{Multiply by the conversion factors.}$$

$$= \frac{.35\ \cancel{daL}}{100} \cdot \frac{10\ \cancel{L}}{1\ \cancel{daL}} \cdot \frac{10\ dL}{1\ \cancel{L}} \qquad \text{Cancel out the units.}$$

$$= 35\ dL \qquad \text{Multiply and divide.}$$

CONVERTING BETWEEN U.S. AND METRIC SYSTEMS

Occasionally, you will need to convert between U.S. and Metric units. Because this involves a conversion between units of different systems, the conversions are approximations. Below are tables of length, weight and volume conversions:

Equivalent lengths	
US to metric	Metric to US
1 in ≈ 2.54 cm	1 cm ≈ .3937 in
1 ft ≈ 0.3048 m	1 m ≈ 3.2808 ft
1 mi ≈ 1.6093 km	1 km ≈ 0.6214 mi

Equivalent weights	
US to metric	Metric to US
1 oz ≈ 28.35 g	1 g ≈ 0.035 oz
1 lb ≈ 0.454 kg	1 kg ≈ 2.2 lb

Equivalent volumes	
US to metric	Metric to US
1 fl oz ≈ 0.030 L	1 L ≈ 33.8 fl oz
1 gal ≈ 3.785 L	1 L ≈ 0.264 gal

Example 3-12: Convert 25 miles into kilometers, rounding to the nearest tenth.

Solution: Use the conversion factor $1\ mi \approx 1.6093\ km$ from the table above.

$25\ mi$ = 25 • 1 *mile*

= 25 • (1.6093 *km*)   Substitute 1 mile with 1.6093 km.

= 40.2 *km*   Multiply and round to the nearest tenth.

Example 3-13: Which is heavier – a 2 lb tub of butter or a 1 kg tub of margarine?

Solution: Convert the 2 lb of butter into kg and then compare the value to 1 kg.

2 lb   = 2 • 1 *lb*

           = 2 • (0.454 *kg*)   Substitute 0.454 kg for 1 lb.

           = 0.908 *kg*   Multiply.

Since the 2 lb tub of butter weighs approx. 0.908 kg, the **1 kg tub of margarine is heavier.**

Example 3-14: You have a 5-gallon container for water. What is the maximum number of 1-liter bottles of water that can be poured into it?

Solution: Convert the 5 gallons into liters and then truncate the result to find the maximum number of 1-liter bottles of water that can fit.

5 *gallon*   = 5 • 1 *gal*

              = 5 • (3.785 *L*)   Substitute 3.785 L for 1 gallon.

              = 18.925 *L*   Multiply.

Since 5 gallons is less than 19 L, the **5-gallon container can hold 18 1-liter bottles.**

5-4: INTEREST

When money is invested, the investor is paid for use of the money by the institution he/she is investing the money with. This money earned by the investor is called **interest** and can be calculated in a variety of ways. Simple interest is the easiest to understand and will be explained first.

Likewise, when someone borrows money, they usually have to pay additional money for the right to borrow the money. This cost is also called **interest** and is paid from the person borrowing the money to the person or company lending the money. A loan with interest will cost the borrower more than the initial value of the loan once the loan has been repaid.

SIMPLE INTEREST

Key terms for understanding simple interest:

Principal: The amount of money that is invested or loaned.

Interest Rate: A rate (percent) that is used to calculate the amount of interest to be paid on the investment or the loan.

Time: the length of time that the money is invested or loaned. Usually expressed in years.

Simple Interest Formula

$I = Prt$

I = Interest earned on the principal
P = Principal investment (or initial value of money borrowed)
r = Rate per time period
t = Number of time periods for which money is invested or borrowed

---

You can see from the simple interest formula that the amount of interest earned will depend on the initial investment, the rate which the investment will earn, and length of time the money is invested. The longer you invest money, for example, the more interest you will earn. Likewise, if you invest a large sum of money, you will receive more interest than someone who invests a smaller sum. When looking for a 'good' investment, consumers will look for the highest interest rate, assuming other factors are equal.

Example 4-1: $5,000 is invested for 1 year at a simple interest rate of 3% per year. Calculate the interest earned.

Solution: Use the simple interest formula to calculate the interest earned. The principle is the initial investment ($5,000), the rate is 3% per year and the time is 1 year.

$I = Prt$
$= 5,000 \cdot 0.03 \cdot 1$ Substitute values for P, r, and t. 3% = 0.03 in decimal form.
$= 150$ Multiply.

The interest earned after 1 year is $150.

Remember that the units of time for the investment interval and the rate over which the interest is calculated must match. Rates are usually expressed in percent per year and if the investment is shorter than 1 year, then convert the investment time to a fraction.

Example 4-2: $7,500 is invested for 4 months at a simple interest rate of 1.3% per year. Calculate the interest earned.

Solution: Use the simple interest formula to calculate the interest earned.

$I = Prt$

$= 7,500 \cdot 0.013 \cdot \dfrac{4}{12}$ Substitute values for P, r, and t. Convert interest rate to decimal form and investment period from months to years.

$= 32.5$ Multiply.

The interest earned after 4 months is $32.50.

Example 4-3: $20,000 is borrowed for 6.5 years at a simple interest rate of 6% per year. Calculate the interest owed.

Solution: Interest on loans is calculated the same way as interest on investments. Use the simple interest formula to calculate the interest owed.

$I = Prt$

$= 20,000 \cdot 0.06 \cdot 6.5$ Substitute values for P, r, and t.

$= 7800$ Multiply.

The interest owed after 6.5 years is $7800.

When making an investment, you will usually want to know how much money your investment is worth at the end of the investment period. You can calculate this by adding the interest earned to the initial investment. The formula is shown below.

Final Investment Value Formula (Simple Interest)

$A = P \cdot (1 + rt)$

A = Final investment value
P = Principal investment (or initial value of money borrowed)
r = Rate per time period
t = Number of time periods for which money is invested or borrowed

Example 4-4: $50,000 is invested in the stock market at a simple interest rate of 4.5% per year. Calculate the total value of the investment after 15 years.

Solution: Use the final interest formula to calculate the final value of investment.

$$A = P \cdot (1 + rt)$$
$$= 50{,}000 \cdot (1 + 0.045 \cdot 15) \quad \text{Substitute values for } P, r, \text{ and } t.$$
$$= 83{,}750 \quad \text{Multiply.}$$

The final value of the investment after 15 years is $83,750.

Example 4-5: $8,200 is borrowed to purchase a car at a simple interest rate of 3.9% per year. Calculate the total amount repaid to the lender after 24 months.

Solution: Use the final interest formula to calculate the final value of the loan, or the total amount repaid.

$$24 \text{ months} = 2 \text{ years} \quad \text{First, remember to convert months to years since interest rate is per year.}$$

$$A = P \cdot (1 + rt)$$
$$= 8{,}200 \cdot (1 + 0.039 \cdot 2) \quad \text{Substitute values for } P, r, \text{ and } t.$$
$$= 8{,}839.60 \quad \text{Multiply.}$$

The total amount repaid is $8,839.60.

COMPOUND INTEREST

In practice, most savings accounts will compound interest rather than using simple interest. This means that once interest is accumulated on your account, it is added to the balance, and then interest is earned on the interest.

Key terms:

Compounding period – period of time between when interest is calculated and added to the principal.

Interest can be compounded annually, semiannually, quarterly, monthly or daily.

If an initial investment of $1000 is deposited into an account earning 5% interest compounded annually, then we can use the simple interest formula to illustrate how compounding works to find the value of the account after 3 years.

Year	Value of investment at beginning of the year	Interest earned $I = Prt$	Value at the end of the year = Value at the beginning of the year + interest earned
1	$1000	$I = 1000 \cdot .05 \cdot 1 = 50$	$1000 + $50 = $1050

The value at the start of year 2 is equal to the value at the end of year 1. Add this to the table and calculate the interest earned during year 2 and the total value at the end of year 2.

Year	Value of investment at beginning of the year	Interest earned $I = Prt$	Value at the end of the year = Value at the beginning of the year + interest earned
1	$1000	$I = 1000 \cdot .05 \cdot 1 = 50$	$1000 + $50 = $1050
2	$1050	$I = 1050 \cdot .05 \cdot 1 = 52.50$	$1050 + $52.50 = $1102.50

Since the investment was made for 3 years, continue this process and add one more row to the table for year 3 and calculate the interest earned and the total value at the end of year 3. The value at the start of year 3 is equal to the value of the investment at the end of year 2, or $1102.50.

Year	Value of investment at beginning of the year	Interest earned $I = Prt$	Value at the end of the year = Value at the beginning of the year + interest earned
1	$1000	$I = 1000 \cdot .05 \cdot 1 = 50$	$1000 + $50 = $1050
2	$1050	$I = 1050 \cdot .05 \cdot 1 = 52.50$	$1050 + $52.50 = $1102.50
3	$1102.50	$I = 1102.5 \cdot .05 \cdot 1 = 55.13$	$1102.50 + $55.13 = $1157.63

As you can see, each year the investment will earn more interest than the previous year because the interest is being calculated on both the initial investment plus the accumulated interest.

If the final value of the investment had been calculated using only simple interest, the value would be $I = Prt = 1000 \cdot .05 \cdot 3 = \$1150$. You can see that with compounded interest, the value is worth more.

To efficiently calculate compound interest without needing to calculate intermediate values, the compounding formula is shown in the table below.

Final Investment Value Formula (Compound Interest)

$$A = P \cdot \left(1 + \frac{r}{n}\right)^{nt}$$

A = Final investment value
P = Principal investment (loan)
r = Rate per number of time periods
n = number of times per period interest is compounded
t = Number of time periods

Example 4-6: $18,600 is invested in a savings account which pays a 4% interest rate, compounded annually. Calculate the value of the account after 10 years.

Solution: Use the formula in the table above for compounded interest to calculate the final value. The investment is compounded annually for 10 years so there are 10 compounding intervals and the number of times per period (year) the interest is compounded is once.

$$A = P \cdot \left(1 + \frac{r}{n}\right)^{nt}$$

$$= 18{,}600 \cdot \left(1 + \frac{.04}{1}\right)^{1 \times 10} \quad \text{Substitute values for } P, r, n, \text{ and } t.$$

$$= 27{,}532.54 \quad \text{Multiply.}$$

Example 4-7: $50,000 is invested in a retirement account which pays a 6.8% interest rate, compounded monthly. Calculate the value of the account after 25 years.

Solution: Use the Final Investment formula to calculate the final value. Since the investment is compounded monthly, that means there are 12 compounding intervals per year (n = 12)

$$A = P \cdot \left(1 + \frac{r}{n}\right)^{nt}$$

$$= 50{,}000 \cdot \left(1 + \frac{.068}{12}\right)^{12 \times 25} \quad \text{Substitute values for } P, r, n, \text{ and } t.$$

$$= 272{,}387.17 \quad \text{Multiply.}$$

The final value is $272,387.17.

Sample Test Questions

UNIT CONVERSION QUESTIONS

1. Convert 6 ½ yards to inches

   A. 234 in
   B. 216 in
   C. 78 in
   D. 19.5 in

2. How many fluid ounces are in 2 quarts?

   A. 8 fl oz
   B. 16 fl oz
   C. 32 fl oz
   D. 64 fl oz

3. Which weighs more and by how much: a 2.3 ton elephant or a 4,500 pound car?

   A. Car weighs more by 100 lbs
   B. Elephant weighs more by 100 lbs
   C. Elephant weighs more by 10 lbs
   D. They are the same weight

4. Convert 352 g to kg

   A. 0.352 kg
   B. 3.52 kg
   C. 35.2 kg
   D. 352 kg

5. Convert 2.15 dm to mm

   A. 0.0215 mm
   B. 2.15 mm
   C. 215 mm
   D. 2,150 mm

6. Which is longer and by how much: a 12 inch ruler or 25 centimeter stick?

   A. Stick is longer by 4.72 cm
   B. Stick is longer by 5.48 cm
   C. Ruler is longer by 4.72 cm
   D. Ruler is longer by 5.48 cm

INTEREST QUESTIONS

1. A homeowner borrows $8,000 to pay for kitchen remodeling. The terms of the loan are 9.2% annual interest to be repaid in 2 years. How much interest will be paid on the loan?

   A. $147,200
   B. $1,472
   C. $7,360
   D. $14,720

2. If Joe invests $14,250 in the stock market and receives a 5% return, compounded quarterly, on his investment, what is the value of his investment after 7 years?

   A. $20,177.89
   B. $55,861.84
   C. $20,051.18
   D. $15,675

3. If $10,000 is deposited in a savings account that earns 2.7% simple interest, how much interest is earned at the end of 5 months?

   A. $1,350
   B. $1,125
   C. $112.50
   D. $135,000

4. To purchase a car, a man takes out a loan for $2,000 at an interest rate of 8% per year. How much will he have paid in total for the car at the end of a 120 day loan period?

   A. $21,200
   B. $2,052.60
   C. $2,526.03
   D. $2,160

5. Investment A pays 3.5% interest, compounded daily and Investment B pays 4% simple interest. Which investment will earn more money if $12,500 is invested for 6.5 years and by how much?

   A. Investment A worth $61.98 more
   B. Investment A worth $117.72 more
   C. Investment A worth $56.95 more
   D. Investment B worth $56.95 more

6. If a $100,000 investment earns 8.2% interested, compounded annually, what is the final value of the investment after 16 years.

   A. $352,887.42
   B. $231,200
   C. $108,200
   D. $13,120,000

UNIT CONVERSION KEY

1. A

$$6.5 \text{ yds} = \frac{13 \text{ yds}}{2} \cdot \frac{3 \text{ ft}}{1 \text{ yd}} \cdot \frac{12 \text{ in}}{1 \text{ ft}}$$

$$= 234 \text{ in}$$

2. D

$$2 \text{ qt} = \frac{2 \text{ qt}}{1} \cdot \frac{2 \text{ pt}}{1 \text{ qt}} \cdot \frac{2 \text{ c}}{1 \text{ pt}} \cdot \frac{8 \text{ fl oz}}{1 \text{ c}}$$

$$= 64 \text{ fl oz}$$

3. D

$$2.3 \text{ ton} = \frac{2.3 \text{ ton}}{1} \cdot \frac{2000 \text{ lb}}{1 \text{ ton}}$$

$$= 4600 \text{ lb.}$$ **The elephant is heavier by 100 lbs.**

4. A
5. C
6. D

$$12 \text{ in} = 12 \cdot (2.54 \text{ cm})$$

$$= 30.48 \text{ cm.}$$ **Therefore, the ruler is longer.**

INTEREST KEY

1. B

$$I = Prt$$
$$= 8{,}000 \cdot 0.092 \cdot 2$$
$$= 1472$$

The interest paid after 2 years is $1472.

2. A

$$A = P \cdot \left(1 + \frac{r}{n}\right)^{nt}$$
$$= 14{,}250 \cdot \left(1 + \frac{.05}{1}\right)^{4 \cdot 7}$$
$$= 20{,}177.89$$

Final value of investment is $20,177.89.

3. C

$$I = Prt$$
$$= 10{,}000 \cdot 0.027 \cdot \frac{5}{12}$$
$$= 112.5$$

The interest earned after 5 months is $112.50.

4. B

$$A = P \cdot (1 + rt)$$
$$= 2{,}000 \cdot \left(1 + 0.08 \cdot \frac{120}{365}\right)$$
$$= 2052.60$$

The total paid after 5 months is $2052.60.

5. D

<u>Investment A</u>

$$A = P \cdot \left(1 + \frac{r}{n}\right)^{nt}$$
$$= 12{,}500 \cdot \left(1 + \frac{.035}{365}\right)^{365 \cdot 6.5}$$
$$= 15{,}693.05$$

Investment A is worth $15,693.05.

<u>Investment B</u>

$$A = P \cdot (1 + rt)$$
$$= 12{,}500 \cdot (1 + 0.04 \cdot 6.5)$$
$$= 15{,}750$$

Investment B is worth $15,750.

Therefore, Investment B earned $56.95 more.

6. A

$$A = P \cdot \left(1 + \frac{r}{n}\right)^{nt}$$
$$= 100{,}000 \cdot \left(1 + \frac{.082}{1}\right)^{1 \cdot 16}$$
$$= 352{,}887.42$$

Final value of investment is $352,887.42.

 Test-Taking Strategies

Here are some test-taking strategies that are specific to this test and to other DSST tests in general:
- Keep your eyes on the time. Pay attention to how much time you have left.
- Read the entire question and read all the answers. Many questions are not as hard to answer as they may seem. Sometimes, a difficult sounding question really only is asking you how to read an accompanying chart. Chart and graph questions are on most DANTES/DSST tests and should be an easy free point.
- If you don't know the answer immediately, the new computer-based testing lets you mark questions and come back to them later if you have time.
- Read the wording carefully. Some words can give you hints to the right answer. There are no exceptions to an answer when there are words in the question such as always, all or none. If one of the answer choices includes most or some of the right answers, but not all, then that is not the answer. Here is an example:

    The primary colors include all of the following:
    A) Red, Yellow, Blue, Green
    B) Red, Green, Yellow
    C) Red, Orange, Yellow
    D) Red, Yellow, Blue

- Although item A includes all the right answers, it also includes an incorrect answer, making it incorrect. If you didn't read it carefully, were in a hurry, or didn't know the material well, you might fall for this.
- Make a guess on a question that you do not know the answer to. There is no penalty for an incorrect answer. Eliminate the answer choices that you know are incorrect. For example, this will let your guess be a 1 in 3 chance instead.

Test Preparation

How much you need to study depends on your knowledge of a subject. If you are interested in literature, took it in school, or enjoy reading then your study and preparation for the literature or humanities test will not need to be as intensive as that of someone who is new to literature.

This book is much different than the regular DANTES study guides. This book actually teaches you the information that you need to know to pass the test. If you are particularly interested in an area, or feel that you want more information, do a quick search online. We've tried not to include too much depth in areas that are not as essential on the test. Everything in this book will be on the test. It is important to understand all major theories and concepts listed in the table of contents. It is also important to know any bolded words.

Don't worry if you do not understand or know a lot about the area With minimal study, you can complete and pass the test.

One of the fallacies of other test books is test questions. People assume that the content of the questions are similar to what will be on the test. That is not the case. They are only there to test your "test taking skills" so for those who know to read a question carefully, there is not much added value from taking a "fake" test.

To prepare for the test, make a series of goals. Allot a certain amount of time to review the information you have already studied and to learn additional material. Take notes as you study; it will help you learn the material.

Legal Note

All rights reserved. This Study Guide, Book and Flashcards are protected under US Copyright Law. No part of this book or study guide or flashcards may be reproduced, distributed or stored in a retrieval system, or transmitted in any form or by any means, electronic, mechanical, photocopying, recording, or otherwise, without the prior written permission of the publisher Breely Crush Publishing LLC.

FLASHCARDS

This section contains flashcards for you to use to further your understanding of the material and test yourself on important concepts, names or dates. Read the term or question then flip the page over to check the answer on the back. Keep in mind that this information may not be covered in the text of the study guide. Take your time to study the flashcards, you will need to know and understand these concepts to pass the test.

Terms	**Algebraic expression**
Like or unlike terms? 2y, 14y	**Like or unlike terms?** 2y, -14x
Like or unlike terms? 14, -14	**Like or unlike terms?** 3x2, 3x
Coefficient of the variable	**Polynomial**

Collection of terms that are separated by arithmetic operations	Numbers and variables
Unlike	Like
Unlike	Like
Expression containing the sum of a finite number of terms	The number multiplied by the variable

FOIL	Factor
Simplify	Algebraic equation
Balance in equations	Quadratic equation
What is the solution to a quadratic equation?	Vertex

Two numbers or terms that when multiplied together yield the original term	First, out, inner, last
Must contain an equal sign	Solve or reduce
$$\dfrac{-b \pm \sqrt{b^2 - 4ac}}{2a}$$	The value of each side of the equation is the same
The lowest point on the parabola	The root of the polynomial $ax^2+bx+c=0$

In graphing the term x runs horizontal or vertical?	**In graphing the term y runs horizontal or vertical?**
What is absolute value?	$\|\ \|$
$\neq$	$\leq$
$\geq$	$<$

Vertical	Horizontal
Notation for absolute value	The distance between a number and 0 on the number line
Notation of less than or equal to	Notation for not equal to
Notation for less than	Notation for greater than or equal to

>	Parallel lines
Perpendicular lines	⊥
∥	Logarithms
Natural logarithms	When are logarithms and exponents used?

Two lines are parallel if they lie on the same plane and never intersect	Notation for greater than
Notation for perpendicular	Two lines are perpendicular if their intersection forms a right angle
The exponent of a positive number	Notation for parallel
To calculate simple & compound interest and exponential growth	Have a base "e" which is a constant

I = Prt	In I=Prt what does P stand for?
In I=Prt what does r stand for?	In I=Prt what does I stand for?
In I=Prt what does t stand for?	Set
{ }	Another name for empty set

| Principle | Simple interest |

| Interest rate | Annual interest rate |

| Collection of elements | Time |

| Null set | Empty set |